KU-531-436

# new flavours

photography by **Jean Cazals**

over **300** tried-and-tested recipes

# new
# flavours

everyday **cooking** with a **difference**

BBC

Published by
**BBC Worldwide Ltd**
Woodlands
80 Wood Lane
London W12 OTT

Designed and produced by
**Quadrille Publishing Limited**
Alhambra House
27-31 Charing Cross Road
London WC2H OLS

First published in 2000
Text and photographs © 1999
Quadrille Publishing Limited
and BBC Worldwide
Design and layout © 2000
Quadrille Publishing Limited

All rights reserved. No part of this book may be
reproduced in any form or by any means without
permission in writing from the publisher, except
by a reviewer who may quote brief passages.

ISBN 0 563 55175 5

BBC Good Food Editor **Orlando Murrin**
Deputy Editor **Mary Cadogan**
Chief Sub-editor **Melanie Leyshon**

Photographer **Jean Cazals**
Food Stylists **Maxine Clark, Joanna Farrow,
Marie Ange Lapierre, Louise Pickford,
Bridget Sargeson, Linda Tubby**
Photographic Stylists **Kasha Harmer Hirst,
Maya Babic**

Quadrille Art Director **Mary Evans**
Editorial Director **Jane O'Shea**
Editor and Project Manager **Janet Illsley**
Original design **Vanessa Courtier**
Design Assistant **Jim Smith**
Editorial Assistant **Caroline Perkins**
Production **Julie Hadingham, Rachel Wells**

Printed and bound by **Dai Nippon Printing, Hong Kong**

Recipes written by:

**Sara Buenfeld**

**Maxine Clark**

**Joanna Farrow**

**Louise Pickford**

**Bridget Sargeson**

**Linda Tubby**

**Sunil Vijayakar**

706499
MORAY COUNCIL
Department of Technical
& Leisure Services
641.5

**Cookery notes**
- All recipes serve four unless otherwise stated.
- All spoon measures are level unless otherwise indicated.
- Follow either metric or imperial measures, not a mixture
  of both as they are not necessarily interchangeable.
- Use fresh herbs and freshly ground black pepper unless
  otherwise suggested.

# contents

# stimulating soups & starters

**Full of colour and piquancy**, these sensational soups and starters are the perfect way to **start off a special meal in style. Elegant fish starters**, such as grilled mussels with coconut and coriander pesto, and crab and papaya salad will **complement most menus**. If you are following with a light main course, opt for one of the more **substantial chicken**, **meat** or **pasta starters**. Soups are an excellent first course choice, as they can be prepared in advance. **Exquisite vegetable starters**, including Japanese sushi and **fragrant warm salads**, are easy to prepare and guaranteed to stimulate appetites.

## Grilled mussels with coconut and coriander pesto

Mussels on their half shell are topped with a creamy coconut and coriander pesto, then sprinkled with Parmesan and grilled.

32 large fresh mussels in shells
2 tbsp freshly grated Parmesan
olive oil, for drizzling
*for the pesto*
25g/1oz fresh coriander leaves
1 small garlic clove, crushed
2 tbsp ground almonds
2 tbsp coconut cream
2 tbsp olive oil
pinch of cayenne pepper
salt and pepper

**1** Scrub the mussels thoroughly in several changes of cold water and pull away any 'beards' which are attached to the shells.
**2** Put the mussels in a large pan, with just the water clinging to the shells after washing. Cover the pan with a tight fitting lid and steam for 4 minutes until the shells have opened. Discard any that remain closed.
**3** Refresh the mussels in cold water, drain well and discard the empty half shells. Invert the mussels in their half shells on to kitchen paper to drain thoroughly.
**4** For the pesto, put all the ingredients in a food processor and work to a rough paste.
**5** Place the mussels, open side up, in a grill pan. Spoon a little pesto on top of each one, then sprinkle with the cheese. Drizzle with a little olive oil and grill for 3-4 minutes until bubbling and golden. Let cool for a minute or so before serving, with warm bread.

**NOTE** You can use ready made basil pesto as a tasty, quick alternative to this coconut and coriander pesto.

## Indian spiced monkfish chappatis

Grilled monkfish fillets infused with tandoori spices are served between crisp fried chappatis, with a cooling cucumber raita.

2 monkfish fillets, each 225g/8oz, skinned
1 garlic clove, crushed
1 tsp grated fresh root ginger
1 tbsp tandoori spice mix
1 tbsp tomato purée
1 tbsp sunflower oil
1½ tbsp lemon juice
*for the raita*
100g/4oz yogurt
¼ tsp salt
¼ tsp sugar
pinch of cayenne pepper
50g/2oz cucumber, peeled and grated
1 tbsp chopped fresh mint
*to finish*
2 chappatis, cut into triangles
sunflower oil, for shallow frying
lemon wedges and mint leaves, to garnish

**1** Place the monkfish in a dish. In a small bowl, mix together the garlic, ginger, tandoori spice, tomato purée, oil and lemon juice. Add to the monkfish, turn to coat and leave to marinate in a cool place for at least 1 hour.
**2** Meanwhile, mix together the ingredients for the raita. Set aside.
**3** Preheat the grill. Lay the monkfish on the grill rack and grill for 6-8 minutes, turning halfway, until cooked through. Leave to rest in a warm place for 5 minutes.
**4** Meanwhile, heat a thin layer of oil in a frying pan and fry the chappati triangles for 1 minute until crisp. Drain on kitchen paper.
**5** Slice the monkfish and sandwich between the chappati triangles. Serve garnished with lemon and mint, accompanied by the raita.

## Fish timbales with wasabi dressing

A stylish, special occasion starter. *Serves 6*

250g/9oz skinless halibut or cod fillet
2 egg whites
450g/1lb skinless salmon or trout fillet
300ml/½ pint double cream, chilled
salt and white pepper
*for the dressing*
6 tsp wasabi paste
6 tsp mirin
4 tbsp rice wine vinegar
250ml/9fl oz sunflower oil

**1** Mince the halibut in a food processor. Add a third of the egg white, a little at a time, mixing well between each addition. Transfer to a bowl. Repeat this process with the salmon, adding all of the remaining egg white. Chill both mixtures for 5 minutes.
**2** Gradually stir a third of the cream into the halibut mixture; add the rest to the salmon, a little at a time. Season both mixtures.
**3** Butter six 150ml/¼ pint timbales, or other ovenproof moulds. Divide half of the salmon mix between them. Cover with the halibut mixture, then top with the remaining salmon, to create layers. Chill for up to 3 hours.
**4** For the dressing, shake the ingredients together in a screw-topped jar to emulsify.
**5** Remove timbales from fridge 15 minutes before cooking. Preheat oven to 180C/fan oven 160C/Gas 4. Stand the moulds in a deep roasting tin and surround with a 3mm/⅛in depth of hot water. Cover with a dampened double layer of greaseproof paper. Bake for 15 minutes or until the tops are firm to the touch. Remove from tin and let stand, covered, for 10-15 minutes.
**6** Unmould the timbales on to kitchen paper then lift on to plates. Drizzle the wasabi dressing around the timbales to serve.

### Scallops with broad bean purée

A creamy minted bean purée is the perfect
partner to sweet, char-griddled scallops.

12 large scallops, cleaned
3 tbsp extra virgin olive oil
salt and pepper
1 tbsp lemon juice
*for the broad bean purée*
100g/4oz broad beans
½ garlic clove, crushed
1 tbsp freshly grated Parmesan
1 tbsp chopped fresh mint
2 tbsp extra virgin olive oil
4 tbsp double cream
*for the garnish*
mint sprigs

**1** Cut away the tough muscle at the side of
each scallop and any dark vein, then wash
and dry well. Toss with 1 tbsp of the oil,
season liberally and set aside.
**2** To make the broad bean purée, cook the
beans in lightly salted boiling water for 3-4
minutes until tender. Drain well and transfer
to a blender. Add the remaining ingredients,
except the cream, and purée until smooth.
Transfer to a small pan, add the cream and
warm through. Keep warm.
**3** Heat a ridged griddle or heavy-based pan
until smoking, add the scallops and cook for
1 minute, then turn and cook for the other
side for 1 minute. Transfer to a warm plate
and rest for a further 1 minute.
**4** For the dressing, mix the remaining 2 tbsp
oil with the lemon juice and seasoning.
Arrange the scallops on individual plates
with the bean purée. Drizzle with the
dressing and garnish with mint to serve.

**NOTE** The bean purée can be made ahead.
To serve, add the cream and heat through.

### Crab and papaya salad

Either buy a freshly dressed crab or use
vacuum packed fresh crab meat for this
tangy crab salad.

350g/12oz fresh white crab meat (see note)
2 ripe tomatoes, skinned, seeded
and diced
1 red chilli, seeded and finely chopped
2 tbsp chopped fresh coriander leaves
2 tbsp extra virgin olive oil
3 tbsp lime juice
few drops of Tabasco sauce
1 small papaya
salt and pepper
2 trevise or chicory bulbs
a little extra virgin olive oil
squeeze of lime juice
coriander leaves and lime wedges,
to garnish

**1** Carefully pick over the crab meat
discarding any small pieces of shell or
cartilage, then place in a bowl.
**2** Stir in the tomatoes, chilli, coriander, olive
oil, lime juice and Tabasco sauce. Cover
and leave to infuse in the refrigerator for
at least 1 hour.
**3** Just before serving, peel the papaya
and scoop out the seeds. Dice the papaya
flesh and stir into the crab meat. Check
the seasoning.
**4** Separate the trevise or chicory leaves
and dress with a little olive oil and lime juice.
Arrange on individual serving plates. Spoon
the crab salad on top and garnish with
coriander leaves. Serve immediately, with
lime wedges and warm French bread.

**NOTE** If you prefer to buy a whole crab,
choose one that weighs at least 1.5kg/3lb
to obtain the required amount of white meat.

### Piadina with red mullet and aioli

Piadina are Italian flat griddle breads,
often served with a topping. Make them in
advance and reheat in the oven. *Serves 6*

*for the piadina*
225g/8oz plain flour
salt and pepper
15g/½oz butter
150ml/¼ pint warm water
*for the aioli*
2 egg yolks
1 tbsp lemon juice
300ml/½ pint olive oil
2 garlic cloves, crushed
*for the topping*
2 tbsp extra virgin olive oil
6 small red mullet, filleted, or 6 trout fillets
squeeze of lemon juice
few rocket leaves

**1** Sift the flour and ½ tsp salt into a bowl,
rub in the butter, then work in the water to
form a soft dough. Knead for 10 minutes on
a lightly floured surface until smooth. Wrap
in plastic film and rest for 30 minutes.
**2** To make the aioli, put the egg yolks, lemon
juice and seasoning in a food processor and
pulse briefly. With the motor running, slowly
add the oil through the funnel until glossy
and thick. Turn into a bowl; stir in the garlic.
**3** Divide dough into 6 pieces. Roll out on a
floured surface to 18cm/7in rounds. Preheat
a griddle or heavy frying pan and fry the
breads, one at a time, for 1 minute. Turn and
cook underside for 30 seconds; keep warm.
**4** Heat the oil in a frying pan and cook the
fish fillets for 1-2 minutes each side. Season
and flavour with a little lemon juice.
**5** Top each piadina with 2 red mullet fillets
(or 1 trout fillet), a spoonful of aioli and a
few rocket leaves. Serve at once.

## Smoked fish tartlets

Smoked fish works beautifully in these melt
in the mouth tartlets. *Serves 8*

450g/1lb ready-made shortcrust pastry
450g/1lb undyed smoked haddock fillet,
skinned
200ml/7fl oz milk
2 strips of lemon zest
200ml/7fl oz double cream
2 medium eggs, lightly beaten
1 tbsp chopped fresh tarragon
pinch of cayenne pepper
salt and pepper
tarragon leaves, to garnish
salad leaves, to serve

**1** Preheat oven to 200C/fan oven 180C/Gas 6.
Divide the pastry into 8 pieces. Roll out on
a lightly floured surface into thin rounds and
use to line eight 10cm/4in individual flan
tins. Prick the bases with a fork and chill
in the refrigerator for 30 minutes.
**2** Line the pastry cases with greaseproof
paper and baking beans and bake blind
for 15 minutes; remove the paper and beans
and bake for a further 10-15 minutes until
the pastry is crisp and golden. Set aside
to cool.
**3** Place the fish in a shallow pan with the
milk and lemon strips. Bring to a gentle
simmer, cover and poach gently for
7 minutes. Cool slightly, then flake the
fish discarding any bones. Leave to cool.
**4** Put the fish in a bowl with the cream,
eggs, tarragon, cayenne and salt and
pepper. Stir gently to mix.
**5** Spoon the filling into the flan cases and
bake for 25 minutes until risen and set.
Leave to cool slightly for a few minutes.
Serve warm on a bed of mixed salad
leaves, garnished with tarragon sprigs.

## Garlic prawn and mozzarella salad

Hot garlic prawns are piled on to sliced
tomatoes and buffalo mozzarella, then
dressed with an emerald basil oil.

20 large raw prawns, peeled
3 tbsp extra virgin olive oil
2 garlic cloves, crushed
1 red chilli, seeded and chopped
225g/8oz buffalo mozzarella, sliced
4 ripe plum tomatoes, sliced
*for the basil oil*
15g/½oz fresh basil leaves
4 tbsp extra virgin olive oil
½ tsp lemon juice
salt and pepper
*for the garnish*
basil leaves

**1** Start by making the basil oil. Roughly
tear the leaves and place in a blender
with the oil, lemon juice and 1½ tsp boiling
water. Work until smooth, then transfer to a
bowl. Season with salt and pepper to taste.
**2** Devein the prawns, rinse and pat dry with
kitchen paper. Heat the oil in a large frying
pan. Add the prawns, garlic and chilli. Fry,
stirring, over a medium heat for 4-5 minutes
until the prawns are cooked through.
**3** Arrange the mozzarella and tomato slices
on individual serving plates and top with the
hot prawns and their pan juices. Garnish
with basil leaves and serve immediately,
drizzled with the basil oil.

**NOTE** Mozzarella made from cow's milk can
be used, but authentic buffalo mozzarella
lends a superior flavour and texture.

## Smoked salmon parcels

Jewel-like salmon eggs and toasted
brioche elevate these simple parcels
to a decadent starter.

450g/1lb sliced smoked salmon
100g/4oz cooked peeled prawns
175g/6oz ricotta cheese
50g/2oz crème fraîche
1 tbsp chopped fresh chervil
1 tbsp chopped fresh chives
1 tbsp lemon juice
salt and pepper
*for the garnish*
salmon caviar
crème fraîche
chervil sprigs
*to serve*
toasted slices of brioche

**1** Line 4 timbales or ramekins with the
best smoked salmon slices, using about
300g/10oz; allow sufficient overhang to
cover the tops. Roughly chop the remaining
smoked salmon.
**2** Put the chopped salmon and prawns in
a food processor. Add the ricotta, crème
fraîche, herbs, lemon juice, pepper and
a little salt; process until fairly smooth.
**3** Spoon the ricotta mixture into the lined
timbales or ramekins and spread evenly.
Carefully fold the excess smoked salmon
over the top to enclose the filling. Wrap the
ramekins tightly with plastic film and chill in
the refrigerator for several hours.
**4** To serve, unmould the salmon mousses
on to individual serving plates and garnish
with a little extra crème fraîche, salmon
caviar and chervil sprigs. Serve with warm
toasted brioche.

## Warm artichoke and hazelnut salad

4 large globe artichokes, stalks removed

2 tbsp extra virgin olive oil

salt and pepper

175g/6oz French beans, trimmed

*for the dressing*

1 small garlic clove, crushed

4 tbsp hazelnut oil

2 tbsp extra virgin olive oil

1 tbsp white wine vinegar

2 tsp wholegrain mustard

*to serve*

25g/1oz hazelnuts, toasted and chopped

pecorino or Parmesan shavings

**1** Put the artichokes in a large pan of cold water and bring to the boil. Simmer, partially covered, for 20 minutes. Lift out and immediately plunge into cold water; drain.

**2** Trim away the artichoke leaves to reveal the heart. Using a spoon, scoop out the prickly choke and discard. Toss the artichoke bases in olive oil and season well.

**3** Preheat a ridged griddle (or grill). Cook the artichoke hearts for 5 minutes each side, basting with oil, until tender. Cool slightly.

**4** Meanwhile, whisk together the ingredients for the dressing, seasoning to taste.

**5** Cook the beans in boiling salted water for 3 minutes or until just tender; drain well.

**6** Lay the artichoke bases on warmed plates and arrange the beans on top. Scatter over the nuts and cheese shavings. Serve drizzled with the dressing.

## Roasted cherry tomatoes on griddled chick pea cakes

Similar to set polenta but with a smoother texture, chick pea wedges are the ideal base for juicy, roasted tomatoes. *Serves 6*

115g/4oz gram (chick pea) flour

1 tsp salt

450ml/16fl oz cold water

3 tbsp olive oil, plus extra for frying

24 large cherry tomatoes

1 garlic clove, crushed

4 fresh thyme sprigs

pinch of sugar

salt and pepper

1 tbsp balsamic vinegar

extra virgin olive oil, to serve

**1** Preheat oven to 230C/fan oven 210C/Gas 8. Sift the flour and salt into a bowl. Gradually whisk in the water with 1 tbsp olive oil until smooth.

**2** Turn into a non-stick pan and slowly bring to the boil, stirring constantly until the mixture is thickened enough to leave the side of the pan. Spoon into an oiled 23cm (9in) shallow cake tin. Set aside to cool.

**3** Put the tomatoes, garlic, thyme and sugar in a small roasting tin; season with salt and pepper. Drizzle with remaining oil and roast for 20 minutes until softened. Sprinkle with the balsamic vinegar.

**4** Turn out the chick pea 'cake' and cut into 6 wedges. Heat a little oil in a large frying pan and fry the chick pea wedges for 1-2 minutes each side until golden. Serve the chick pea wedges topped with the tomatoes and their juices, and a generous drizzle of extra virgin olive oil.

## Mixed vegetable sushi

Now that the main ingredients are available from larger supermarkets as well as oriental food stores, it is surprisingly easy to make your own sushi. *(Illustrated on pages 6-7)*
*Serves 8*

225g/8oz sushi rice
3 tbsp rice wine vinegar
2 tbsp caster sugar
salt and pepper
2 eggs, lightly beaten
a little sunflower oil
8 sheets nori seaweed
140g/5oz mixed vegetables, including
carrot, cucumber, cooked baby corn
and cooked beetroot, cut into strips
*to serve*
wasabi paste
pickled ginger
Japanese soy sauce

**1** Cook rice according to pack instructions.
**2** Warm the vinegar, sugar and 1¹/2 tsp salt together in a small pan until dissolved.
**3** Transfer the rice to a bowl and stir in the vinegar. Cover with a tea towel; let cool.
**4** In another bowl, beat the eggs with a little salt and pepper. Brush an omelette pan with a little oil. Heat gently, pour in the egg and cook for 2 minutes until set. Cool, then cut into strips the same size as the vegetables.
**5** Lay 1 sheet of seaweed on a bamboo mat or board and trim off the top third. Spread about 50g/2oz rice along the front end, flatten slightly, then place a line of omelette and vegetable strips on top. Roll up tightly to form a log. Cut into 5 or 6 slices.
**6** Repeat with the remaining rice and vegetable strips to make a selection of different sushi fillings.
**7** Arrange the sushi in individual bowls and serve accompanied by the wasabi, pickled ginger and soy sauce.

## Asparagus with quail's eggs and prosciutto

Grilling asparagus brings out the full, sweet flavour of this wonderful vegetable. Delicate quail's eggs and crisp grilled pancetta are perfect partners.

350g/12oz thin asparagus spears, trimmed
1 tbsp olive oil
salt and pepper
12 quail's eggs
4 slices prosciutto, or Parma ham
2 plum tomatoes, skinned, seeded and diced
*for the dressing*
3 tbsp extra virgin olive oil
2 tsp lemon juice
truffle oil, for drizzling (optional)

**1** Peel the asparagus stalks, leaving the tips intact. Preheat a ridged griddle (or grill). Brush the asparagus spears with olive oil and cook, turning, for 3-4 minutes, until tender and charred. Season lightly and set aside until cold.
**2** Cook the quail's eggs in boiling water for 2 minutes; drain and plunge into cold water. Once cool, peel and carefully halve the eggs.
**3** Grill the prosciutto slices until crisp and golden; leave to cool, then break in half.
**4** For the dressing, whisk together the olive oil, lemon juice, and salt and pepper.
**5** To serve, arrange the asparagus, quail's eggs and prosciutto slices on 4 large serving plates. Scatter over the diced tomatoes. Spoon over the dressing and add a generous drizzle of truffle oil if using.

## Sweetcorn and coconut fritters

These fritters make a delicious starter or snack. Try serving with iceberg lettuce and fresh herbs, such as coriander and basil. To eat, roll the fritter and a few herb leaves in a lettuce leaf and dip into the sauce.

85g/3oz plain flour
¹/2 tsp baking powder
1 egg, lightly beaten
2 tbsp coconut cream
1 tbsp light soy sauce
1 tbsp lemon juice
185g can sweetcorn kernels, drained
4 lime leaves, finely shredded (see note)
1 tbsp chopped fresh coriander
vegetable oil, for deep frying
*for the dipping sauce*
50g/2oz palm or caster sugar
4 tbsp rice wine vinegar
2 tbsp Thai fish sauce
2 tsp chilli sauce

**1** First make the dipping sauce. Warm the ingredients together in a small pan to dissolve the sugar. Set aside to cool.
**2** Sift the flour and baking powder into a bowl and gradually beat in the egg, coconut cream, soy sauce and lemon juice. Stir in the sweetcorn, lime leaves and coriander.
**3** Heat a 5cm/2in depth of vegetable oil in a wok or deep, wide pan until it registers 180C on a sugar thermometer. Drop in spoonfuls of the batter and fry in batches for 2-3 minutes until crisp and golden.
**4** Drain on kitchen paper and keep warm in a low oven while cooking the rest of the fritters. Serve hot, with the dipping sauce.

**NOTE** Before shredding lime leaves, remove the thick central vein which is often tough.

### Chicken liver and blueberry salad

Flavourful blueberries, salted almonds and a warm, fruity dressing perfectly offset rich chicken livers.

4 tbsp extra virgin olive oil
50g/2oz whole unblanched almonds
sea salt and pepper
350g/12oz chicken livers, trimmed and halved if large
175g/6oz blueberries
1 tbsp raspberry vinegar
100g/4oz mixed salad leaves
50g/2oz French beans, blanched
few fresh herb leaves (eg basil, mint, parsley)

**1** Heat 2 tbsp olive oil in a frying pan, add the almonds and fry gently for about 1 minute until evenly browned. Remove with a slotted spoon, dust with sea salt and set aside.
**2** Increase the heat. Add the chicken livers to the pan and fry for 1 minute. Turn the livers over and fry for a further 1 minute until browned on the outside, but still slightly pink in the middle. Remove and allow to rest for a few minutes.
**3** Return the pan to the heat, add the blueberries and warm through for 30 seconds. Remove from the heat and add the remaining oil and raspberry vinegar.
**4** Arrange the salad leaves, beans, herbs and almonds on serving plates. Add the chicken livers, then spoon over the blueberries and pan juices. Serve at once, with warm bread.

### Chicken with pawpaw and rice noodles

This salad of hot, spicy chicken tossed with cool pawpaw, carrot and rice noodles epitomises the fresh tastes of Thai food.

225g/8oz skinless chicken breast fillets
100g/4oz rice vermicelli noodles
1 small carrot, cut into julienne
1 small pawpaw, peeled, seeded and diced
2 tbsp fresh coriander leaves, roughly torn
*for the marinade*
1 tbsp Thai fish sauce
1 tsp sesame oil
1 tsp Thai red curry paste
1 tsp clear honey
*for the dressing*
3 tbsp sunflower oil
1 tbsp caster sugar
3 tbsp lime juice
1 1/2 tbsp Thai fish sauce or soy sauce
1 red chilli, seeded and chopped

**1** First mix the marinade ingredients in a dish. Cut the chicken into strips, toss in the marinade and leave for 1 hour.
**2** Soak the noodles in boiling water for 4-5 minutes or according to pack instructions. Drain, dry well and place in a large bowl. Add the carrot, pawpaw and coriander.
**3** Mix the dressing ingredients together, toss half with the noodles and chill until required.
**4** Heat a wok or large frying pan until smoking. Add the chicken with the marinade and stir-fry over a high heat until cooked through. Divide the chicken and noodles between 4 bowls and serve drizzled with the remaining dressing.

### Griddled chicken and fig bruschetta

Ridged griddle pans give food an authentic char-grill flavour. Here chicken and figs are bathed in a sweetened balsamic sauce, then griddled until charred and tender.

2 large chicken breast fillets (with skin)
2 tbsp balsamic vinegar
1 tsp clear honey
2 tbsp extra virgin olive oil, plus extra for drizzling
salt and pepper
4 large, firm but ripe figs, halved
4 large slices rustic bread
1 peeled garlic clove, halved
4 slices prosciutto, or Parma ham
handful of rocket leaves

**1** Make several slashes through the skin side of each chicken breast. Mix together the balsamic vinegar, honey, oil and seasoning. Set aside half of the mixture; brush the rest over the chicken and figs.
**2** Heat a ridged griddle or heavy-based frying pan until smoking. Add the chicken and fry for 4-5 minutes each side until charred on the outside and cooked through. Lift out and leave to rest for 5 minutes. Add the figs to the pan and cook for 1-2 minutes until softened.
**3** Meanwhile, lightly toast the bread on both sides under the grill, then rub all over with garlic and drizzle with olive oil; keep warm. Grill the prosciutto for about 1 minute each side until crisp.
**4** Slice the chicken and arrange on the bruschetta with the figs, prosciutto and rocket leaves. Season and drizzle over the remaining balsamic sauce to serve.

Japanese chicken skewers (left);
Mini chicken kiev (below)

## Japanese chicken skewers

Poised to become the food for the millennium, Japanese cooking uses few ingredients, flavours are light, and dishes are healthy and often quick to prepare.

4 tbsp Japanese soy sauce
2 tbsp saké or medium dry sherry
1 tbsp caster sugar
8 boneless chicken thighs, skinned
*for the cucumber salad*
1 small cucumber
½ tsp salt
15g/½oz arame or hijiki seaweed (optional)
2.5cm/1in piece fresh root ginger, peeled
2 tbsp rice wine vinegar
1 tbsp caster sugar

**1** Put the soy sauce, saké or sherry and sugar in a small pan and heat gently until the sugar is dissolved. Set aside to cool.
**2** Cut the chicken into bite size cubes, place in a shallow dish, add the soy mixture and leave to marinate for about 2 hours. Pre-soak 4 bamboo skewers in cold water for 20 minutes.
**3** Thinly slice the cucumber lengthways, using a vegetable peeler. Sprinkle with the salt and leave to drain for 30 minutes. Rinse well, dry on kitchen paper and place in a bowl. (If using seaweed, pour on boiling water and soak for 10 minutes; drain, dry well and add to the cucumber.)
**4** Using a garlic crusher, squeeze out as much juice from the ginger as possible and mix the ginger juice with the vinegar and sugar. Add to the cucumber, toss well and set aside until required.
**5** Preheat the grill. Remove the chicken from the marinade and thread onto the bamboo skewers. Grill for 6-7 minutes, turning and basting with the marinade until the chicken is cooked through.
**6** Serve the chicken skewers hot with the cucumber salad.

**NOTE** Saké, or Japanese rice wine, is available from oriental food stores and wine merchants. If unavailable, medium dry sherry may be substituted.

## Mini chicken kiev

Serve these croquettes as a snack lunch or supper with a crisp salad, or as a starter.
*Serves 2 as a snack; 4 as a starter*

2 large skinless chicken breast fillets
4 tbsp seasoned flour
1 large egg, lightly beaten
115g/4oz dried plain breadcrumbs
1 tbsp sesame seeds
sunflower oil, for shallow frying
*for the spiced butter*
50g/2oz butter, at room temperature
1 small red chilli, seeded and diced
1/2 tsp ground cumin
1 tbsp chopped fresh coriander
grated rind and juice of 1/2 lime
salt and pepper
*to serve*
lime wedges

**1** Start by making the spiced butter. Place all the ingredients in a bowl and beat until well blended. Roll into a small log, wrap in foil and freeze for at least 1 hour.
**2** Lay each chicken breast flat and slice in half horizontally to give 4 thin escalopes. Place between sheets of plastic film and beat flat with a rolling pin.
**3** Cut the chilled butter into 4 slices. Place 1 slice in the middle of each escalope and fold the chicken over the butter to enclose and seal. Secure with cocktail sticks.
**4** Dust each parcel with flour, then dip into the egg. Mix the breadcrumbs and sesame seeds together. Carefully toss the chicken parcels in the crumb mixture to coat well. Chill for several hours, or overnight.
**5** Heat a shallow layer of oil in a frying pan and gently fry the parcels for 15-20 minutes, turning several times, to brown evenly. Drain on kitchen paper and remove the cocktail sticks. Serve with lime wedges.

## Smoked chicken and sweet onion wrap

The sandwich of the moment, 'the wrap' is simply a tasty filling wrapped up in a Mexican soft flour tortilla. Serve as a snack or substantial starter.

1 tbsp olive oil
1 large red onion, sliced
1 red chilli, seeded and sliced
1/2 tsp salt
50g/2oz redcurrant jelly
1 tbsp red wine vinegar
4 large flour tortillas
mizuna or other salad leaves
225g/8oz smoked chicken (or cooked breast fillet), shredded
1 small ripe avocado, peeled, stoned and sliced
4 tbsp crème fraîche

**1** Heat the oil in a frying pan, add the onion and chilli and fry over a medium heat for 10 minutes until browned. Add the salt, redcurrant jelly, vinegar and 1 tbsp water; cook gently for a further 15 minutes until thickened. Leave to cool.
**2** Lay the tortillas flat and top each one with a few salad leaves, the shredded chicken, avocado slices, a spoonful of the onion jam and a dollop of crème fraîche.
**3** Carefully fold the tortilla around the filling to form a cone shape and wrap up firmly. Serve at once or wrap securely in napkins or waxed paper and keep in a cool place until ready to serve.

## Roasted chicken and spinach wrap

Finely slice 225g/8oz ordinary roasted chicken. Top each of 4 large floured tortillas with a handful of spinach leaves, the chicken and 1/2 fresh peach, sliced. Add a spoonful of mayonnaise mixed with a little chopped fresh basil. Grate over fresh Parmesan to taste and wrap up in the tortilla.

## Duck and mango salad with star anise

If you cannot buy ground star anise, use a coffee or spice grinder to grind whole ones.

2 small duck breasts, each about 125g/4oz
juice of 1/2 orange
1 1/2 tbsp dark soy sauce
1 1/2 tbsp clear honey
1/2 tsp ground cinnamon
1/4 tsp ground star anise
125g/4oz mangetout
125g/4oz mixed salad leaves
1 small mango, peeled, stoned and sliced
1 tbsp sesame seeds, toasted
*for the dressing*
6 tbsp groundnut oil
4 tsp sesame oil
1 1/2 tbsp rice wine vinegar
2 tbsp chopped fresh coriander

**1** Pat the duck breasts dry with kitchen paper, then score the fat. Lay them in a shallow dish. Mix the orange juice, soy sauce, honey and spices together, pour over the duck and leave to marinate in a cool place for 30 minutes.
**2** Lift the duck breasts on to the grill rack, fat side down, reserving 2 tbsp marinade. Grill for 2 minutes, then turn and grill for a further 5-6 minutes or until the duck is crisp on the outside, but still slightly pink in the centre. Cover loosely with foil and leave to rest in a warm place for 5 minutes.
**3** Meanwhile, blanch the mangetout in lightly salted boiling water for 1 minute. Drain, refresh under cold water and pat dry.
**4** Whisk the dressing ingredients together in a bowl. Toss the salad leaves with a little of the dressing and arrange on plates.
**5** Put the reserved marinade and remaining dressing in a small pan. Bring to the boil; remove from heat.
**6** Thinly slice the duck breasts and arrange on the salad leaves with the mangetout and mango slices. Drizzle over the warm dressing and serve scattered with sesame seeds.

## Pork and liver pâté with apple relish

A simple pâté set under a layer of butter, served with a tangy apple and ginger relish.

100g/4oz chicken livers, diced
3 tbsp marsala
175g/6oz unsalted butter
3 shallots, finely chopped
2 garlic cloves, crushed
1 tbsp chopped fresh sage
$1/4$ tsp cayenne pepper
100ml/$3^1/2$fl oz pork or chicken stock
25g/1oz fresh breadcrumbs
225g/8oz cooked pork, diced
100g/4oz cooked ham, diced
salt and pepper
1 fresh sage sprig
*for the apple relish*
1 small onion, sliced
$1/2$ tsp grated fresh root ginger
1 large cooking apple, peeled, cored and diced
4 tbsp cider vinegar
4 tbsp water
5 tbsp light muscovado sugar

**1** Put the chicken livers and marsala in a bowl and leave to marinate for 15 minutes.
**2** Melt 50g/2oz of the butter in a frying pan, add the shallots, garlic and sage and fry gently for 5 minutes. Add the chicken livers and marsala. Fry over a high heat for 1 minute, then stir in the cayenne and stock. Simmer for 3-4 minutes until the livers are cooked. Leave to cool completely.
**3** Put the cooled mixture in a food processor with the breadcrumbs, pork and ham; work briefly to chop finely. Season to taste.
**4** Spoon the mixture into a pâté dish and smooth the surface. Melt remaining butter over a low heat, let cool for 5 minutes, then carefully pour over the pâté. Position the sage sprig on top, pressing gently down into the butter. Chill for several hours.
**5** Meanwhile, make the relish. Put all the ingredients in a pan and bring to the boil. Lower heat and simmer for 35-40 minutes until thickened. Cool and season to taste.
**6** Serve the pâté with the relish and crisp French sticks.

## Frisée, pancetta and aubergine salad

Crisp fried aubergine slices add a new dimension to this classic salad.

100g/4oz sliced smoked pancetta, derinded
4 tbsp olive oil
4 slices white bread, about 100g/4oz, crusts removed, cut into cubes
2 garlic cloves, crushed
vegetable oil, for deep-frying
1 aubergine, thinly sliced
100g/4oz frisée leaves
*for the dressing*
6 tbsp extra virgin olive oil
$1^1/2$ tbsp balsamic vinegar
salt and pepper

**1** Grill the pancetta for 2-3 minutes each side until crisp and golden. Cool, then crumble into bite size pieces.
**2** Heat the olive oil in a frying pan. Fry the bread cubes for a few minutes until golden all over, adding the garlic for the last minute. Drain on kitchen paper.
**3** Heat a 5cm/2in depth of oil in a heavy pan to 160C. Deep-fry the aubergine slices in batches for 1-2 minutes until crisp. Drain on kitchen paper; keep warm in the oven.
**4** Put the frisée in a large bowl and add the bacon and croûtons. Whisk the dressing ingredients together, then pour over the salad and toss lightly. Serve in individual bowls, topped with the aubergine crisps.

**NOTE** Smoked pancetta is available from Italian delicatessens and selected super-markets. If unobtainable, use lightly smoked bacon instead.

## Smoked duck antipasta

Thinly slice 1 large smoked duck breast and arrange on individual serving plates. Top each serving with a handful of mizuna or rocket leaves, a few bean sprouts, a few coriander leaves and a sprinkling of toasted sesame seeds. For the dressing, whisk together 2 tbsp sunflower oil, $1/2$ tsp sesame oil, 1 tbsp lime juice, $1^1/2$ tsp caster sugar, 1 finely chopped seeded red chilli and a pinch of salt. Drizzle the dressing over the salads to serve.

## Bresaola antipasta

Cured beef, crisp capers and sweet/sharp pecorino cheese combine beautifully in this Italian starter.

50g/2oz good quality, large salted capers
1 tbsp plain flour
3 tbsp olive oil
3 tbsp fresh parsley leaves
squeeze of lemon juice
16 slices good quality bresaola
85g/3oz mixed mâche and rocket leaves
25g/1oz pecorino cheese shavings
*for the dressing*
$1/2$ small shallot, finely chopped
1 tsp white wine vinegar
$1/2$ tsp Dijon mustard
$1/2$ tsp sugar
4 tbsp extra virgin olive oil
salt and pepper

**1** Soak the capers in cold water for 30 minutes. Drain and pat dry with kitchen paper, then dust with the flour.
**2** Heat the oil in a small frying pan and fry the capers for 2-3 minutes until crisp and golden. Add the parsley leaves and fry for 30 seconds. Drain on kitchen paper, then toss the mixture with the lemon juice.
**3** Whisk the dressing ingredients together in a bowl.
**4** Arrange the bresaola on serving plates. Top with the salad leaves, caper mixture and pecorino shavings. Drizzle with the dressing and serve.

## Spaghetti with broccoli and garlic breadcrumbs

Sprouting broccoli is ideal for this simple pasta dish. Otherwise you can use calabrese, cavolo nero or spring greens.

50g/2oz butter
2 garlic cloves, crushed
50g/2oz fresh white breadcrumbs
300g/10oz broccoli, divided into sprigs
salt and pepper
225g/8oz dried spaghetti
6 tbsp extra virgin olive oil
1 red chilli, seeded and diced
juice of 1/2 lemon
1 tbsp chopped fresh parsley
freshly grated Parmesan, to serve

**1** Melt the butter in a large frying pan. Add the garlic and breadcrumbs and stir-fry over a medium heat until golden. Remove and set aside.
**2** Add the broccoli to a pan of boiling water and blanch for 2 minutes; drain and refresh under cold water.
**3** Add the spaghetti to a large pan of boiling salted water and cook until *al dente*.
**4** Meanwhile, heat half the oil in a clean frying pan, add the chilli and broccoli and stir-fry for 3 minutes until tender. Add the lemon juice, remaining oil and parsley.
**5** Drain the spaghetti, retaining 4 tbsp cooking water. Add to the broccoli and toss over a low heat for 1 minute. Serve topped with the garlic breadcrumbs and a little grated Parmesan.

## Penne with roasted beetroot and feta

Sweet roasted beetroot and salty feta combine well in this pretty pasta dish. The rocket leaves just wilt as they are stirred into the hot pasta.

450g/1lb baby beetroot, trimmed (see note)
1 garlic clove, crushed
2 tbsp walnut oil, plus extra to drizzle
salt and pepper
300g/10oz dried penne or other pasta shapes
50g/2oz rocket leaves
100g/4oz feta cheese, crumbled
2 tbsp toasted pine nuts

**1** Preheat oven to 220C/fan oven 200C/Gas 7. Put the beetroot in a small roasting tin with the garlic, oil, salt and pepper. Add 2 tbsp water and roast in the oven for 50-60 minutes until tender. Keep warm.
**2** Add the pasta to a large pan of boiling salted water and cook until *al dente*.
**3** Drain the pasta thoroughly and immediately toss with the rocket leaves, roasted beetroot, pepper and a little extra walnut oil.
**4** Spoon the pasta mixture into warmed bowls and scatter over the crumbled feta and toasted pine nuts. Drizzle with walnut oil to serve.

**NOTE** To ensure the baby beets are similar in size, halve any larger ones.

## Macaroni bakes with balsamic sauce

Macaroni baked in a savoury cheese custard in timbales, then turned out and served with a piquant tomato sauce.

100g/4oz dried elbow macaroni
salt and pepper
300ml/1/2 pint double cream
50g/2oz gruyère, grated
25g/1oz Parmesan, freshly grated
3 eggs, beaten
*for the dressing*
1 shallot, finely diced
2 ripe tomatoes, peeled, seeded and diced
6 tbsp extra virgin olive oil
few fresh thyme leaves
1 tbsp balsamic vinegar

**1** Preheat oven to 180C/fan oven 160C/Gas 4. Oil and base line 4 timbales or ovenproof cups.
**2** Cook the pasta in boiling salted water until *al dente*. Drain thoroughly and divide between the timbales or cups.
**3** Slowly bring the cream to the boil in a pan. Remove from the heat, season and stir in the cheeses until melted. Stir into the beaten eggs. Pour the savoury custard over the macaroni.
**4** Stand the moulds in a roasting tin, half filled with boiling water. Bake for 25 minutes.
**5** Remove the moulds from the bain-marie; let rest for 5 minutes. Warm the dressing ingredients together in a small pan for 5 minutes or until the shallots are softened; season with salt and pepper to taste.
**6** Turn out the pasta moulds onto warmed plates and surround with the tomato dressing. Garnish with thyme to serve.

## Pea soup with minted gremolata

Gremolata – an Italian mix of mint, lemon zest and garlic – adds a real zing to this creamy, fresh tasting soup.

25g/1oz butter
1 onion, diced
1 potato, peeled and diced
450g/1lb shelled fresh peas (see note)
700ml/1¼ pints vegetable or chicken stock
2 fresh mint sprigs
salt and pepper
*for the gremolata*
2 tbsp shredded fresh mint leaves
grated rind of 1-2 lemons
1 garlic clove, crushed
*to serve*
extra virgin olive oil

**1** Melt the butter in a pan, add the onion and potato and fry gently for 10 minutes until softened and lightly golden. Add the peas, stock, mint and seasoning. Bring to the boil, lower the heat, cover and simmer gently for 20 minutes.
**2** Meanwhile, mix the gremolata ingredients together in a bowl.
**3** Transfer the soup to a blender and purée until very smooth. Return to the pan and heat through. Adjust the seasoning to taste.
**4** Spoon the soup into warm bowls and serve topped with the gremolata and a drizzle of olive oil.

**NOTE** Use frozen peas when fresh ones are out of season.

## Chilled tomato soup with Thai flavours

This adaptation of the classic Spanish gazpacho uses Thai ingredients. It is best appreciated during the summer months when the heat demands a cooling starter, and tomatoes are full of flavour. *Serves 6*

700g/1½lb ripe tomatoes
2 garlic cloves, crushed
1 tsp grated fresh root ginger
4 lime leaves, shredded
2-4 red chillies, seeded and diced
2 spring onions, trimmed and chopped
2 tbsp chopped fresh coriander
300ml/½ pint iced water
150ml/¼ pint tomato juice
2 tbsp light soy sauce
2 tbsp rice wine vinegar
1 tbsp sesame oil
salt and pepper
*to serve*
ice cubes
torn coriander leaves
sesame oil

**1** Roughly chop the tomatoes and place in a blender with the garlic, ginger, lime leaves, chillies, spring onions and coriander. Purée until fairly smooth.
**2** Transfer to a large bowl and whisk in the water, tomato juice, soy sauce, wine vinegar and sesame oil. Season with salt and pepper to taste. Cover and chill in the refrigerator for several hours.
**3** Serve with ice cubes, garnished with coriander and a drizzle of sesame oil.

## Prawn wonton soup

You can buy the wonton wrappers for this fragrant soup from oriental food stores.

1.2 litres/2 pints vegetable stock
4 red chillies, bruised
2 slices fresh root ginger
2 tbsp rice vinegar
2 tbsp light soy sauce
2 tsp sugar
1 tsp sesame oil
*for the wontons*
175g/6oz small raw prawns, peeled
125g/4oz fresh cod fillet, skinned and diced
2 spring onions, chopped
1 garlic clove, crushed
grated rind and juice of ½ lime
1 tbsp chopped fresh coriander leaves
salt and pepper
20 wonton wrappers
1 small egg, beaten
*for the garnish*
coriander sprigs

**1** Put the stock into a pan with the chillies, ginger, rice vinegar, soy sauce, sugar and sesame oil. Bring to the boil, cover and simmer gently for about 20 minutes.
**2** Devein the prawns, wash and pat dry. Put in a food processor with the cod, spring onions, garlic, lime rind and juice, and the coriander. Purée until fairly smooth, then season with a little salt and pepper.
**3** Brush each wonton wrapper with a little beaten egg and place a spoonful of the prawn mixture in the centre. Draw up the edges over the filling and pinch together at the top to form small parcels.
**4** Drop the wontons into the soup, return to a rolling boil, then simmer for 3-4 minutes.
**5** Ladle the soup into warmed bowls and serve garnished with coriander sprigs.

## Mediterranean fish soup

Parmesan crisps give this version of a classic *soupe de poisson* a new twist. *Serves 4-6*

900g/2lb mixed fish, such as monkfish,
red mullet and mackerel, cleaned
225g/8oz raw tiger prawns
6 tbsp extra virgin olive oil
2 red onions, roughly chopped
2 garlic cloves, crushed
2 carrots, diced
1 celery stick, diced
4 tbsp brandy
1.2 litres/2 pints water
400g can chopped tomatoes
4 fresh rosemary sprigs
2 fresh bay leaves
¼ tsp saffron strands
salt and pepper
*for the Parmesan crisps*
100g/4oz Parmesan, freshly grated
*to finish*
4-6 tbsp crème fraîche (optional)
paprika, for sprinkling

**1** Preheat oven to 200C/fan oven 180C/Gas 6. Wash and dry the fish and cut into chunks, discarding the heads. Devein the prawns, and rinse well.
**2** Heat 3 tbsp of the oil in a frying pan and fry the fish chunks and prawns in batches over a high heat until golden. Using a slotted spoon, transfer to a large saucepan.
**3** Heat the remaining oil in the frying pan. Add the onions, garlic, carrots and celery, and fry gently for 10 minutes. Pour in the brandy and let bubble until evaporated.
**4** Add the sautéed vegetables to the fish, with the water, tomatoes, herbs and saffron. Slowly bring to the boil, skim the surface, then cover and simmer for 30 minutes.
**5** Meanwhile, make the Parmesan crisps. Sprinkle 4 small circles of grated cheese on a well oiled non-stick baking sheet. Bake for 3-4 minutes until crisp and golden. Leave on the baking sheet for 5 minutes, then carefully peel off using a palette knife. Repeat to make 16 crisps in total.
**6** Purée the soup, including the seafood, in batches in a blender or food processor until smooth. Pass through a fine sieve into a clean pan. Season with salt and pepper to taste and heat through.
**7** Ladle the soup into warmed bowls. Drizzle with crème fraîche if wished, and sprinkle with paprika. Serve with the Parmesan crisps.

## Fennel broth with anchovy croûtes

A fragrant fennel and fish broth topped with savoury anchovy croûtes. *Serves 6*

2 tbsp olive oil
1 onion, sliced
4 garlic cloves, crushed
grated rind of ¹/₂ orange
1 tbsp chopped fresh thyme
2 fennel bulbs, thinly sliced
2 tbsp Pernod
400g can chopped tomatoes
900ml/1¹/₂ pints fish stock
*for the croûtes*
6 thin slices French bread
50g/2oz can anchovy fillets, drained and chopped
25g/1oz pine nuts
1 garlic clove, crushed
2 tsp lemon juice
pepper
*to finish*
4 tbsp crème fraîche
fennel fronds or dill, to garnish

**1** Preheat oven to 200C/fan oven 180C/Gas 6. Heat the olive oil in a saucepan, add the onion, garlic, orange rind, thyme and fennel, and fry gently for 10 minutes until the onion is softened and lightly golden. Add the Pernod and allow to bubble until it is evaporated.
**2** Add the chopped tomatoes and stock, bring to the boil, cover and simmer gently for 30 minutes.
**3** Meanwhile make the croûtes. Put the slices of French bread on a baking sheet and bake for 10 minutes until crisp and golden. Set aside.
**4** Put the anchovy fillets, pine nuts, garlic, lemon juice and pepper in a blender or food processor and purée until fairly smooth. Spread the anchovy paste on top of the croûtes.
**5** Spoon the fennel soup into warmed bowls and top each serving with an anchovy croûte. Add a spoonful of crème fraîche and garnish with a sprinkling of chopped fennel fronds or dill.

## Vietnamese tamarind and prawn soup

350g/12oz small raw tiger prawns
900ml/1¹/₂ pints vegetable stock
2 lemon grass stalks, roughly chopped
2 slices fresh galangal or root ginger
2 shallots, diced
2 red chillies
50g/2oz flat rice noodles
1 celery stick, sliced
1 tbsp caster sugar
1 tbsp Thai fish sauce
2 tbsp tamarind juice (see note)
1 tbsp each chopped fresh coriander, mint and basil
4 cooked prawns in shells, to garnish

**1** Remove, rinse and reserve the heads and shells from the prawns. De-vein the prawns and set aside. Put the prawn shells and heads in a pan with the stock, lemon grass, galangal or ginger, shallots and 1 whole chilli. Bring to the boil, cover and simmer gently for 30 minutes. Strain the flavoured stock into a clean pan.
**2** Put the noodles in a bowl, pour on boiling water and leave to soak for 5 minutes.
**3** Meanwhile, seed and chop the remaining chilli. Add to the stock with the prawns, celery, sugar, fish sauce and tamarind juice. Simmer gently for 2-3 minutes until the prawns are cooked. Stir in the herbs.
**4** Drain the noodles thoroughly and divide between warm soup bowls. Spoon the soup over the noodles and garnish with the whole prawns to serve.

**NOTE** Dried tamarind pulp is available from Indian food stores and some supermarkets. To make tamarind juice, dissolve 50g/2oz tamarind pulp in 150ml/¹/₄ pint boiling water, then press through a sieve.

## Roasted tomato soup with ricotta

Roasted tomatoes give this hearty Italian tomato soup a great depth of flavour. *Serves 6*

8 tbsp olive oil
1 onion, finely chopped
900g/2lb ripe tomatoes, halved
12 garlic cloves, peeled
15g/¹/₂oz fresh mint leaves
1 tsp caster sugar
salt and pepper
600ml/1 pint vegetable stock
100g/4oz dried pastina (small soup pasta)
*for the garnish*
50g/2oz ricotta cheese, crumbled
mint leaves
olive oil, to drizzle

**1** Preheat oven to 220C/fan oven 200C/Gas 7. Heat half the oil in a shallow flameproof casserole and fry the onion for 10 minutes. Add the tomatoes, garlic cloves, mint, sugar, salt and pepper. Bring to the boil.
**2** Transfer to the oven and roast, uncovered, for 20 minutes. Let cool slightly, then purée the tomato mixture with the remaining oil in a blender or food processor; return to the pan.
**3** Stir in the stock and bring to the boil. Add the pasta and simmer gently for 10 minutes until *al dente*. Adjust the seasoning to taste.
**4** Spoon into warmed bowls and top with crumbled ricotta, mint leaves and a generous drizzling of olive oil. Serve with Italian bread.

# flavourful pasta

**Today's ultimate convenience food**, pasta is quick to cook, sustaining and endlessly versatile. Take **a fresh look at flavouring pasta** with this collection of inventive recipes. For ultra fast suppers, turn to our **fresh tasting no-cook sauces** or great **new flavours for spaghetti**. Prepare ahead pasta dishes are perfect for family suppers and casual entertaining. Make the most of those **colourful, flavoured pastas** on sale in supermarkets and delicatessens. Create **gourmet pasta dishes** for special occasions and, when you have a little time to spare, try our foolproof **homemade pasta** - it has a **sublime taste and texture**.

## Seafood spaghetti

Serve this luxurious pasta dish with a leafy green salad, dressed with lemon juice and light olive oil. *Serves 4-6*

1kg/2lb 4oz mussels in shells, cleaned
250g/9oz peeled, raw tiger prawns
25g/1oz butter
100ml/3½fl oz white wine
1 tsp finely grated lemon rind
2 tsp mild curry paste
300ml/½ pint single cream
175g/6oz smoked salmon trimmings, sliced
salt and pepper
500g/1lb 2oz dried spaghetti
lemon wedges, to serve

**1** Discard any damaged mussels or open ones that do not close when tapped sharply. Halve the prawns lengthwise and de-vein.
**2** Melt the butter in a large pan with the wine and 4 tbsp water. Add the mussels, cover tightly and cook briskly for 4 minutes, or until the shells open, shaking the pan from time to time. Discard any mussels which have not opened.
**3** Lift out the mussels with a slotted spoon and set aside 12 for the garnish. Remove the rest of the mussels from their shells.
**4** Add the prawns to the pan. Cook, stirring, for 4-5 minutes until they turn pink. Stir in the lemon rind, curry paste and cream, then add the smoked salmon and shelled mussels. Heat through gently and season with salt and pepper to taste.
**5** Meanwhile, cook the spaghetti in a large pan of boiling salted water until *al dente*. Drain and toss with the seafood sauce. Serve immediately, garnished with the reserved mussels and accompanied by lemon wedges.

**NOTE** Always add pasta to a large saucepan containing plenty of boiling water. Cook at a fast boil to prevent sticking.

## Spaghetti with leeks and pancetta

A deliciously rich, creamy dish. *Serves 4-6*

2 tbsp olive oil
2 medium leeks, thinly sliced
175g/6oz pancetta, thinly sliced
100ml/3½fl oz white wine
300ml/½ pint single cream
500g/1lb 2oz dried spaghetti
3 tbsp freshly grated Parmesan

**1** Heat the oil in a pan and fry the leeks gently for 3-4 minutes to soften. Add the pancetta and cook for 4-5 minutes until beginning to brown.
**2** Add the wine, stir to deglaze, and bring nearly to the boil. Add the cream and warm through.
**3** Meanwhile, cook the spaghetti in a large pan of boiling salted water until *al dente*. Drain and toss with the sauce and Parmesan to serve.

## Spaghetti with aubergines

Serve with a rocket salad. *Serves 4-6*

900g/2lb aubergines, cut into 1cm/½in dice
salt and pepper
5 tbsp olive oil
2-3 tbsp crushed sun-dried tomatoes in oil
1 tbsp finely shredded fresh basil
500g/1lb 2oz dried spaghetti
75g/2½oz pine nuts, toasted
freshly grated pecorino cheese or
Parmesan, to serve

**1** Put the aubergines in a colander and sprinkle generously with salt. Leave to drain for 30 minutes. Rinse well and pat dry on a tea towel.
**2** Heat the oil in a pan and fry the aubergines for about 15 minutes, until tender and brown. Add the sun-dried tomatoes, basil and pepper.
**3** Meanwhile, cook the spaghetti in a large pan of boiling salted water until *al dente*. Drain and toss with the aubergine mixture and pine nuts. Serve at once, with grated pecorino or Parmesan.

**NOTE** It is worth salting the aubergines for this dish to draw out their bitter juices.

## Walnut and mixed olive spaghetti

*Serves 4-6*

230g jar mixed olives in extra virgin olive oil
75g/2½oz walnuts (ideally freshly shelled)
juice of ½ orange (3-4 tbsp)
500g/1lb 2oz dried wholewheat spaghetti
salt and pepper (black or 5 pepper mix)
freshly grated Parmesan, to serve

**1** Strain the olives and reserve the oil. Stone and slice the olives. Grate the walnuts, using a mouli grater or food processor.
**2** For the dressing, mix together the orange juice and olive oil.
**3** Cook the spaghetti in a large pan of boiling salted water until *al dente*. Return to the warm pan and add the olive slices, grated walnuts, dressing and seasoning; toss lightly together. Serve at once, with grated Parmesan and a salad.

## Spaghetti with oven-dried tomatoes, mint and peas

Oven-dried cherry tomatoes bring a sweet intensity to this dish. *Serves 4-6*

500g/1lb 2oz dried spaghetti
salt and pepper
450g/1lb frozen or fresh peas or petits pois
1 batch oven-dried tomatoes (see below)
2 tbsp finely shredded fresh mint

**1** Cook the spaghetti in a large pan of boiling salted water until *al dente*.
**2** Meanwhile, cook the peas in a separate pan of boiling water until tender.
**3** Drain the pasta and peas, return to the warm pasta pan and add the oven-dried tomatoes with 2-3 tbsp of the oil, and the mint. Toss lightly, season and serve.

**OVEN-DRIED TOMATOES** Preheat oven to 130C/fan oven 110C/Gas 1. Lay 400g/14oz halved cherry tomatoes on a non-stick baking tray, cut-side up. Sprinkle with salt, pepper and sugar. Bake for 1½ hours or until dry but not brown. Cool slightly, then put into a bowl and add extra virgin olive oil to cover. When cold, store in jars covered with a layer of olive oil. Use as required.

## Tuna tapenade

175g/6oz black olives (preferably Greek), stoned
2 tbsp capers in brine, rinsed
10 canned anchovy fillets in oil, drained
125g/4$^1$/$_2$oz canned tuna fish in oil, drained
100ml/3$^1$/$_2$fl oz olive oil
1 canned red pepper (capsicum), rinsed, seeded and diced
2 tbsp shredded fresh basil
lemon juice, to taste
salt and pepper
450g/1lb dried pasta shapes, such as ballerine, radiattore, casarecce, capelletti

**1** Chop the olives, capers, anchovies and tuna in a food processor.
**2** With the motor running, add the oil in a steady stream and mix briefly.
**3** Transfer to a bowl and stir in the diced pepper and chopped basil. Flavour with lemon juice and season with salt and pepper to taste.
**4** Bring a large pan of salted water to the boil. Add the pasta and cook until *al dente*. Drain, keeping back 2 tbsp water in the pan. Immediately toss the pasta with the sauce. Cover and leave to stand for 2-3 minutes before serving.

**NOTE** The no-cook sauces featured on this page all rely on the heat of the pasta to melt, wilt or simply warm the ingredients through. After dressing the pasta it is important to cover and leave for a few minutes, to warm the sauce and develop the flavours.

## Mediterranean sauce

175g/6oz soft fresh goat's cheese
2 tbsp capers in vinegar, drained
225g/8oz mixed green and black olives, stoned and chopped
8 sun-dried tomatoes in oil, drained and chopped
1 tsp dried oregano (preferably freeze-dried)
salt and pepper
450g/1lb dried pasta shapes, such as ballerine, radiattore, casarecce, capelletti

**1** In a bowl, mix the goat's cheese with the capers, olives, sun-dried tomatoes, oregano and seasoning to taste.
**2** Cook the pasta in a large pan of salted water until *al dente*. Drain, keeping back 2 tbsp water in the pan. Immediately toss the pasta with the sauce. Cover and leave to stand for 3 minutes before serving.

## Cherry tomato and basil sauce

450g/1lb ripe cherry tomatoes, quartered
2 garlic cloves, finely chopped
4 tbsp shredded fresh basil
150ml/$^1$/$_4$ pint extra virgin olive oil
salt and pepper
450g/1lb dried chunky pasta shapes, such as rigatoni, penne, farfalle
100g/4oz feta cheese, thinly sliced

**1** In a bowl, mix the tomatoes with the garlic, basil, olive oil and seasoning. Cover and leave to infuse for at least 30 minutes; do not refrigerate.
**2** Bring a large pan of salted water to the boil. Add the pasta and cook until *al dente*. Drain, keeping back 2 tbsp water in the pan. Immediately toss the pasta with the sauce. Cover with a lid and leave to stand for 3 minutes.
**3** Remove the lid, stir and serve topped with slices of feta.

## Walnut, parsley and gorgonzola sauce

2 slices wholemeal bread, crusts removed
200ml/7fl oz milk
225g/8oz walnut pieces
1 garlic clove, crushed
125g/4$^1$/$_2$oz Gorgonzola cheese, in pieces
4 tbsp extra virgin olive oil
100ml/3$^1$/$_2$fl oz crème fraîche
6 tbsp chopped fresh parsley
salt and pepper
450g/1lb dried ribbon pasta, such as pappardelle, tagliatelle, or fettucine

**1** Preheat oven to 190C/fan oven 170C/Gas 5. Soak the bread in the milk for 10 minutes or until all the milk is absorbed.
**2** Spread the walnuts on a baking sheet and toast in the oven for 5 minutes. Transfer to a plate and allow to cool.
**3** Put the soaked bread, walnuts, garlic, gorgonzola and olive oil in a food processor and work until almost smooth.
**4** Transfer to a bowl and stir in the crème fraîche and chopped parsley. Season generously with pepper, and a little salt if required.
**5** Bring a large pan of salted water to the boil. Add the pasta and cook until *al dente*. Drain, keeping back 2 tbsp water in the pan. Immediately toss the pasta with the sauce. Cover with a lid and leave to stand for 3 minutes before serving.

### Pasta with chilli pesto

This robust pasta dish is spiked with a fiery homemade chilli pesto – to delicious effect. Store any leftover pesto in a jar, covered with a layer of olive oil, in the fridge for up to 2 weeks. It is excellent with grilled chicken.

1 large red pepper
50g/2oz fresh basil leaves
1 garlic clove, crushed
2 ripe tomatoes, skinned
2 tbsp pine nuts
3 tbsp sun-dried tomato paste
3 tbsp tomato purée
1 tsp mild chilli powder
few drops of Tabasco sauce
50g/2oz Parmesan, freshly grated
150ml/¼ pint light olive oil
450g/1lb dried casarecce or spaghetti

**1** Grill the pepper, turning occasionally, until charred. Cool slightly, then skin, halve and de-seed. Place in a food processor with the other ingredients, except the oil and pasta. Work until almost smooth. Turn into a bowl and stir in the oil.
**2** Bring a large pan of salted water to the boil. Add the pasta and cook until *al dente*.
**3** Drain the pasta, keeping back 2 tbsp water in the pan. Immediately toss with chilli pesto to taste, allowing approximately 2 tbsp per serving.

**NOTE** Holding back a few tablespoonfuls of the cooking water with the pasta helps the sauce to cling to the pasta and adds a certain creaminess.

### Pasta with bacon and wilted spinach

Bacon, garlic and spinach are mellowed in a cream sauce. Don't overcook the fresh spinach – it should still be vivid green and full of flavour.

450g/1lb dried spaghetti, tagliatelle or linguine
salt and pepper
4 tbsp olive oil
8 slices pancetta or unsmoked streaky bacon, chopped
2 garlic cloves, finely chopped
900g/2lb spinach leaves, stalks removed
150ml/¼ pint double cream
freshly grated nutmeg
3 tbsp pine nuts, toasted

**1** Bring a large pan of salted water to the boil. Add the pasta and cook until *al dente*.
**2** Meanwhile heat the oil in a large pan, add the pancetta or bacon and fry until just turning golden. Add the garlic and cook for 1 minute.
**3** Stir in the spinach and cook over a high heat for a few minutes or until the leaves are just wilted. Pour in the cream, turning the spinach to ensure it is well coated. Season with salt, pepper and nutmeg to taste. Heat until boiling.
**4** Drain the pasta, keeping back 2 tbsp water in the pan. Immediately toss the pasta with the hot sauce. Serve sprinkled with the pine nuts.

### Pasta with mushrooms, thyme and grated courgettes

Mushrooms and courgettes are perfect partners. Sautéed with garlic and thyme, they make a wonderful aromatic sauce.

450g/1lb dried curly pasta shapes, such as spiralli or casarecce, or shells
salt and pepper
50g/2oz butter
1 garlic clove, chopped
4-6 large flat mushrooms, sliced
1 tbsp chopped fresh thyme
4 small courgettes, coarsely grated
pecorino cheese or Parmesan shavings, to serve

**1** Bring a large pan of salted water to the boil. Add the pasta and cook until *al dente*.
**2** Meanwhile, melt the butter in a frying pan. Add the garlic and cook gently for 2-3 minutes until golden.
**3** Add the sliced mushrooms and fry for about 2 minutes until softened and beginning to brown.
**4** Stir in the thyme and grated courgettes. Increase the heat and cook, stirring constantly, for about 5 minutes or until the courgettes are tender. Season with salt and pepper to taste.
**5** Drain the pasta, keeping back 2 tbsp water in the pan. Immediately toss the pasta with the sauce and serve topped with pecorino or Parmesan shavings.

**NOTE** For speed, use a food processor fitted with a coarse grating disc to prepare the courgettes, or dice them if you prefer.

**VARIATION** Use 175g (6oz) button or chestnut mushrooms instead of flat mushrooms.

## Pasta with avocado and coriander pesto

This wonderfully pungent pesto sauce is particularly good with buckwheat noodles.

2 small, ripe avocados
3 spring onions, finely chopped
50g/2oz fresh coriander leaves
1 tbsp lime juice
few drops of Jalapeno or Tabasco sauce
2 tbsp crème fraîche
1 large tomato, skinned and diced
salt and pepper
450g/1lb dried buckwheat noodles, or whole-wheat spaghetti
coriander leaves, to garnish

**1** Halve, stone and peel the avocados. Put them in a food processor with the spring onions, coriander leaves, lime juice and Jalapeno or Tabasco sauce. Pulse until the ingredients are evenly mixed and finely chopped.
**2** Turn into a bowl and stir in the crème fraîche, then the diced tomato. Season with salt and pepper to taste.
**3** Bring a large pan of salted water to the boil. Add the noodles or spaghetti and cook until *al dente*.
**4** Drain the pasta, keeping back 2 tbsp water in the pan. Immediately toss with the sauce and serve scattered with coriander leaves.

**NOTE** In general, chunky sauces are best with chunky pasta, such as spirals, penne, shells or rigatoni. Soft, fluid sauces suit long pasta, such as noodles or spaghetti.

## Pasta with roast peppers and shallots

For this chunky sauce, shallots are roasted until lightly caramelised and mixed with smoky roasted peppers. For a treat, serve topped with a dollop of mascarpone flavoured with cracked black peppercorns.

2 red peppers
8 shallots, thickly sliced
4 tbsp olive oil
450g/1lb dried chunky pasta shapes, such as rigatoni or shells
salt and pepper
2 tbsp balsamic vinegar
freshly grated Parmesan, to serve

**1** Preheat oven to 200C/fan oven 180C/ Gas 6. Place the whole red peppers and sliced shallots in a small roasting tin and drizzle with the oil. Turn the peppers and shallots to coat with the oil.
**2** Roast in the oven for 10-15 minutes until the shallots are golden brown. Using a slotted spoon, transfer the shallots to a saucepan.
**3** Roast the peppers, turning occasionally, for a further 15-20 minutes until charred. Leave until cool enough to handle, then skin. Halve the peppers, discard the seeds and cut the flesh into strips. Add the pepper strips and any juices to the shallots.
**4** Bring a large pan of salted water to the boil. Add the pasta and cook until *al dente*.
**5** Meanwhile, reheat the shallot mixture and stir in the balsamic vinegar. Cook over a high heat for 1 minute. Season with salt and pepper to taste.
**6** Drain the pasta, keeping back 2 tbsp water in the pan. Immediately toss with the sauce. Serve accompanied by freshly grated Parmesan.

## Pasta with garlic and anchovy sauce

Pasta in a classic tomato sauce infused with the savoury saltiness of melted anchovies. Serve topped with a tangle of peppery rocket for contrast.

3 tbsp olive oil
3 garlic cloves, chopped
1 small can anchovies in oil, drained and chopped
400g can chopped tomatoes
pepper
450g/1lb dried bucatini, macaroni or pasta shapes
10 large fresh basil leaves, shredded
100g/4oz fresh rocket leaves

**1** Heat the olive oil in a saucepan. Add the garlic and fry until just colouring. Stir in the anchovies and cook gently until they begin to dissolve.
**2** Stir in the chopped tomatoes and bring to the boil. Season to taste with pepper (salt won't be needed as the anchovies are quite salty). Cover and simmer gently for 10 minutes.
**3** Meanwhile, bring a large pan of salted water to the boil. Add the pasta and cook until *al dente*. Drain the pasta, keeping back 2 tbsp water in the pan.
**4** Stir the shredded basil into the tomato and anchovy sauce. Immediately add to the pasta and toss well. Serve each portion topped with a tangle of rocket leaves.

## Smoked haddock frittata

Smoked haddock, mellow Churnton cheese and a hint of onion give this omelette a wonderful flavour while the pasta makes it a little more substantial.

40g/1½oz butter
300g/10oz skinless smoked haddock fillet
8 large eggs
4 tbsp milk
salt and pepper
2 tbsp finely chopped spring onion
2 tbsp snipped chives
85g/3oz cooked pasta twists or shells
(ie 25g/1oz dried weight)
100g/4oz mature Churnton cheese or
Cheddar, grated
snipped chives, to garnish

**1** Heat half the butter in a large frying pan. Add the smoked haddock, cover tightly and cook for 3 minutes. Lift the fish out of the pan and flake roughly.
**2** Beat the eggs with the milk, seasoning, spring onion, chives and the cooked pasta. Preheat the grill.
**3** Melt the remaining butter in the frying pan, then pour in the egg mixture and scatter over half of the flaked fish. Move the mixture round the pan with a wooden spatula until half set.
**4** Remove from the heat and top with the remaining smoked haddock. Sprinkle with the cheese and extra chives. Grill for about 2 minutes until set and puffy. Serve with a salad and crusty bread.

**NOTE** Make sure you use a cast-iron pan or other frying pan which is suitable for placing under the grill.

**VARIATION** Replace the smoked haddock with a 200g/7oz packet of wafer-thin smoked ham. Scrunch up the ham and scatter over the frittata before sprinkling with cheese.

## Buckwheat noodles with Savoy cabbage

Japanese noodles tossed with pancetta and cabbage in a creamy cheese sauce.

2 tbsp olive oil
125g/4¹/₂oz pancetta or lightly smoked bacon, diced
2 red onions, sliced
225g/8oz Savoy cabbage, shredded
3 garlic cloves, chopped
225g/8oz buckwheat (soba) noodles, or egg tagliatelle
salt and pepper
250g tub mascarpone
140g/5oz dolcelatte cheese, diced

**1** Heat the oil in a large deep frying pan, add the pancetta or bacon and onions and fry for 5 minutes, stirring occasionally.
**2** Stir in the cabbage and garlic, cover and cook for 8-10 minutes until the cabbage is tender.
**3** Meanwhile, cook the noodles in a large pan of boiling salted water until *al dente*.
**4** Drain the noodles thoroughly and toss with the cabbage; season. Add the mascarpone and dolcelatte and heat gently until melted to a creamy sauce. Serve immediately.

## Farfalle with potted shrimps

This simple dish is an ideal speedy supper for one. Accompany with a tomato and avocado salad, and warm bread. *Serves 1*

85g/3oz dried farfalle or other pasta shapes
salt and pepper
55g tub potted shrimps (see note)
freshly grated nutmeg (optional)
1 tbsp finely chopped fresh parsley

**1** Cook the pasta in a large pan of boiling salted water until *al dente*.
**2** Drain the pasta, return to the pan and toss in the shrimps with their butter. Warm through until the butter melts.
**3** Add grated nutmeg to taste, toss in the chopped parsley and serve.

**NOTE** Potted shrimps are packed in butter flavoured with cayenne, nutmeg and mace. For additional spice, add extra nutmeg.

## Spaghetti with pepper butter sauce

Red peppers, whizzed in a food processor, give this sauce a wonderful silky texture and sweet flavour, while Tabasco adds a touch of heat. Serve with a rocket salad.

3 large red peppers
250g/9oz dried spaghetti
salt and pepper
85g/3oz butter
dash of Tabasco sauce
2 tbsp chopped fresh basil
4 tbsp milk
shredded basil leaves, to garnish
freshly grated Parmesan cheese, to serve

**1** Peel the red peppers, using a potato peeler, then halve and remove the core and seeds. Place the pepper flesh in a food processor and work to a purée.
**2** Cook the spaghetti in a large pan of boiling salted water until *al dente*.
**3** Meanwhile, transfer the red pepper purée to a saucepan and add the butter, Tabasco, chopped basil and milk. Season generously with salt and pepper. Cover and simmer gently, stirring frequently, for 8-10 minutes.
**4** Drain the spaghetti and return to the warm pan. Add the pepper butter sauce and toss to mix.
**5** Divide the pasta between warmed serving plates. Sprinkle with basil and serve with grated Parmesan.

## All-in-one curried noodles

Tiger prawns tossed with noodles and plenty of vegetables in a curried coconut sauce.

175g/6oz rice stick or egg thread noodles
1 tbsp sunflower oil
1 red pepper, cored, seeded and cut into thin sticks
1 red onion, cut into wedges
100g/4oz baby corn cobs, halved lengthways
100g/4oz sugar snaps, halved
100g/4oz close cup mushrooms, halved
2 tbsp madras curry paste
400g can coconut milk
2 tbsp light soy sauce
200g/7oz extra large cooked tiger prawns (thawed and dried if frozen)
4 tbsp chopped fresh coriander
coriander sprigs, to garnish

**1** Put the noodles in a bowl, pour on boiling water and leave to soak for 5 minutes or according to packet directions.
**2** Heat the oil in a large pan or wok. Add the red pepper and onion and stir-fry for a few minutes until starting to soften.
**3** Toss in the baby corn and stir-fry for 2 minutes, then add the sugar snaps and mushrooms, and stir-fry for a further few minutes.
**4** Stir in the curry paste, then pour in the coconut milk and soy sauce. Add the prawns and chopped coriander; toss well. Divide the noodles between warmed bowls, add the curried sauce and serve garnished with coriander.

**NOTE** Baby corn cobs and sugar snaps are available in 200g/7oz mixed packets from some supermarkets.

## Individual salmon lasagnes

Creamed horseradish marries this flavour combination of fresh and smoked salmon perfectly. Don't overcook the lasagnes or the salmon will toughen and spoil the dish.

850ml/1½ pints milk
85g/3oz butter
85g/3oz plain flour
1 fresh bay leaf
salt and pepper
2 tbsp creamed horseradish
squeeze of lemon juice (optional)
500g/1lb 2oz boneless skinless salmon fillets, cut into small cubes
8 sheets dried (no-need to pre-cook) lasagne
6 smoked salmon slices
*for the topping*
85g/3oz Emmental cheese, grated

**1** Pour the milk into a pan. Add the butter, flour, bay leaf and seasoning. Whisk over a medium heat, until the sauce is smooth and thickened.
**2** Pour half of the sauce into a bowl and add the horseradish with a squeeze of lemon juice to taste. Stir in the fresh salmon cubes; set aside. Leave the bay leaf in the remaining sauce, to infuse.
**3** Par-cook the lasagne in a large pan of boiling salted water with 2 tbsp oil added for 5 minutes (to shorten the baking time).
**4** Spoon a third of the salmon mixture into the base of four individual pie dishes, cover with a sheet of lasagne, then spoon over the rest of the salmon mixture.
**5** Cover with the remaining lasagne sheets and top with a slice of smoked salmon. Discard the bay leaf, then spoon the sauce over the smoked salmon.
**6** Halve the other 2 smoked salmon slices and place one piece on each portion. Scatter with the cheese. If preparing ahead, cover and chill for up to 24 hours.
**7** To serve, preheat oven to 190C/fan oven 170C/Gas 5. Bake the lasagnes for 30 minutes until bubbling. If necessary, brown under the grill. Serve with a fennel, baby spinach and orange salad.

**NOTE** Providing frozen salmon isn't used, the lasagnes may be frozen before baking.

## Fusilli lunghi with peppers and anchovy olives

Anchovy olives provide a piquant flavour, while mascarpone and Parmesan melt to an irresistible creamy topping.

3 tbsp olive oil
1 large onion, thinly sliced
3 garlic cloves, thinly sliced
2 red peppers, cored, seeded and sliced
3 courgettes, cut into sticks
two 400g cans peeled tomatoes in rich juice
2 tbsp chopped fresh basil
salt and pepper
300g/10oz dried fusilli lunghi, or lasagnette
100g/4oz anchovy stuffed olives, halved
*for the topping*
250g tub mascarpone
50g/2oz fresh Parmesan, coarsely grated
25g/1oz pine nuts
basil leaves, to garnish

**1** Heat the oil in a large frying pan and fry the onion until golden. Add the garlic, peppers and courgettes, and stir-fry over a high heat for 5 minutes.
**2** Stir in the tomatoes with their juice and the chopped basil. Season and simmer gently for 10 minutes until the vegetables are tender.
**3** Meanwhile, cook the pasta in a large pan of boiling salted water until *al dente*. Drain the pasta and refresh under cold running water; drain thoroughly.
**4** Stir the pasta into the tomato mixture with the olives. Turn in to a large ovenproof dish and top with spoonfuls of mascarpone. Sprinkle with the grated Parmesan and pine nuts. If preparing ahead, cover with plastic film and chill.
**5** To serve, preheat the oven to 200C/fan oven 180C/Gas 6. Bake the pasta dish for 30 minutes or until bubbling. Let stand for a few minutes, then scatter with basil leaves and serve with crusty bread.

**NOTE** For a vegetarian dish use pimento rather than anchovy stuffed olives.

## Pork and prosciutto meatballs with madeira

These meatballs are surprisingly quick to make and taste superb.

350g/12oz pork mince
70g/2½oz prosciutto, or Parma ham
1 large garlic clove, crushed
25g/1oz white bread
salt and pepper
1 medium egg
2 tbsp sunflower oil
4 tbsp Madeira
125ml/4fl oz pork or chicken stock
6 sage leaves, shredded
150ml/¼ pint double cream
450g/1lb dried linguine or spaghetti

**1** Put the pork mince and prosciutto in a food processor and pulse briefly to chop the ham. Add the garlic, bread, ½ tsp salt, a generous grinding of pepper and the egg. Process until well mixed.
**2** Divide the mixture into 4 pieces, then shape 6 meatballs from each portion.
**3** Heat the oil in a large frying pan and fry the meatballs, turning, until golden. Add the madeira and bubble until reduced by half.
**4** Pour in the stock, stir in the sage and season. Simmer gently for 5 minutes, then stir in the cream. If preparing ahead, cool and refrigerate for up to 2 days.
**5** To serve, reheat gently on the hob until bubbling. Meanwhile, cook the linguine in a large pan of boiling salted water for 10 minutes until *al dente*. Drain and toss with the meatballs and sauce. Serve with steamed Savoy cabbage.

## Stuffed beefsteak tomatoes

Juicy giant baked tomatoes with a tasty filling of mushrooms, tiny pasta, Parmesan and oregano. *Serves 2, or 4 as a starter*

4 large beefsteak or marmande tomatoes
85g/3oz dried pastina (small soup pasta)
salt and pepper
1 tbsp olive oil
1 red onion, diced
1 garlic clove, crushed
2 tsp finely chopped fresh oregano
100g/4oz mushrooms, diced
25g/1oz Parmesan or pecorino cheese, finely grated

**1** Preheat oven to 180C/fan oven 160C/Gas 4. Cut off the tops of the tomatoes; set aside for 'lids'. Using a teaspoon, scoop out the tomato seeds and cores to leave 1cm/1/2in thick shells.
**2** Add the pasta to a pan of boiling salted water and cook until *al dente*. Drain and rinse in cold water to arrest cooking; drain thoroughly.
**3** Heat the olive oil in a pan, add the onion and cook gently for about 5 minutes until softened but not coloured. Add the garlic and cook for 2-3 minutes. Add the oregano and mushrooms and fry for a further 3-5 minutes. Allow to cool slightly. Add the grated cheese, pasta and seasoning to taste; mix well.
**4** Spoon the mushroom filling into the hollowed-out tomatoes, then replace the tomato lids. Carefully transfer to an oven-proof dish and bake for about 30 minutes until the tomatoes are quite soft but still holding their shape. Serve hot.

## Fettucine with vegetable julienne

For this delicately flavoured pasta dish, vegetables are cooked briefly in a tasty stock, then combined with noodles.

600ml/1 pint homemade or bought fresh chicken stock
200g/7oz carrots, cut into julienne strips
200g/7oz leeks, cut into julienne strips
3 tomatoes, skinned, seeded and sliced
pepper
300g/10oz dried fettucine or tagliatelle
freshly grated Parmesan, to serve (optional)

**1** Bring the stock to the boil in a pan. Add the carrots and poach for about 2 minutes; remove with a slotted spoon and place in a bowl. Repeat with the leeks; add to the bowl. Boil the stock to reduce by about half.
**2** Meanwhile cook the pasta in a large pan of boiling salted water until *al dente*.
**3** Add the leeks, carrots and tomatoes to the stock and just warm through.
**4** Drain the pasta and add to the vegetable julienne and stock to serve.

## Plaice and caper stuffed conchiglioni

250g/9oz dried conchiglioni (about 40 very large, unbroken pasta shells)
salt and pepper
425ml/3/4 pint vegetable stock
1 large or 2 small fennel bulbs, thinly sliced
500g/1lb 2oz plaice fillet, skinned
1 tbsp capers, rinsed
25g/1oz butter, chilled

**1** Preheat oven to 180C/fan oven 160C/Gas 4. Cook the pasta shells in a large pan of boiling salted water until *al dente*. Drain and immediately rinse in cold water; drain.
**2** Heat the stock in a pan, add the fennel and poach for 15 minutes until tender. Drain and spread in a shallow ovenproof dish.
**3** Cut the plaice into about 40 pieces and pop one piece into each pasta shell. Place the shells, stuffed side up, on top of the fennel. Sprinkle with the capers and season generously with pepper. Place a tiny dot of butter in each shell.
**4** Cover the dish with foil and bake for 30 minutes or until the fish is opaque.

## Lemon pasta salad with mushrooms and coriander

This tangy fresh pasta salad is best served freshly made, while it is still warm.
*Serves 3-4; or 6 as part of a meal*

1 tbsp olive oil
350g/12oz flat mushrooms, cut into wedges
1 tsp coriander seeds, crushed
2 tsp finely chopped fresh sage
1/2 tsp grated lemon rind
3 tbsp lemon juice
250g/9oz fresh ballerine, or farfalle pasta
salt and pepper
sage leaves, to garnish

**1** Heat the oil in a frying pan and stir-fry the mushrooms for 2-3 minutes, then add the coriander and sage. Cook for 2-3 minutes until the mushroom juices start to run. Remove from the heat and add the lemon rind and juice.
**2** Add the pasta to a large pan of boiling salted water and cook for a few minutes only, until *al dente*. Drain, briefly refresh in cold water and drain well.
**3** Toss the warm mushrooms and pasta together. Season with salt and pepper to taste. Serve garnished with sage.

**VARIATION** Replace the mushrooms with 3 red or orange peppers, skinned, seeded and sliced.

## Seafood pasta with a coconut cream sauce

A delicious fusion of prawns and crabmeat, flavoured with spring onions, chilli and coriander in a coconut cream sauce.

100ml/3¹/₂fl oz double cream
100ml/3¹/₂fl oz coconut milk
1-2 tbsp sun-dried tomato paste
450g/1lb dried spinach tagliatelle, smoked salmon tagliatelle, or egg pappardelle
salt and pepper
1 tbsp olive oil
3 spring onions, thinly sliced
1 garlic clove, crushed
1 tsp grated fresh root ginger
1 red chilli, seeded and finely chopped
300g/10oz cooked peeled tiger prawns
200g/7oz white crabmeat
3 tbsp chopped fresh coriander leaves
coriander leaves, to garnish

**1** In a bowl, whisk together the cream, coconut milk and sun-dried tomato paste; set aside.
**2** Cook the pasta in a large pan of boiling salted water until *al dente*.
**3** Meanwhile, heat the oil in a large pan. Add the spring onions, garlic, ginger and chilli. Stir-fry for 2 minutes, then add the prawns and crabmeat. Heat through, stirring, for 1 minute.
**4** Add the cream mixture and slowly bring to a simmer, stirring. Add the chopped coriander, stir well and season with salt and pepper to taste.
**5** Drain the pasta and toss with the seafood sauce. Serve immediately, scattered with coriander leaves.

## Fusilli with tomatoes and mozzarella

500g/1lb 2oz plum tomatoes, roughly chopped
1 garlic clove, crushed
2 tbsp chopped fresh basil
2 tsp chopped fresh marjoram
4 anchovy fillets, finely chopped
juice of ¹/₂ lemon
4 tbsp extra virgin olive oil
salt and pepper
450g/1lb dried tricolore fusilli or pasta shells
350g/12oz mozzarella, diced

**1** Place the tomatoes, garlic, herbs, anchovies, lemon juice and olive oil in a bowl. Season with pepper and a little salt, mix well and set aside.
**2** Cook the pasta in a large pan of boiling salted water until *al dente*.
**3** Drain the pasta and turn into a large warm serving bowl. Stir in the diced mozzarella, then add the tomato sauce and toss well to mix. Check the seasoning and serve immediately.

## Spinach tagliatelle with minted peas

450g/1lb dried spinach tagliatelle
salt and pepper
85g/3oz butter
4 spring onions, thinly sliced
550g/1¹/₄lb peas (shelled fresh or frozen)
2 tbsp chopped fresh mint
2 tsp finely grated orange rind
1 tbsp orange juice
freshly grated Parmesan, to serve

**1** Cook the tagliatelle in a large pan of boiling salted water until *al dente*.
**2** Meanwhile, melt 50g/2oz of the butter in a pan. Add the spring onions and cook gently for 3-4 minutes or until tender.
**3** Add the peas and 100ml/3¹/₂fl oz water; cook for 3-4 minutes or until tender. Stir in the mint.
**4** Put the remaining butter, orange rind and juice in a large, warm serving dish. Drain the pasta and add to the dish with the pea sauce. Toss well and season with salt and peper to taste.
**5** Serve topped with grated Parmesan.

## Tomato spaghetti with coriander and avocado

The heat of the cooked spaghetti brings out the full flavours of creamy, ripe avocados and cherry tomatoes.

500g/1lb 2oz cherry tomatoes, quartered
2 tbsp torn fresh coriander leaves
grated rind and juice of ¹/₂ lemon
1 garlic clove, crushed
3 tbsp extra virgin olive oil
3 small avocados (preferably hass), peeled, stoned and cut into 1cm/¹/₂in dice
salt and pepper
450g/1lb dried tomato spaghetti

**1** Combine the tomatoes, coriander, lemon rind and juice, garlic and olive oil in a large bowl. Add the diced avocados and toss gently to mix. Season with salt and pepper to taste and set aside.
**2** Cook the pasta in a large pan of boiling salted water until *al dente*.
**3** Drain the pasta and toss gently with the sauce to serve.

**NOTE** Don't prepare this sauce too far in advance, or the avocado may discolour and spoil the appearance of the dish.

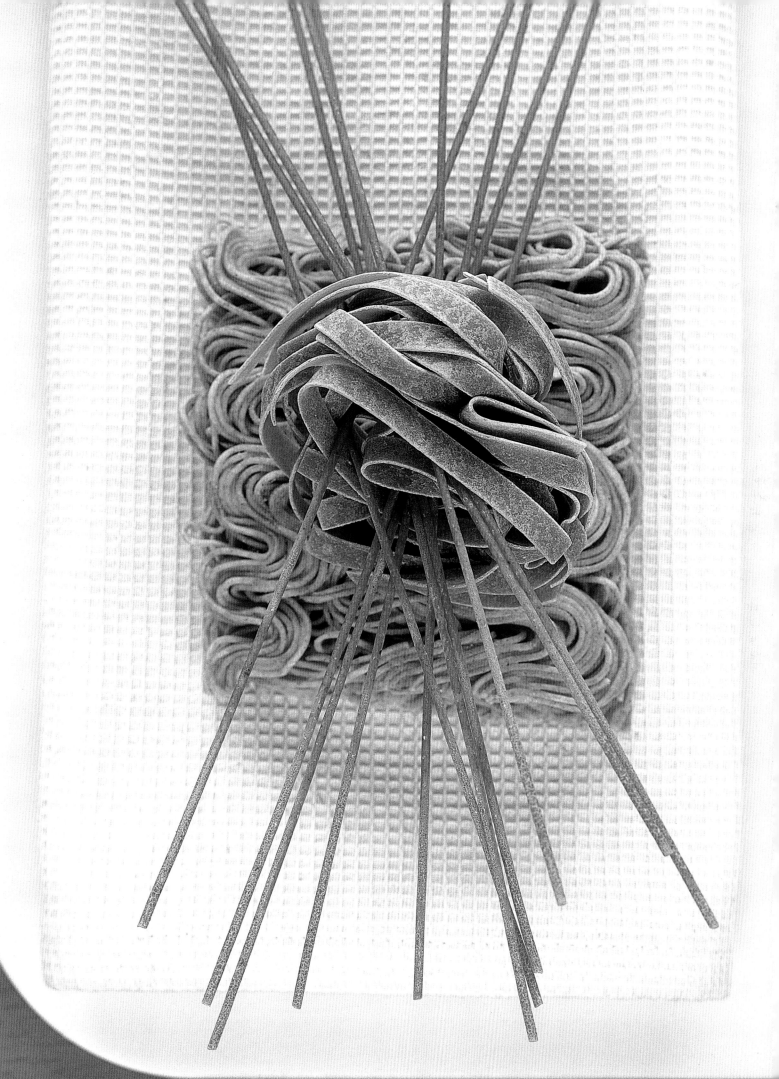

## Squid ink pasta with a spicy seafood sauce

Squid, prawns, chilli, white wine and tomatoes, with a hint of garlic, are a classic mix. Combine with black squid ink pasta for a dramatic dish.

3 tbsp extra virgin olive oil
4 garlic cloves, finely chopped
450g/1lb dried squid ink pasta
salt and pepper
300g/10oz cleaned baby squid, cut into rings
300g/10oz raw tiger prawns, peeled and deveined
1-2 red chillies, seeded and finely sliced
150ml/¼ pint dry white wine
400g can chopped tomatoes
3 tbsp chopped flat leaf parsley
flat leaf parsley sprigs, to garnish

**1** Heat the oil in a large, heavy-based frying pan and gently sauté the garlic until softened.
**2** Meanwhile, cook the pasta in a large pan of boiling salted water until *al dente*.
**3** Add the squid and prawns to the garlic. Stir-fry over a high heat for 2-3 minutes, then add the chilli and wine. Lower heat to medium and cook for 3-4 minutes. Add the tomatoes and parsley and cook for a further 3-4 minutes. Season to taste.
**4** Drain the pasta, toss with the seafood sauce and serve, garnished with parsley.

## Tortelloni with creamy dolcelatte sauce

This is excellent with any bought tortelloni. The dolcelatte must be young, not aged.

500g/1lb 2oz dried tortelloni
salt and pepper
50g/2oz butter
140g/5oz dolcelatte cheese, cut into small cubes
175ml/6fl oz double cream
85g/3oz fresh Parmesan, finely grated
chopped flat leaf parsley, to garnish

**1** Cook the tortelloni according to packet instructions or until *al dente*.
**2** Meanwhile melt the butter in a small, heavy-based pan over a low heat. Add the dolcelatte and stir until completely melted. Add the cream and slowly bring to a simmer, stirring. When the sauce is thick enough to coat the spoon, stir in the Parmesan. Season to taste.
**3** Drain the tortelloni and toss with the sauce. Serve sprinkled with chopped parsley and accompanied by a salad.

## Fettucine with asparagus, pancetta and chives

Spinach flavoured tagliatelle tossed in a creamy saffron sauce with fresh asparagus, spring onions, pancetta and chives.

¼ tsp saffron threads
140g/5oz pancetta, diced
450g/1lb asparagus
450g/1lb dried spinach fettucine
salt and pepper
85g/3oz butter
4 spring onions, thinly sliced
125ml/4fl oz dry white wine
250ml/8fl oz double cream
3 tbsp snipped fresh chives
50g/2oz fresh Parmesan, finely grated

**1** Soak the saffron in 2 tbsp hot water.
**2** Preheat a heavy-based frying pan, then add the pancetta and fry, stirring, until golden and crisp. Set aside.
**3** Cut asparagus into short lengths, keeping the tips whole. Par-boil for 5 minutes; drain.
**4** Cook the fettucine in a large pan of boiling salted water until *al dente*.
**5** Meanwhile, melt the butter in a large frying pan. Add the spring onions and cook for 1 minute, then add the asparagus and sauté for 1-2 minutes. Pour in the wine and cook for 3 minutes. Stir in the cream, saffron and soaking liquid. Bring to a simmer.
**6** Drain the pasta and add to the saffron sauce with the chives, Parmesan and pancetta. Toss well, season and serve.

## Corn pasta with fennel and red onion

Fresh fennel, dill, red onion, tomatoes and herbs give this uncooked sauce a wonderfully refreshing taste sensation.

1 fennel bulb, cored and finely diced
500g/1lb 2oz ripe plum tomatoes, seeded and finely diced
1 red onion, finely diced
2 tbsp chopped fresh basil
2 tbsp chopped fresh dill
3 tbsp extra virgin olive oil
juice of 1 lemon
salt and pepper
450g/1lb dried corn pasta (preferably fusilli)
basil leaves and red onion slices, to garnish
freshly grated Parmesan, to serve

**1** In a bowl, mix together the fennel, tomatoes, red onion, herbs, olive oil and lemon juice. Season with salt and pepper to taste and set aside.
**2** Cook the pasta in a large pan of boiling salted water until *al dente*.
**3** Drain the pasta, and return to the pan. Add the fennel sauce and toss to mix. Check the seasoning. Cover with a lid and leave to stand for 2-3 minutes to allow the flavours to infuse.
**4** Serve garnished with basil and red onion slices. Accompany with grated Parmesan.

## Caserecce gratin with taleggio, prosciutto and baby spinach

A slightly twisted pasta, caserecce is ideal for gratins. Taleggio has a delicious tang, though gruyère may be used. *Serves 6*

425ml/³/₄ pint milk
25g/1oz plain flour
25g/1oz butter
salt and pepper
freshly grated nutmeg
2 tbsp sunflower oil
350g/12oz young leaf spinach
500g/1lb 2oz dried caserecce, or spirals
140g/5oz prosciutto, or Parma ham, cut into strips
250g/9oz taleggio cheese, finely diced

**1** Preheat oven to 200C/fan oven 180C/Gas 6. Grease a 20x25cm (10x8in) gratin dish.
**2** Place the milk, flour and butter in a heavy-based pan over a medium heat and whisk until thick. Season with pepper, nutmeg and a little salt.
**3** Heat the oil in a large wok or pan, add the spinach and cook over a high heat for 1 minute only, turning continuously. Transfer to a colander and leave to drain.
**4** Add the pasta to a large pan of boiling salted water. Cook for 2 minutes less than the suggested time on the packet. Drain the pasta thoroughly and tip into the gratin dish.
**5** Add the spinach, prosciutto, two thirds of the cheese, and the sauce. Season with pepper. Toss well. Dot the surface with the remaining cheese and dust with nutmeg.
**6** Cover the dish with foil and bake for 10 minutes. Uncover and bake for a further 5 minutes or until golden and bubbling.

**NOTE** For convenience, assemble this gratin a few hours in advance. Keep covered in the fridge but bring to room temperature before baking, allowing an extra 10 minutes in the oven.

## Saffron pasta dough

Wonderfully therapeutic to prepare, and not difficult, homemade pasta is worth the effort for a special dinner. *Makes 350g/12oz*

¹/₄ tsp saffron strands
2 eggs (preferably organic, for yolk colour)
200g/7oz type '00' pasta flour
extra flour, for dusting

**1** Crush the saffron strands, using a mortar and pestle, add the eggs and mix well.
**2** Put the egg mixture into a food processor, add the flour and pulse until the mixture forms lumpy grains.
**3** Turn on to a lightly floured surface (not marble, as this is too cold), and knead until smooth. Wrap in plastic film and leave to rest in the refrigerator for at least 3 hours.
**4** Use a pasta machine to roll the dough into thin sheets to make ravioli (see right). For tagliatelle or spaghetti, fit the appropriate cutters to the machine after rolling.

### VARIATIONS

*Sun-dried tomato pasta:* Replace the saffron with 25g/1oz chopped sun-dried tomatoes (not in oil). Process to a purée with the eggs.

*Mushroom pasta:* Replace the saffron with 20g/³/₄oz dried porcini, ground to a powder.

*Spinach pasta:* Wilt 125g spinach in 1 tbsp oil, drain well and squeeze out all moisture. Purée in the processor with the eggs.

**NOTE** For convenience, you can make the pasta 1-2 days in advance. Keep tightly wrapped in plastic film, in the fridge, until required. If you are making ravioli (see right) prepare these a day ahead, freeze overnight and cook from frozen. (They are best frozen for a short time only).

## Saffron ravioli with butternut squash

Homemade ravioli served with a warm dressing of garlic, olives and thyme.

750g/1lb 10oz butternut squash, quartered
4 tbsp sunflower oil
salt and pepper
60g/2¹/₄oz pecorino cheese or Parmesan, grated
1 quantity saffron pasta dough (see left)
1 egg white
*for the dressing*
4 garlic cloves, thinly sliced
150ml/¹/₄ pint extra virgin olive oil
85g/3oz black olives, stoned and sliced
4 tsp fresh thyme leaves, roughly chopped
85g/3oz pecorino cheese or Parmesan

**1** Preheat oven to 200C/fan oven 180C/Gas 6. Place the squash quarters on a baking sheet and drizzle with 2 tbsp oil; season lightly. Roast for 55 minutes until very soft. Discard seeds. Scoop the squash flesh into a food processor. Add the cheese and ¹/₂ tsp pepper. Whizz to a purée.
**2** Cut the pasta into manageable portions; keep wrapped. Roll out, one piece at a time, using a pasta machine. Pass dough through the widest setting at least 3 times, then gradually narrow the setting as you roll out, until you have a thin pliable sheet of pasta. Pass through the thinnest setting 3 times. Repeat with remaining dough.
**3** Place a pasta sheet on a board and stamp out discs, with a 6cm/2¹/₂in fluted cutter. Lay half the discs on a sheet of plastic film and paint edges with egg white. Put a teaspoon of squash filling in the centre of each and top with the other discs, sticking the edges together without squashing the filling.
**4** Repeat with the rest of the pasta to make about 35 ravioli. Place on trays lined with plastic film, spacing apart. Freeze or use within 1 hour.
**5** To make the dressing, put the garlic and oil in a small pan and heat very gently until just beginning to turn golden. Add the olives, thyme and pepper to taste. Set aside to infuse.
**6** When ready to serve, bring a large saucepan of salted water to the boil and add 2 tbsp oil. Cook the ravioli for 4-6 minutes until *al dente*; drain. Serve the ravioli with the warm dressing poured over and topped with pecorino shavings.

Making saffron pasta
dough (far left);
shaping ravioli (left)

### Tagliatelle with wild mushroom sauce

Locate a good selection of mushrooms, including wild ones if possible. Use mushroom flavoured tagliatelle if preferred.

20g/³/₄oz dried porcini mushrooms
150ml/¹/₄ pint dry white wine
3 garlic cloves, peeled
300ml/¹/₂ pint double cream
50g/2oz walnuts
2 tbsp olive oil
400g/14oz mixed oyster, chestnut and wild or field mushrooms, halved if large
salt and pepper
375g/13oz dried egg tagliatelle
cep powder, to sprinkle (optional, see note)
chervil sprigs, to garnish

**1** Soak the dried porcini in the wine for 30 minutes to soften. Strain the soaking liquid into a small heavy-based pan, squeezing out all excess liquid from the porcini.
**2** Add the garlic to the pan and simmer until softened and the liquid is reduced by half; take out the garlic and set aside. Stir the cream into the liquid; remove from the heat.
**3** Chop the garlic, nuts and porcini together, to a coarse paste. Heat the oil in a wok or deep frying pan and stir-fry the mushrooms over a high heat, adding firmer ones first. Season well. Lower the heat and stir in the walnut paste, then the sauce; heat through.
**4** Add the tagliatelle to a large pan of boiling salted water and cook until *al dente*. Drain well and toss the pasta with the mushroom sauce. Serve dusted with cep powder if wished, and scattered with chervil.

**NOTE** Cep powder adds a special finishing touch. It is available in a shaker from larger supermarkets or, to make your own, grind dried ceps to a powder in a coffee grinder.

### Corn spaghetti with seared squid and salmon

Corn pasta has a wonderful colour and looks great with pink salmon. *Serves 6*

7.5cm/3in piece fresh root ginger, peeled
oil for deep-frying
650g/1lb 7oz salmon fillet, skinned and cut into 2.5cm/1in pieces
2 tbsp olive oil
salt and pepper
350g/12oz baby squid, cleaned and cut into 1cm/¹/₂in pieces
500g/1lb 2oz dried corn spaghetti
*for the dressing*
150ml/¹/₄ pint olive oil
3 tbsp dry white wine
2 tbsp lemon juice
2 tbsp chopped fresh dill
*for the garnish*
dill sprigs

**1** Finely slice the ginger lengthways, then cut into fine julienne. Heat a 5cm/2in depth of oil in a deep pan to 170C. Deep-fry the ginger until golden. Drain on kitchen paper.
**2** Toss the salmon in 1 tbsp oil and season well. Repeat with the squid. Preheat oven to 150C/fan oven 130C/Gas 2.
**3** Heat a non-stick frying pan until very hot. Add the salmon and sear for 30 seconds each side. Remove and keep warm in a covered dish in the oven. Repeat with squid.
**4** Add the spaghetti to a large pan of boiling salted water and cook until *al dente*.
**5** Meanwhile, whisk the dressing ingredients, except the dill, in a pan; warm through.
**6** Drain the pasta well and place in a bowl. Add the chopped dill and dressing; toss well. Fold in the salmon and squid.
**7** Top with dill sprigs, a generous grinding of pepper, and the ginger julienne to serve.

### Pappardelle with artichokes and aubergines in a sun-dried tomato sauce

This delicious sauce can be made in advance and reheated as the pasta is cooking. *Serves 4-6*

50g/2oz sun-dried aubergines (see note)
3 garlic cloves, peeled
4 tbsp sun-dried tomato paste
250g/9oz grilled artichoke hearts in olive oil (see note)
salt and pepper
500g/1lb 2oz dried pappardelle
4 tbsp roughly torn fresh parsley
50g/2oz pine nuts, toasted

**1** Simmer the sun-dried aubergines in water to cover for 2 minutes. Drain and refresh in cold water; dry on kitchen paper. Cut each slice into 3 long strips.
**2** Simmer the garlic in water to cover for 7-8 minutes until softened. Drain and crush the garlic with the back of a knife, then mix with the sun-dried tomato paste.
**3** Drain the artichokes, reserving 4 tbsp oil; halve any larger ones. Heat the reserved oil in a large frying pan and stir-fry the aubergine until cooked. Add the artichokes and heat through. Add the garlic mixture and season; keep warm.
**4** Cook the pasta in a large pan of boiling salted water until *al dente*. Add 4 tbsp of the cooking liquid to the sauce. Drain the pasta and toss with the hot sauce, parsley and pine nuts to serve.

**NOTE** Packs of char-grilled sun-dried aubergines and jars of grilled artichoke hearts in oil are sold in major supermarkets. Alternatively, substitute 1 large fresh aubergine, thinly sliced, and a jar of artichoke hearts in oil, drained. Brush the aubergine slices with oil and grill on both sides until charred. Fry the artichokes in 2 tbsp olive oil until tinged brown. Add both to the sauce.

## Herb and parmesan pasta

Parsley leaves are sandwiched between layers of homemade pasta and served in a vivid pepper sauce with rocket. Make both pasta and sauce in advance. *Serves 4-6*

*for the pasta*

190g/6$^1$/2oz type '00' pasta flour

20g/$^3$/4oz fresh Parmesan, finely grated

2 medium eggs (preferably organic, for yolk colour)

48 flat leaf parsley leaves, stalks removed

*for the sauce*

8 tbsp extra virgin olive oil

2 onions, finely chopped

4 red peppers, halved, cored and seeded

salt and pepper

*to finish*

3 tbsp oil

100g/4oz rocket leaves

**1** To make the pasta, put all the ingredients in a food processor and pulse until the mixture forms lumpy grains. Tip on to a lightly floured surface (not marble) and knead together until smooth. Wrap in plastic film and refrigerate for at least 3 hours.

**2** Cut the pasta into manageable portions; keep wrapped. Roll out, one piece at a time, using a pasta machine. Pass dough through the widest setting at least 3 times, then gradually narrow the setting as you roll out, until you have a thin pliable sheet of pasta.

**3** Lay parsley leaves on one pasta sheet at 2.5cm/1in intervals and place another sheet of pasta on top to sandwich the leaves. Roll through the machine on a medium setting, then once on a narrow setting. Cut into rectangles around the leaves, with a pasta wheel or a knife. Leave to dry slightly on greaseproof paper for 3 hours (or overnight).

**4** To make the sauce, heat 4 tbsp of the oil in a heavy-based frying pan and gently fry the onions over a low heat for 10 minutes, turning occasionally. Grill the peppers until charred, let cool slightly, then skin. Dice the pepper flesh and add to the onions with the remaining oil. Cook on a low heat for 20 minutes until soft, but not brown.

**5** Add the pasta to a large pan of boiling salted water with 2 tbsp oil and cook for 3-4 minutes until *al dente*. Meanwhile heat 1 tbsp oil in a large pan, add the rocket and cook briefly until just wilted. Drain the pasta and serve at once on the wilted rocket, topped with the hot sauce.

# fragrant fish

**Savour the real taste** of fresh fish with this diverse collection of original recipes. Sample **wonderful new flavours** for salmon, **effortless ways to cook shellfish**, and tasty ideas for **fast fish suppers**. Choose from the wide variety of species on display at supermarket fresh fish counters and good fishmongers. Most are sold cleaned and ready to cook. **Impress guests** with our **gourmet fish dishes**, such as roasted monkfish with saffron aioli, and Chinese-style sea bass. Or **capture the rich flavours** and **colours of Mediterranean seafood** with unforgettable dishes from Spain, Italy, Greece and Morocco.

## Peppered salmon with juniper and vermouth

An easy dish with intriguing flavours –
delicious with herby mashed potatoes.

1 tsp dried green peppercorns
16 juniper berries
1 tsp salt
4 salmon steaks or fillets, skinned
25g/1oz unsalted butter
8 tbsp dry vermouth (preferably Noilly Prat)
2-3 tbsp double cream or crème fraîche

**1** Crush together the peppercorns, juniper
berries and salt, using a pestle and mortar
(or end of a rolling pin and strong bowl).
Sprinkle over the salmon and press well
to adhere.
**2** Melt the butter in a frying pan over a
medium heat and fry the seasoned fish for
about 10-12 minutes for steaks, a little less
for salmon fillets, turning once.
**3** Lift the salmon on to a warm serving dish;
keep warm while you finish the sauce.
**4** Deglaze the pan with the vermouth and
let bubble for 2-3 minutes until syrupy. Stir
in the cream or crème fraîche and let bubble
for 2 minutes. Spoon the sauce over the
salmon to serve.

**NOTE** If buying salmon by the piece to cut
into portions, choose the middle or tail end
as this is less oily than the head end.

## Salmon and potato slice

Salmon fillet is baked between layers of
potato and celery seed, keeping it moist.

700g/1lb 9oz potatoes, skin on, thinly sliced
85g/3oz butter, melted
1 tsp celery or fennel seeds
salt and pepper
700g/1lb 9oz skinless salmon fillet (tail end)
3 tbsp single cream
chopped flat leaf parsley, to garnish

**1** Preheat oven to 200C/fan oven 180C/Gas 6.
Parcook the potatoes in water or stock for
4-5 minutes; the slices must remain whole.
Drain and refresh under cold water; drain.
**2** Line a buttered shallow 18x25cm/7x10in
ovenproof dish with half of the potatoes,
brushing with butter and sprinkling with
celery or fennel seed, salt and pepper.
**3** Cut the fish into chunks and lay over the
potato; season and drizzle over the cream.
Top with the remaining potato slices,
seasoning as before. Bake for 40 minutes
until the topping is crisp. Scatter with
chopped parsley to serve.

## Salmon baguette

An original meal in a baguette! *Serves 2*

Preheat oven to 220C/fan oven 200C/Gas 7.
Split a baguette, about 5cm/2in across,
22cm/8-9in in length, without cutting right
through. Spread both cut faces with 2-3 tbsp
pesto. Finely slice 250g/9oz fresh salmon
fillet into 5mm/1/4in slices. Fill the baguette
with the salmon, overlapping the slices, and
season with pepper. Wrap in oiled foil and
bake for about 30 minutes. Open the foil to
let out steam and return to the oven for a
few minutes. Cut in half and serve in napkins.

## Salmon with ginger and coriander

Very fresh salmon is essential for this raw
marinated dish. *Serves 3-4; or 8 as a starter*

500g/1lb 2oz salmon fillet (tail end), with skin
25g/1oz fresh root ginger, peeled
40g/1 1/2oz fresh coriander leaves, chopped
1 tsp coriander seeds
1 tbsp sea salt
1 tbsp caster sugar
freshly ground black pepper

**1** Trim the salmon, removing any bones.
**2** Coarsely chop the ginger and squeeze
out the juice on to the salmon, using a garlic
press. Mix remaining ingredients together
and press on to both sides of the fish.
**3** Lay the fish, skin side down, in a shallow
dish large enough to hold it flat. Cover with
baking parchment, place a board on top
and weight down. Leave to marinate in the
fridge for 3-4 days, turning fish each day.
**4** Blot excess oil from the fish with kitchen
paper. Thinly slice the salmon, on the
diagonal, off the skin. Serve with a rocket
salad and rye bread.

## Salmon with anchovies and capers

Piquant whole baked salmon. *Serves 4-6*

Preheat oven to 220C/fan oven 200C/Gas 7.
Make 4 or 5 diagonal slits on each side of a
cleaned 1.5-1.6kg/3 1/4-3 1/2lb whole salmon.
Finely chop 8 anchovy fillets, 1 tbsp capers
and 2-3 tbsp fresh parsley. Mix together with
1 tsp grated lemon rind and the juice of
1/2 lemon. Press this paste into the cuts in
the fish. Season with pepper, wrap in oiled
foil and seal loosely. Bake for 45 minutes.
Leave, wrapped, to rest and complete
cooking in its own steam for 15 minutes.

## Prawns on crackling rice pancakes

An impressive dish to rustle up from the storecupboard, using instant risotto rice.

250g packet instant risotto, preferably saffron flavoured (see note)
1 garlic clove, finely chopped
1cm/3/4in piece fresh root ginger, peeled and grated
2 tbsp chopped fresh chives
4 spring onions, finely chopped
salt and pepper
750g/1lb 10oz medium raw prawns in shells
25g/1oz butter
2 tbsp sunflower oil
2 tbsp Thai red curry paste
chives, to garnish

**1** To make the risotto, cook the rice according to the packet instructions, together with the garlic, ginger, chives, spring onions and seasoning. Tip on to a tray; allow to cool. When cold, shape into 8 cakes, with wet hands.
**2** Shell the prawns, leaving the tail shells on.
**3** Melt the butter in a frying pan and cook the pancakes carefully, a few at a time, until golden and crispy on one side; turn and cook the other side. Avoid moving during cooking or they might break up. Keep warm.
**4** Heat the oil in a wok or frying pan, add the curry paste and cook, stirring, for 1 minute. Add the prawns and stir-fry for 3-4 minutes until cooked. Serve at once, on the rice cakes. Garnish with chives.

**NOTE** Instant '12 minute' risotto rice (eg Riso Gallo) is available from supermarkets.

## Scallop, pancetta and mushroom bruschetta

Sautéed scallops, cubes of pancetta and chunky mushrooms piled on to slices of grilled country bread rubbed with garlic and olive oil.

8 large scallops, cleaned
4 large thick slices country bread
1 garlic clove, peeled and halved
3-4 tbsp olive oil
50g/2oz cubed pancetta or bacon lardons
4 large flat mushrooms, cut into wedges
salt and pepper
2 tbsp sherry or balsamic vinegar

**1** Cut away the tough muscle at the side of each scallop and any dark vein, then wash and dry. If the scallops are very large, halve them horizontally.
**2** Grill the bread slices on both sides then rub with the garlic and drizzle with olive oil; keep warm.
**3** Heat 2 tbsp oil in a frying pan, add the pancetta or bacon and fry until beginning to brown. Increase the heat, add the scallops and toss over a high heat for 2 minutes or until just opaque. Lift out with a slotted spoon and set aside.
**4** Add the mushrooms to the pan and fry for 2 minutes until softened, adding a little extra oil if needed.
**5** Return the scallops to the pan and stir over a high heat for a few seconds to warm through. Season well, then pile on to the warm bread. Deglaze the pan with the vinegar and pour the juices over the scallops to serve.

## Mussels steamed in a paper bag

Mussels are quick and easy, especially if you buy ready cleaned ones and cook them in this unusual way.

1.5kg/3lb 5oz fresh mussels in shells
2 tbsp olive oil
1 garlic clove, chopped
2 celery sticks, cut into fine julienne strips
1 red pepper, cored, seeded and finely sliced
1 red chilli, seeded and finely diced
1 tsp Szechuan peppercorns, crushed
4 tbsp teriyaki marinade

**1** To clean the mussels if necessary, scrub in several changes of water, discarding any that do not close when sharply tapped. Pull off any 'beards' which are still attached.
**2** Preheat oven to 230C/fan oven 210C/Gas 8. Heat the oil in a frying pan and add the garlic, celery, red pepper and chilli. Stir-fry over a brisk heat for 1 minute. Add the crushed peppercorns and take off the heat.
**3** Cut four 30cm/12in squares of baking parchment. Divide the mussels between the paper squares, piling them in the centre. Top with the stir-fried vegetables and pour 15ml/1 tbsp teriyaki marinade over each portion. Bring the sides of the paper up over the mussels to enclose them like a bag; tie with cotton string. Place on a baking tray.
**4** Place in the oven for 10 minutes or until the mussels open (squeeze bags to check). Serve immediately, in the paper bags!

**NOTE** Make sure guests discard any mussels which have not opened.

## Smoked salmon and leek risotto

A luxurious risotto flavoured with wine, sautéed leeks and lashings of smoked salmon. For a special supper, top with a spoonful of crème fraîche and a little lumpfish roe or salmon caviar.

5 tbsp olive oil
450g/1lb medium leeks, thinly sliced
2 garlic cloves, finely chopped
500g/1lb 2oz arborio or other risotto rice
300ml/1/2 pint medium white wine
1 litre/2 pints well flavoured fish stock (approximately)
225g/8oz sliced smoked salmon, roughly chopped
salt and pepper
*to serve*
crème fraîche
lumpfish roe or salmon caviar (optional)

**1** Heat the oil in a heavy-based pan. Add the leeks and sauté for a few minutes until lightly coloured and beginning to soften. Stir in the garlic and cook for 2-3 minutes.
**2** Add the rice and stir well to coat with oil. Add the wine and boil until totally reduced.
**3** Meanwhile, bring the stock to a simmer in another pan.
**4** Add a large ladleful of stock to the rice and stir until it is absorbed. Continue to add the stock in this way, ensuring each addition is absorbed before adding more, until the rice is tender and creamy, but firm to the bite.
**5** Gently fold in the smoked salmon. Season generously with pepper and salt to taste. Cover and leave to rest for 1 minute. Serve topped with crème fraîche, and lumpfish roe or salmon caviar if wished.

## Smoked mackerel and spinach frittata

This Italian omelette is cooked slowly over a low heat. The filling is stirred into the eggs or scattered on top. It is served just set, never folded. *Serves 3-4 as a snack*

450g/1lb ready-prepared young fresh spinach
2 tbsp olive oil
225g/8oz smoked mackerel fillets
175g/6oz small new potatoes
salt and pepper
100g/4oz butter
6 large eggs
50g/2oz Parmesan, freshly grated

**1** Remove any tough stems from the spinach. Heat the oil in a frying pan, add the spinach and toss until just wilted; transfer to a plate. Remove the skin from the mackerel fillets and roughly flake the flesh.
**2** Cook the potatoes in boiling salted water for 15-20 minutes until just tender. Drain and allow to cool slightly, then slice thickly.
**3** Heat half the butter in a non-stick frying pan and sauté the potatoes for 5 minutes or until beginning to colour.
**4** In a bowl, beat the eggs with half of the Parmesan, a good pinch of salt and plenty of pepper. Stir in the spinach and potatoes.
**5** Melt the remaining butter in a 25cm/10in heavy non-stick frying pan. When foaming, pour in the egg mixture. Turn down the heat as low as possible. Cook for about 15 minutes until set, with the top still a little runny. Scatter over the flaked mackerel and sprinkle with the remaining Parmesan.
**6** Place briefly under a hot grill to lightly brown the cheese and just set the top; do not over brown or the frittata will dry out. Slide onto a warm plate and cut into wedges. Serve with a crisp salad.

## Pan-seared gravad lax on a celeriac and potato mash

Thin slices of gravad lax are quickly fried in butter and served on a pile of celeriac and potato mash flavoured with dill mustard, chopped dill pickles and spring onions.

225g/8oz celeriac
225g/8oz potatoes
salt and pepper
150ml/1/4 pint milk
2 tbsp olive oil
1-2 tbsp sweet dill mustard
2 large dill pickles, chopped
8 spring onions, finely sliced
25g/1oz butter
450g/1lb gravad lax (see note)

**1** Peel the celeriac and potatoes and cut into even sized pieces. Add to a pan of cold salted water, bring to the boil and cook for 15-20 minutes until tender. Drain thoroughly, then mash well.
**2** Heat the milk with the olive oil, mustard, dill pickles and spring onions. Beat into the celeriac and potato mash: keep warm.
**3** Heat the butter in a heavy-based frying pan until sizzling. Fry the gravad lax, in two batches, over a high heat until just starting to colour.
**4** Pile the mash on to warmed serving plates and top with the gravad lax. Pour on any pan juices and serve immediately.

**NOTE** Packets of Swedish gravad lax – sliced marinated salmon flavoured with dill – can be found alongside the smoked salmon in supermarkets.

## Potted crab with ginger and garlic

Fresh, ready prepared crab mixed with a spiced clarified butter and set in little pots. Serve with warm, toasted pitta bread.

4 small dressed crabs, each about 175g/6oz
100g/4oz unsalted butter
1cm/³/₄in piece fresh root ginger, peeled and grated
1 garlic clove, crushed
1 tsp sweet paprika
salt and pepper

**1** Scoop the white and dark meat out of the crab shells.
**2** Melt the butter slowly in a small saucepan. Add the ginger and garlic and cook over a gentle heat for 3-5 minutes until soft but not coloured.
**3** Add the paprika and crab. Stir to coat with the butter and heat through; season with salt and pepper to taste.
**4** Spoon the crab mixture into small pots or ramekins and smooth the tops. Allow to cool, then chill in the refrigerator for at least 1 hour to set.
**5** Serve the potted crab with warm toasted pitta bread fingers.

**NOTE** Small ready prepared fresh crabs are obtainable from most supermarket fresh fish counters.

## Herring with mustard lemon butter

4 large herring fillets
100ml/3¹/₂fl oz milk
100g/4oz pinhead oatmeal
1 lemon, thinly sliced
50g/2oz butter
juice of 1 lemon
1 tbsp wholegrain mustard
2 tbsp chopped fresh parsley
salt and pepper

**1** Dip herring in milk, then coat with oatmeal.
**2** Melt the butter in a frying pan. Fry the herring with the lemon slices for about 2 minutes each side; transfer to warm plates.
**3** Add the lemon juice, mustard and parsley to the pan and heat until bubbling; season. Pour over the herring and serve.

## Cod with creamy white bean stew

2 tbsp olive oil
2 garlic cloves, finely chopped
2 tbsp finely shredded fresh sage
1 red chilli, seeded and finely chopped
400g can cannellini beans, drained
150ml/¹/₄ pint fish or vegetable stock
50g/2oz butter
2 onions, halved and thinly sliced
4 cod steaks, each about 175g/6oz

**1** Heat half the oil in a pan; fry the garlic until golden. Add the sage and chilli; cook for 1 minute. Add the beans and stock, bring to the boil and simmer for 20 minutes; season.
**2** Meanwhile, melt the butter in a small pan. Stir in the onions, add 2 tbsp water and cover tightly. Simmer gently for 20-25 minutes until very soft, stirring occasionally.
**3** Brush the cod steaks with oil, season and grill for 2-3 minutes on each side. Serve on the bean stew, topped with the onions.

## Tagliatelle with smoked salmon and parsley pesto

Tagliatelle is tossed with a chopped pesto of toasted almonds, garlic, parsley, Parmesan and olive oil, and served topped with a generous tangle of sliced smoked salmon.

100g/4oz blanched whole almonds
1 garlic clove, finely chopped
2 tbsp freshly grated Parmesan
50g/2oz fresh parsley leaves, roughly chopped
150ml/¹/₄ pint light olive oil
2 tbsp curd cheese
salt and pepper
500g/1lb 2oz dried tagliatelle
225g/8oz sliced smoked salmon, cut into strips
flat leaf parsley, to garnish

**1** Spread the almonds on a baking sheet and place under the grill for 1-2 minutes, turning frequently, until toasted and golden. Allow to cool, then chop roughly. Beat together with the garlic, Parmesan, parsley, olive oil and curd cheese. Season with salt and pepper to taste.
**2** Add the tagliatelle to a large pan of boiling salted water and cook according to the packet directions until *al dente* (cooked, but still firm to the bite). Drain, keeping back 2-3 tbsp of the cooking water.
**3** Add the parsley pesto to the pasta and toss well to mix. Pile into warmed bowls and top each serving with a tangle of smoked salmon. Garnish with flat leaf parsley and serve at once.

**NOTE** Don't be tempted to whizz the pesto ingredients in a food processor until smooth. A coarse textured pesto gives a better result for this recipe.

## Plaice with anchovies and Parmesan

8 plaice fillets, skinned
4 anchovy fillets, finely chopped
200ml/7fl oz double cream
5 tbsp fresh brown breadcrumbs
2 tbsp finely chopped parsley
8 tbsp finely grated fresh Parmesan

1 Preheat oven to 220C/fan oven 200C/Gas 7. Halve each plaice fillet lengthways along the natural line. Dot with the anchovies.
2 Roll up each fillet from the thickest end. Arrange the fish, spiral side uppermost, in 4 individual gratin dishes and spoon over the cream.
3 Mix the breadcrumbs with the parsley and Parmesan and scatter over the plaice. Bake for 8-10 minutes until the fish is cooked and the topping is golden. Serve with a salad, or grilled tomatoes and baby potatoes.

## Hoki, ham and gruyère grills

Hoki, a relative of the hake, is fished from the seas around New Zealand and makes an excellent alternative to cod.

4 thick skinless hoki or cod fillets, each about 200g/7oz
salt and pepper
50g/2oz pitted green olives, sliced
100g/4oz gruyère cheese, finely grated
50g/2oz wafer-thin smoked ham

1 Preheat the grill. Lay the fish fillets in a grillproof dish, season, then grill for 2-3 minutes. Mix the olives and cheese together.
2 Turn the fish steaks over and top with the ham. Scatter with the cheese and olives.
3 Grill for a further 4-5 minutes until the cheese is golden and bubbling and the fish fillets are cooked through to the middle. Serve with a salad and crusty bread.

## Trout with dill cucumber and capers

Pan fried trout with a piquant sauce. *Serves 2*

2 whole trout, cleaned
2 tbsp seasoned flour
25g/1oz unsalted butter
juice of 1/2 small lemon
1/2 dill cucumber, finely chopped
1-2 tsp capers
1-2 tbsp flat leaf parsley, roughly chopped
salt and pepper

1 Coat the trout in seasoned flour. Melt the butter in a large frying pan, then fry the trout for 5 minutes each side or until cooked and the skin is crisp. Lift on to warm plates.
2 Pour the lemon juice into the pan juices. Warm through with the cucumber, capers and parsley. Season to taste, then pour over the trout. Serve with a salad and potatoes.

## Pan-fried monkfish with Dijon mustard

40g/1 1/2oz unsalted butter
2 monkfish fillets, each about 300g/10oz, skinned and thickly sliced
1 garlic clove, crushed
100ml/3 1/2fl oz extra dry white vermouth
1 tbsp Dijon mustard
150ml/1/4 pint double cream
1 tbsp snipped fresh chives (optional)

1 Melt the butter in a large frying pan and briefly fry the monkfish for 1-2 minutes until almost cooked. Lift from the pan.
2 Add the garlic to the pan and fry gently until softened. Add the vermouth and mustard and bubble vigorously to boil off the alcohol.
3 Stir in the cream, and chives if using, then return the fish to the pan to warm through and finish cooking. Serve with tagliatelle and sugar snap peas or mangetout.

## Spicy grilled sardines

Fresh sardines are now widely available. Here they are grilled with a spicy garlic coating and served with a refreshing Moroccan orange salad.

4 garlic cloves, crushed
1/2 tsp hot paprika
1 tsp ground cumin
1 tbsp lemon juice
1 tbsp olive oil
salt and pepper
12-16 fresh sardines, depending on size, cleaned
*for the salad*
5 oranges
1 red onion, very thinly sliced
25g/1oz flat leaf parsley leaves, roughly torn
16 large black olives (optional)
extra virgin olive oil, for drizzling

1 Mix the garlic with the spices, lemon juice, olive oil and seasoning. Rub this mixture all over the sardines to coat thoroughly. Set aside.
2 For the salad, peel and segment the oranges, discarding all white pith, membrane and pips. Place the orange segments in a bowl with the red onion, chopped parsley and black olives if using. Season with salt and pepper to taste and drizzle with a little olive oil.
3 Preheat the grill. Place the sardines on the rack over the grill pan and grill for approximately 2 minutes each side until cooked through. Serve with the orange salad and warm crusty bread.

NOTE Before grilling the sardines, add a little water to the grill pan. This will prevent any juices from the fish burning on the pan base, which causes smoking.

Trout with dill cucumber
and capers (left);
Plaice with anchovies
and Parmesan (far left)

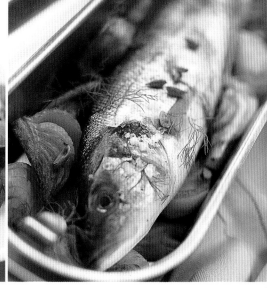

## Monkfish skewers

Firm fleshed monkfish is the perfect choice to thread on to skewers, as it doesn't easily disintegrate. Ask the fishmonger to fillet and skin the fish for you.

4 monkfish fillets, each 200g/7oz, skinned
juice of 1 small lemon
1 tsp fennel seeds
salt and pepper
4 shallots (unpeeled)
1 red pepper, cored, seeded and cut into 12 pieces
a little olive oil, for brushing
lemon wedges, to serve

**1** Cut each monkfish fillet into 5 or 6 pieces and place in a bowl with the lemon juice, fennel seeds, salt and pepper; toss to mix and set aside.
**2** Put the shallots in a pan, cover with cold water and bring to the boil. Simmer gently for 6-8 minutes, then drain and refresh in cold water. Peel and quarter the shallots lengthways.
**3** Preheat the grill to medium. Thread the monkfish chunks onto 4 long skewers, alternating with the red pepper and shallots.
**4** Brush with a little olive oil and grill for 12-15 minutes, turning the skewers occasionally. Serve with lemon wedges, a leafy salad and warm bread.

## Salt baked hake

Hake is an inexpensive white fish with a fine flavour. Here it is encrusted in salt just before baking to seal in the flavour and juices. The flesh stays moist and, perhaps surprisingly, it isn't too salty. *Serves 2*

1 hake, about 600g/1lb 5oz, cleaned
1tbsp Maldon salt flakes
few fresh rosemary branches
lemon wedges, to serve

**1** Preheat oven to 220C/fan oven 200C/Gas 7. Snip the fins off the fish, using kitchen scissors. Wash fish under running cold water. Shake off excess moisture then, holding on to the tail, toss the fish in the salt so that it all adheres.
**2** Lay the rosemary over the base of an ovenproof dish and place the fish on top. Immediately bake for about 20 minutes until cooked through.
**3** To serve, break away and discard the salted fish skin. Serve the fish accompanied by lemon wedges, warm bread and a tomato, olive and red onion salad.

## Warm smoked haddock and butter bean salad

Smokey haddock marries with sweet beetroot and creamy butter beans to make a substantial but low fat meal.

4 small cooked beetroot, diced
2 tsp cider vinegar
500g/1lb 2oz undyed smoked haddock fillet, skinned
1 bunch watercress, trimmed
400g can butter beans, drained
3 spring onions, finely sliced
pepper

**1** Toss the diced beetroot in the cider vinegar; set aside.
**2** Poach the haddock in just sufficient water to cover for 4-5 minutes until opaque; drain.
**3** Meanwhile gently mix the watercress sprigs, butter beans, onions and beetroot together in a shallow serving bowl.
**4** When the fish is cool enough to handle, divide into flakes and scatter over the salad. Season with plenty of pepper.

**NOTE** The beetroot lightly tinges the beans a pretty pale pink. Combine the salad shortly before serving to avoid over-colouring.

## Steamed sea bass with fennel

The delicate flavours in this fragrant one-pot meal are retained during cooking. *Serves 2*

1 tbsp olive oil
3 small fennel bulbs, trimmed and each cut into 8 wedges, feathery fronds reserved
1/2 tsp cardamom seeds (from 3-4 pods)
500ml/18fl oz vegetable stock
1 sea bass, about 750g/1lb 10oz, cleaned
salt and pepper

**1** Heat the oil in a wide, heavy-based deep pot or flameproof casserole, add the fennel with the cardamom seeds and fry until lightly browned and slightly softened.
**2** Add the stock and bring to the boil. Lower the heat, cover and simmer for 10 minutes.
**3** Season the fish and place on its side on top of the fennel. Cover tightly and cook over a medium heat for 15-20 minutes. To make sure the fish is cooked, insert a knife in the thickest part of the back and check that the flesh is opaque.
**4** Carefully lift the fish on to a serving dish and surround with the fennel wedges. Spoon the pan juices over the fish and garnish with the reserved fennel fronds. Serve with warm crusty bread or plain boiled potatoes to mop up the juices.

**NOTE** Most white fish have low fat flesh because their oil is stored in the liver. Oily fish, such as sardines, salmon, tuna and trout, have oil distributed throughout their flesh and are therefore relatively high in fat but full of beneficial fish oils and vitamins.

## Portuguese fish and potato bake

Flavoured with caramelised onions, black olives and garlic, this tasty bake is best enjoyed with a glass of rioja.

750g/1lb 10oz thick cod fillets, skinned
5 tbsp olive oil
3 large onions, halved and thinly sliced
3 garlic cloves, finely chopped
600g/1lb 5oz potatoes (King Edward or Desiree)
3 tbsp finely chopped fresh parsley
16 black olives, stoned and roughly chopped
salt and pepper
150ml/1/4 pint fish or chicken stock
*for the garnish*
4 hard-boiled eggs, quartered
chopped flat leaf parsley

**1** Preheat oven to 180C/fan oven 160C/Gas 4. Place the fish fillets on a lightly oiled baking sheet, brush with olive oil and bake for 7-10 minutes. Let cool slightly.
**2** Meanwhile, heat the remaining oil in a large frying pan, add the onions and sauté for about 20 minutes until golden brown. Add the garlic and sauté for 2 minutes; set aside.
**3** In the meantime, boil the potatoes until tender. Drain and leave to cool slightly, then peel and cut into 1cm/1/2in slices.
**4** When the fish is cool enough to handle, separate into large flakes.
**5** Lightly oil a shallow ovenproof dish, 24-25cm/91/2-10in in diameter. Layer the potatoes, onions, parsley, olives and fish in the dish, seasoning each layer generously and finishing with a layer of onions. Pour in the stock and bake for 20 minutes.
**6** Serve garnished with hard-boiled eggs and chopped parsley. Accompany with green beans or roasted tomatoes.

## Italian seafood risotto

A creamy, wine enriched risotto, liberally flavoured with fresh salmon, tiger prawns and baby squid.

3 tbsp extra virgin olive oil
3 garlic cloves, finely chopped
200g/7oz salmon fillet, skinned and cut into 2.5cm/1in cubes
250g/9oz raw tiger prawns, shelled and deveined
4 baby squid, cleaned and cut into rings
125ml/4fl oz dry white wine
1.5 litres/2 3/4 pints fish stock
40g/1 1/2oz butter
4 shallots, finely chopped
1/2 red pepper, cored, seeded and diced
1 plum tomato, skinned, seeded and chopped
400g/14oz arborio rice
salt and pepper
2 tbsp finely chopped fresh flat leaf parsley

**1** Heat 2 tbsp of the oil in a large saucepan, add the garlic and sauté for 1 minute. Add the salmon, prawns and squid and stir-fry for 3 minutes, then add the wine and bring to a simmer. Remove the fish and shellfish with a slotted spoon and set aside.
**2** Add the fish stock to the pan; set aside.
**3** Melt 25g/1oz of the butter in another large pan with the remaining oil. Add the shallots and cook until golden. Add the red pepper, tomato and rice; cook, stirring, for 2 minutes.
**4** Meanwhile, bring the stock to a simmer. Gradually stir the stock into the rice mixture, about 125ml/4fl oz at a time, ensuring each addition is absorbed before adding more. Continue until the rice is tender. With the last addition of stock, add the seafood and season to taste.
**5** Stir in the remaining butter and chopped parsley. Serve at once.

**NOTE** Cooking time is about 20 minutes from the first addition of the stock. Depending on the variety of rice, you may need to use a little less or more liquid.

## Basque baked fish in parchment

These fish parcels cook quickly and easily in the oven, trapping in the flavours of sweet peppers, onion, garlic and oregano.

4 cod or haddock fillets, each 175-200g/6-7oz, skinned
1/2 green pepper, cored, seeded and diced
1/2 red pepper, cored, seeded and diced
1 onion, finely chopped
1 tbsp fresh oregano leaves, chopped
2 garlic cloves, finely chopped
2 plum tomatoes, skinned, seeded and chopped
juice of 1 lemon
1 tbsp olive oil
4 tbsp dry white wine
salt and pepper
12 black olives (optional)

**1** Preheat oven to 190C/fan oven 170C/Gas 5. Cut 4 sheets of non-stick baking parchment, measuring approximately 30x38cm/12x15in. Place each fish fillet on a piece of paper, positioning it slightly off centre.
**2** In a bowl, mix together the peppers, onion, oregano, garlic, tomatoes, lemon juice, olive oil and wine. Season with salt and pepper.
**3** Spoon the mixture on top of the fish and scatter over the olives, if using. Fold the parchment over the fish to form a triangle. Fold the edges together tightly to form a sealed parcel.
**4** Lift the parcels onto a baking sheet and bake for 15-20 minutes until the fish is cooked through. Place each parcel on a warmed plate and serve at once, with buttery new potatoes and steamed broccoli.

Basque baked fish in parchment

## Mediterranean fish stew

Most Mediterranean countries have their own prized version of a fish stew, containing both white fish and shellfish. Here cod, sea bass and prawns are coupled with fresh fennel, celery, citrus peel and Pernod for good measure.

4 tbsp olive oil
1 onion, finely chopped
5 garlic cloves, finely chopped
1 small fennel bulb, finely chopped
3 celery sticks, finely chopped
400g can chopped tomatoes
1 tbsp fresh thyme leaves
1 bay leaf
grated rind and juice of 1/2 orange
5cm/2in strip of lemon peel
1 tsp saffron strands
700ml/1 1/4 pints fresh fish stock (see note)
3 tbsp Pernod
250g/9oz thick cod fillet
250g/9oz sea bass or hoki fillet
250g/9oz raw tiger prawns, shelled and deveined
3 tbsp finely chopped fresh flat leaf parsley
salt and pepper

**1** Heat the oil in a large saucepan. Add the onion, garlic, fennel and celery and cook on a low heat, stirring occasionally, for 15-20 minutes until the vegetables are soft and just starting to colour.
**2** Add the tomatoes with their juice, thyme, bay leaf, orange rind and juice, lemon peel and saffron. Cook briskly for 5 minutes, then add the fish stock and Pernod and bring to the boil. Turn the heat down to medium and simmer, uncovered, for 20 minutes.
**3** Meanwhile, cut the cod and sea bass into 5cm/2in cubes. Add to the pan and cook for 3 minutes, then add the prawns and cook for a further 3 minutes.
**4** Stir in the chopped parsley and check the seasoning. Serve in warmed bowls with hot bread to mop up the delicious juices. Accompany with a salad.

**NOTE** To make your own stock, ask your fishmonger for the fish bones and trimmings. Put them in a pan with the prawn shells, 2-3 onion slices, a handful of parsley sprigs, a bay leaf and a few peppercorns. Add water to cover, bring to the boil and simmer for 20 minutes. Strain and use as required.

Marinating tuna steaks (above); Seared tuna with fennel and thyme (right)

## Saltimbocca of sole

Lemon sole fillets are wrapped in Parma ham and served with a delicious mild creamy mustard sauce.

2 lemon sole, filleted and skinned
8 slices of Parma ham
16 basil leaves
pepper
50g/2oz unsalted butter
150ml/¼ pint chicken stock
150ml/¼ pint double cream
4 tbsp white wine
1 tsp Dijon mustard
1 tbsp finely chopped fresh flat leaf parsley

**1** Preheat oven to 200C/fan oven 180C/Gas 6. Trim the sole fillets, then cut each in half lengthways.
**2** Lay the slices of Parma ham on a board, place 2 basil leaves on each and cover with a sole fillet. Season with pepper. Starting from the tail end, roll up fairly tightly, making sure the fish is covered by the ham. Repeat to make the remaining rolls.
**3** Melt 25g/1oz of the butter in a large frying pan. When sizzling, carefully add the fish rolls, seam side down, and cook for 1-2 minutes on each side, until golden brown.
**4** Carefully place the rolls, seam side down, on a baking tray lined with greaseproof paper and bake for 8-10 minutes.
**5** Meanwhile, make the sauce. Put the stock, cream, wine and mustard in a small pan and bring to the boil, stirring. Simmer for 4-5 minutes until reduced and slightly thickened, then whisk in the remaining butter. Season with pepper to taste and add the parsley.
**6** To serve, spoon the sauce onto 4 warmed plates and arrange 2 saltimboccas on each plate. Serve at once, with fluffy mashed potatoes and wilted spring greens.

## Greek baked mackerel plaki

4 large mackerel, cleaned and trimmed
salt and pepper
juice of 2 lemons
3 garlic cloves, finely chopped
1 tsp fresh thyme leaves
4 plum tomatoes, skinned, seeded and diced
20 black olives, stoned and chopped
4 tbsp olive oil
5 tbsp dry white wine

**1** Cut 3 slashes on both sides of each fish and place in an oiled large, shallow ovenproof dish; season well. Pour over the lemon juice, cover and leave to marinate in a cool place for 1 hour, turning occasionally.
**2** Preheat oven to 190C/fan oven 170C/Mark 5. Spoon the remaining ingredients over the fish. Bake for 15-20 minutes, until cooked.
**3** Serve with rice and a green salad topped with crumbled feta and thin red onion slices.

## Moroccan grilled cod

Chermoula, a Moroccan spice and herb mix, transforms cod into an exciting dish.

4 cod fillets, each 175-200g/6-7oz, skinned
*for the chermoula*
2 tbsp roughly chopped fresh coriander
1 tbsp chopped fresh mint
1 tbsp chopped fresh flat leaf parsley
2 garlic cloves, chopped
1 red chilli, seeded and chopped
1 tsp paprika
1½ tsp roasted cumin seeds
1 tsp saffron strands
5 tbsp olive oil
juice of 1 lemon
1½ tsp salt

**1** Place the fish fillets in a shallow ceramic or glass dish.
**2** Put the chermoula ingredients in a food processor and blend until smooth. Spoon over the fish and turn to coat. Cover and marinate in the fridge for at least 2 hours, ideally overnight, turning occasionally.
**3** Preheat grill to medium-high. Lift the fish out of the marinade and grill for 5-7 minutes on each side or until lightly browned and cooked through. Check the seasoning. Serve with warm pitta bread and yogurt.

## Seared tuna with fennel and thyme

Hearty fresh tuna or swordfish steaks are marinated with Mediterranean flavours, then quickly seared on a hot griddle. A tomato and basil salsa is the ideal complement.

4 tuna or swordfish steaks, each 200g/7oz
salt and pepper
3 tbsp Pernod
2 tbsp olive oil
zest and juice of 1 lemon
2 tsp fresh thyme leaves
2 tsp fennel seeds, lightly roasted
4 sun-dried tomatoes, finely chopped
1 tsp dried chilli flakes
*for the salsa*
4 plum tomatoes, skinned, seeded and sliced
2 tbsp shredded fresh basil leaves
1 red chilli, seeded and finely sliced
3 tbsp extra virgin olive oil
2 tsp balsamic vinegar
1 tsp caster sugar
*for the garnish*
thyme sprigs

**1** Season the fish and place in a shallow dish. In a bowl, mix together the Pernod, olive oil, lemon zest and juice, thyme, fennel seeds, sun-dried tomatoes and chilli flakes. Pour over the fish, cover and leave to marinate in a cool place for 1-2 hours.
**2** Meanwhile, combine the ingredients for the salsa in a bowl. Season, then cover and set aside to allow the flavours to infuse.
**3** To cook the fish, preheat a lightly oiled griddle or a heavy-based frying pan over a high heat. When very hot, cook the fish steaks for 3-4 minutes on each side; they should still be a little pink in the middle.
**4** Transfer the fish steaks to warmed plates, garnish and serve with the salsa.

## Roasted monkfish with saffron aioli

Prepare the aioli and marinade the day before to allow time for the flavours to develop. The fish can be made oven ready up to 2-3 hours ahead. *Serves 4-6*

2 small monkfish tails, each 600g/1lb 5oz, filleted and skinned (ie 4 fillets in total)
salt and pepper
4 fresh rosemary twigs
4-6 lemon slices
2 tbsp olive oil
*for the marinade*
4 garlic cloves, crushed
1¹/2 tsp finely chopped fresh rosemary
1¹/2 tsp ground coriander
1¹/2 tsp ground cumin
2 tsp sweet paprika
4 tbsp finely chopped fresh coriander leaves
2 tbsp white wine
4 tbsp olive oil
*for the saffron aioli*
2 garlic cloves, peeled
¹/4 tsp saffron strands
1 egg yolk
200ml/7fl oz olive oil
2 tbsp lemon juice (approximately)

**1** To make the marinade, pound the garlic, 1 tsp salt and the rosemary to a paste, using a pestle and mortar. Add the remaining ingredients and mix well. Cover and refrigerate.
**2** To make the aioli, pound the garlic, saffron and ¹/4 tsp salt to a paste, then place in a blender with the egg yolk. With the motor running, slowly add the oil through the feeder tube until the aioli is thick. Transfer to a bowl and stir in lemon juice to taste. Cover and chill.
**3** To prepare the monkfish, smear the flat side of two fillets with the marinade and sandwich them together with the other fillets. Tie at intervals with cotton string and place in a shallow dish. Cover and leave to marinate in a cool place for 2-3 hours.
**4** To cook, preheat oven to 220C/fan oven 200C/Gas 7. Place the fish on a rack in a roasting tin and season well. Thread the rosemary twigs and lemon slices through the string. Drizzle with the 2 tbsp oil and roast for 20 minutes or until cooked through.
**5** Leave to rest for 5-10 minutes before serving, with the aioli and potato chips.

## Skate with nutty brown butter

Skate wings have a delicate texture and a fine flavour. For optimum results, soak the skate in salted water in the fridge for a few hours before poaching to firm up the texture, and take care to avoid overcooking.

¹/2 red onion, finely chopped
6 tbsp cider vinegar
4 cleaned skate wings, each about 200g/7oz
3 pints/1.7 litres court bouillon (see note)
1 tsp yellow mustard seeds
50g/2oz unsalted butter
4 tbsp finely chopped fresh parsley
caper berries or capers, to garnish

**1** Put the chopped red onion into a small bowl, pour on the cider vinegar and set aside to marinate.
**2** Place the skate wings in a large shallow pan and add sufficient court bouillon to just cover them. Slowly bring to the boil, then immediately lower the heat until the liquid is barely moving. Poach the fish for about 10 minutes until the flesh is no longer pink inside. Carefully lift out the skate on to warmed plates; keep warm.
**3** Drain the onion and set aside, reserving the vinegar.
**4** Dry-fry the mustard seeds in a heavy-based frying pan over a high heat until they begin to pop. Immediately add the butter and, as soon as it melts, add the vinegar.
**5** Pour the sizzling butter over the skate wings and scatter with the red onion and parsley. Garnish with caper berries or capers and serve at once.

**NOTE** To make a court bouillon, put 3 pints/ 1.7 litres water in a large pan with ¹/2 red onion, sliced, 6 peppercorns, 2 tsp salt, 6 mustard seeds and 1 tbsp cider vinegar. Bring to the boil, lower the heat and simmer for 5 minutes.

## Deep-fried prawns with harissa salsa

Spicy couscous coated prawns. *Serves 3-4*

24 large raw prawns
400ml/14fl oz well seasoned fish stock
pinch each of turmeric and chilli powder
225g/8oz couscous
8 tbsp chopped fresh coriander leaves
2 red chillies, seeded and finely diced
salt and pepper
oil for deep-frying
seasoned flour, for coating
2 eggs, beaten
*for the harissa salsa*
2 garlic cloves, crushed
1 tsp ground coriander
2 tsp ground caraway seeds
2 tsp mild chilli powder (preferably ancho)
1 tsp sugar
1 tomato, seeded and finely diced
50ml/2fl oz olive oil
juice of 1 lemon
*for the garnish*
deep-fried flat leaf parsley

**1** Shell and devein the prawns, leaving the tail shells on; set aside.
**2** Next, prepare the harissa salsa. Mash the garlic with the spices and a little salt, stir in the remaining ingredients and set aside.
**3** For the prawn coating, bring the stock to the boil, and add the turmeric and chilli powder. Pour over the couscous, cover and leave until the liquid is absorbed. When cool enough to handle, break up the couscous. Add the coriander and chillies; season well.
**4** Heat oil for deep-frying to 160C. Dip the prawns into seasoned flour, then egg, then coat with couscous. Deep-fry, a few at a time, for 3-4 minutes until cooked; drain on kitchen paper. Serve garnished with fried parsley and accompanied by the salsa.

## Seared salmon on lemon pasta salad with saffron salsa

Salmon is seared quickly over a high heat so the outside is crisp and slightly charred, whilst the centre remains rare and moist.

4 small skinless salmon fillets, each about 140g/5oz (see note)
225g/8oz dried fusilli or other pasta shapes
5 tbsp extra virgin olive oil
2 tsp fresh thyme leaves
1 tbsp lemon juice
1 tbsp black peppercorns, crushed
1 tsp cumin seeds
*for the salsa*
1/4 tsp saffron strands
3 tomatoes, peeled, seeded and diced
3 spring onions, finely chopped
1 garlic clove, crushed
1 tbsp shredded fresh basil
salt and pepper
*for the garnish*
basil leaves

**1** First make the salsa. Soak the saffron in 1 tbsp boiling water for 10 minutes, then mix with the other salsa ingredients; set aside.
**2** Cook the pasta in boiling salted water until *al dente*.
**3** Meanwhile, in a small pan, warm 4 tbsp of the oil with the thyme, lemon juice and seasoning. Drain the pasta thoroughly and toss with the dressing. Leave to cool.
**4** Preheat a ridged griddle or heavy-based frying pan until very hot. Combine the peppercorns and cumin seeds and press firmly onto the salmon fillets. Brush with the remaining oil.
**5** Add the salmon to the griddle and sear for 1 1/2 minutes each side. Remove from the pan, let cool slightly, then slice thickly.
**6** Arrange the pasta salad on plates and top with the warm salmon slices. Spoon around the saffron salsa and serve garnished with basil leaves.

**NOTE** Make sure that you use the freshest possible salmon for this dish.

## Seafood with pine nuts and garlic

This deliciously rich Spanish stew is substantial enough to serve as a meal in itself. Accompany with a refreshing watercress salad and plenty of grilled flat bread to mop up the tasty juices. *Serves 4-6*

40g/1 1/2oz raisins
50ml/2fl oz brandy
3 garlic cloves, crushed
85g/3oz pine nuts, lightly toasted
salt and pepper
6 tbsp olive oil
1 large onion, finely chopped
8 tomatoes, skinned and chopped
2 tsp paprika
4 fresh bay leaves
125ml/4fl oz dry white wine
30 mussels in shells, cleaned
24 clams in shells, cleaned (optional)
8-12 whole large raw prawns
700g/1lb 9oz thick cod fillet, cut into 5cm/2in chunks
8-12 small new potatoes, cooked

**1** Soak the raisins in the brandy for 1 hour. Mash the garlic and two thirds of the pine nuts to a paste with a little salt.
**2** Heat 3 tbsp oil in a heavy-based pan and gently fry the onion until soft. Increase the heat and add the tomatoes, paprika, bay leaves, seasoning and wine. Stir well until beginning to thicken. Transfer to a bowl.
**3** Bring 400ml/14 fl oz salted water to the boil in a large pan. Add the mussels, and clams if using. Cover and shake the pan over a medium heat for about 4 minutes, until the shells open. Drain, reserving the liquor; discard any unopened ones. Strain the liquor; stir a little into the garlic paste.
**4** Heat the remaining oil in a deep pan and sauté the prawns for 1 minute. Add the raisins and brandy and cook for 1 minute. Stir in the tomato mixture.
**5** Add the remaining liquor to the pan and bring to a gentle simmer, then remove the prawns with a slotted spoon. Add the cod to the pan and cook for 5 minutes; remove. Increase the heat, then add the garlic paste and potatoes. Simmer for a few minutes.
**6** To serve, add all of the seafood to the pan and heat through gently. Sprinkle with the remaining pine nuts.

## Chinese-style sea bass

An impressive steamed fish to bring to the table whole. Serve with plain rice and a colourful medley of stir-fried vegetables.

1 bunch spring onions, finely shredded
2 sea bass, each about 700g/1lb 9oz, cleaned
1 1/2 tsp Chinese five spice powder
4cm/1 1/2in piece fresh root ginger, shredded
3 garlic cloves, finely sliced
1/2 tsp black, or toasted white sesame seeds
3 tbsp sunflower oil
5 tbsp light soy sauce

**1** Preheat oven to 230C/fan oven 210C/Gas 8. Put the shredded spring onion in a bowl, add cold water to cover and chill in the fridge to curl the onion shreds.
**2** Make deep slashes in both sides of the fish, about 2.5cm/1in apart. Rub the spice powder into the cuts and inside the cavity. Place the sea bass on a large heatproof serving plate.
**3** Drain the spring onion; pat dry. Scatter the onion, ginger, garlic and sesame seeds over the fish. Place some scrunched up balls of foil over the base of a large roasting tin and carefully position the plate of fish on top. Pour over the oil and soy sauce.
**4** Pour a 4cm/1 1/2in depth of boiling water into the roasting tin, then cover with foil to form a tent over the fish; secure the foil under the edge of the tin to hold in the steam during baking.
**5** Carefully place in the oven and bake for about 12-16 minutes, depending on size, until the sea bass is tender. Serve with rice and stir-fried vegetables.

**NOTE** The fish is cooked when the flesh divides into flakes easily.

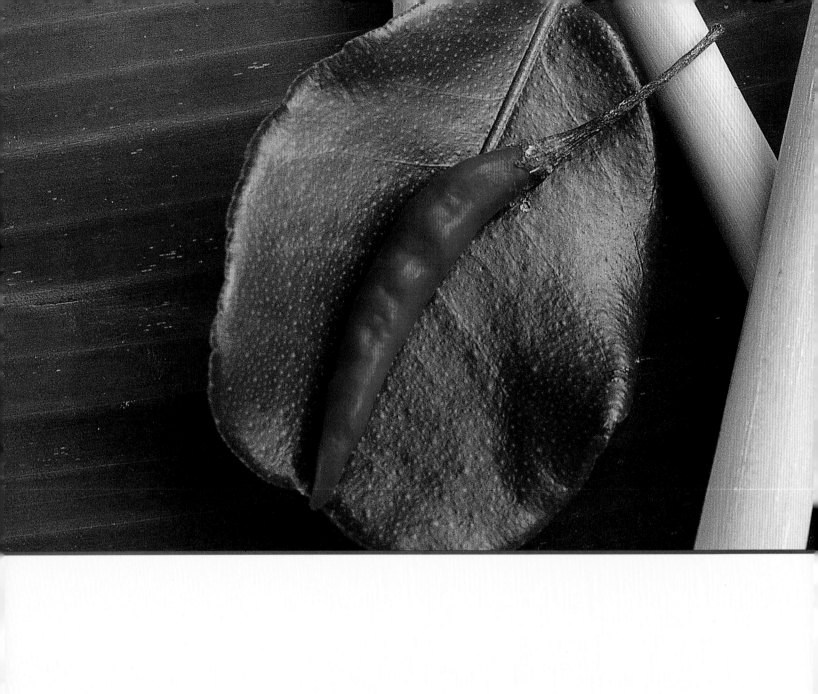

# mouth-watering
# chicken

**Set the tastebuds tingling** with these delicious, original chicken meals. Find new ways to flavour the Sunday roast and **fresh inspiration for fast midweek meals**, including stir-fries, grills and **low fat dishes**. Turn succulent chicken portions into tasty suppers with **robust flavour combinations** from **Tuscany, Provence and North Africa**. For special occasions, **flavourful marinades**, divine dressings and savoury butters transform chicken portions into **dishes of distinction**. Alternatively, treat guests to **fresh-tasting Thai dishes** - scented with lemon grass, sweet basil, coriander and chillies.

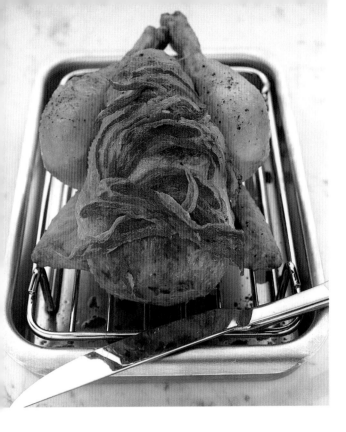

## Pancetta-wrapped roast

Tasty chicken with an Italian stuffing, roasted in a crisp pancetta overcoat.

1 oven-ready chicken, about 1.5kg/3¼lb
200g/7oz Italian-style sausages, skinned
200g/7oz cooked chestnuts (preferably roasted), roughly chopped
salt and pepper
10 thin slices pancetta
oil, for brushing

**1** Preheat oven to 200C/fan oven 180C/Gas 6. Break up the sausage meat with a fork and mix with the chestnuts and plenty of pepper. Use to stuff the neck end of the chicken (not the cavity). Secure the flap under the bird with a cocktail stick.
**2** Season the chicken with plenty of pepper, then lay the pancetta slices, overlapping slightly, over the surface of the chicken.
**3** Put the chicken on a trivet in a roasting dish. Cover with a piece of oiled baking parchment, securing at each 'corner' of the chicken with a cocktail stick. Roast for 50 minutes, then carefully remove the paper. Roast for a further 30-40 minutes until the chicken is cooked.

**NOTES** To calculate roasting time, weigh the chicken and allow 20 minutes per 450g/1lb, plus an extra 20 minutes at 190-200C/fan oven 180C/Gas 5-6.
To test that a roast chicken is cooked, pierce the thickest part of the leg with a skewer and make sure that the juices run clear.

## Citrus roast chicken

1 oven-ready chicken, about 1.6kg/3½lb
olive oil, for brushing
2 tsp five peppercorn mixture, crushed
3 tbsp redcurrant jelly
juice of 1 ruby grapefruit
ruby grapefruit segments, to garnish

**1** Preheat oven to 200C/fan oven 180C/Gas 6. Brush the chicken with oil, then sprinkle with the crushed pepper and salt. Place breast side down in a non-metal shallow ovenproof dish. Roast for 45 minutes.
**2** Melt the redcurrant jelly in a pan over a low heat. Add the grapefruit juice and bring to the boil, stirring. Turn chicken breast side up and spoon over half of the glaze. Lower oven setting to 180C/fan oven 160C/Gas 4 and roast chicken for a further 45 minutes, or until cooked through, basting at intervals.
**3** Serve garnished with grapefruit segments, accompanied by the skimmed pan juices.

## Sesame roast chicken

1 oven-ready chicken, about 1.6kg/3½lb
3 tbsp sesame oil
3 tbsp soy sauce
2-3 tsp grated fresh root ginger
1 tsp sesame seeds

**1** Preheat oven to 200C/fan oven 180C/Gas 6. Mix the oil, soy sauce and ginger together and brush half inside and over the chicken.
**2** Lay breast down in roasting tin and roast for 45 minutes. Turn breast up and brush with more soy mixture. Roast for 20 minutes.
**3** Brush again, sprinkle with sesame seeds and roast for a further 25 minutes or until cooked, reducing setting if browning too fast.

## Saffron roast chicken

1 oven-ready chicken, about 1.6kg/3½lb
*for the saffron butter*
50g/2oz unsalted butter, softened
½ packet saffron threads, crumbled
½ tsp salt
*for the onions*
1 tbsp olive oil
25g/1oz butter
450g/1lb onions, halved and thinly sliced
2 tsp garam masala
2 tsp cumin seeds
6 cardamom pods, lightly crushed
2 tsp finely chopped fresh root ginger
50g/2oz sultanas

**1** Preheat oven to 200C/fan oven 180C/Gas 6. Loosen the skin from the chicken breast by easing your fingers under the neck flap, over the breast and down to the legs, without puncturing the skin.
**2** Mix the ingredients for the saffron butter and spread evenly over the chicken breast under the skin. Secure the neck flap under the bird with a cocktail stick.
**3** Heat the oil and butter in a wide pan and gently fry the onions until softened. Add all the spices and cook for 2-3 minutes. Add the sultanas, then transfer to a roasting dish and place the chicken on top, breast side down. Roast for 45 minutes.
**4** Lower setting to 190C/fan oven 170C/Gas 5 and turn the chicken breast side up. Stir the onions, piling some of the lighter ones on top of the chicken to keep it moist. Roast for a further 45 minutes or until the chicken is cooked through and the onions are crisp.

## Chicken saltimbocca

These prosciutto and sage flavoured parcels are typically served with tagliatelle.

4 slices prosciutto
12 large fresh sage leaves
4 skinless chicken breast fillets
salt and pepper
1 tbsp olive oil
large knob of butter
1 red onion, sliced
dash of white wine
4 tbsp crème fraîche

**1** Lay the prosciutto slices on a surface and place a sage leaf on each. Position the chicken breasts at an angle on top and season with pepper. Top with another sage leaf and wrap the chicken breasts in the prosciutto slices.
**2** Heat the oil and butter in a heavy-based frying pan, add the parcels and fry for 2-3 minutes until lightly browned. Turn the parcels over and add the rest of the sage. Fry for 2 minutes until the sage leaves are frazzled; remove these with a slotted spoon and set aside.
**3** Lower the heat, add the onion to the pan and cook gently until softened. Turn the chicken parcels again. Add the wine, increasing the heat and stirring to deglaze the pan.
**4** Lower the heat, stir in the crème fraîche and simmer gently for 2-3 minutes or until the chicken is cooked through. Serve garnished with the frazzled sage leaves.

## Chicken on a bed of bay leaves

This unusual Italian way of cooking chicken imparts a unique flavour.

2 tbsp olive oil
20 fresh bay leaves
4 skinless chicken breast fillets
salt and pepper

**1** Heat the oil gently in a heavy-based pan or casserole. Cover the base of the pan with a layer of bay leaves, then lay the chicken breast fillets on top. Season, cover tightly and cook for 10-12 minutes.
**2** Turn the chicken breasts over, re-cover and cook for a further 10 minutes or until cooked through. Serve the chicken with the pan juices and vegetables of your choice.

## Stir-fried chicken with pak choi and egg noodles

This aromatic, colourful stir-fry is quick to assemble and cook. If pak choi is not available, use Chinese leaves instead.

2 skinless chicken breast fillets
6 tbsp dark soy sauce
2 garlic cloves, crushed
1 tbsp cornflour
1 tbsp soft brown sugar
2 tsp grated fresh root ginger
250g packet medium Chinese egg noodles
2 tbsp sunflower oil
2 carrots, cut into matchstick strips
4 tbsp dry sherry
8 spring onions, sliced diagonally
200g/7oz pak choi or bok choi, roughly shredded
175g/6oz bean sprouts
4 tbsp chopped fresh coriander

**1** Cut the chicken into strips and mix with the soy sauce, garlic, cornflour, sugar and ginger. Cook the noodles according to the pack instructions.
**2** Heat the oil in a wok and stir-fry the carrot until starting to soften. Add the chicken mixture and stir-fry for 2-3 minutes. Sprinkle in the sherry and allow to bubble until it is totally reduced.
**3** Add the spring onions, pak choi and bean sprouts. Heat through, stirring, then add the drained egg noodles and chopped coriander. Toss well to mix and serve immediately, in warmed bowls.

## Lemon chicken with garlic and potatoes

Try this as an alternative to the traditional Sunday roast – it's all done in one dish!

8-12 chicken pieces (thighs and drumsticks)
salt and pepper
finely grated rind of 1 lemon
2 tbsp chopped fresh thyme
900g/2lb small new potatoes
1 lemon, very thinly sliced
12 large garlic cloves (unpeeled)
150ml/¼ pint olive oil

**1** Preheat oven to 180C/fan oven 160C/Gas 4. Put the chicken in a large bowl, season well and add the lemon rind and thyme. Toss well to coat and spread in a large baking dish.
**2** Crack each potato by tapping sharply with a rolling pin. Add to the chicken. Tuck the lemon slices around. Scatter the garlic cloves over the chicken. Drizzle the olive oil evenly over the top.
**3** Bake for about 45 minutes, stirring occasionally, until golden brown and cooked through. Serve with courgettes or broccoli.

## Tuscan chicken thighs

Rosemary, garlic and plenty of seasoning give these succulent chicken thighs an authentic Tuscan flavour.

4-6 garlic cloves, peeled
2 tsp sea salt
1 tsp freshly ground black pepper
3 tbsp finely chopped fresh rosemary
12 boneless chicken thighs, skinned
12 thin slices pancetta or streaky bacon
12 fresh bay leaves
olive oil, for brushing

**1** Pound the garlic with the salt, pepper and rosemary, using a pestle and mortar or coffee grinder. Rub this paste generously all over the flesh-side of the chicken thighs.
**2** Re-shape and wrap each thigh in a slice of pancetta, tucking in a bay leaf. Secure with fine string. Preheat the grill.
**3** Place the chicken in the grill pan and brush with olive oil. Grill for 15-20 minutes, turning every 5 minutes until golden, crisp and cooked through. Serve drizzled with extra olive oil and accompanied by a salad.

Lemon chicken with garlic and potatoes

## Smoky chicken wings

Grill or barbecue these spicy sweet-sour glazed chicken wings. Serve with warm bread and a tomato salad.

12 large chicken wings
2 tbsp olive oil
juice of 1/2 lemon
2 tsp sweet chilli sauce
1 tsp Pimenton (smoked Spanish paprika) or sweet paprika
1 tbsp sun-dried tomato paste or tomato purée
1 garlic clove, crushed
salt and pepper
thyme sprigs, to garnish

**1** Pre-soak 8 long wooden or bamboo skewers in cold water for 20 minutes. Mix the olive oil, lemon juice, chilli sauce, paprika, tomato paste and garlic together to form a thick sauce.
**2** Preheat the grill (or barbecue). Cut off the very tips of the chicken wings. Thread 3 chicken wings onto 2 parallel skewers; repeat with the remaining wings and skewers.
**3** Grill (or barbecue) for 15 minutes, turning twice, then brush liberally with the sauce. Grill (or barbecue) for a further 10-15 minutes until cooked through and nicely browned, turning and basting with the sauce from time to time.
**4** Season and garnish with thyme to serve. Eat the chicken wings with your fingers!

**NOTE** The secret of these barbecued wings is to brush with the glaze towards the end of cooking rather than at the start, to avoid scorching them.

## Pan-seared chicken with garlic sauce

A real must for garlic lovers – whole cloves are cooked with chicken fillets, then mashed into the sauce.

50g/2oz butter
4 boneless chicken breasts (with skin)
12 garlic cloves, unpeeled
300ml/1/2 pint dry or medium white wine
2 large fresh rosemary sprigs
2 fresh bay leaves
salt and pepper

**1** Melt the butter in a sauté pan. When foaming, add the chicken skin side down and the unpeeled garlic cloves. Fry for about 5 minutes, then turn the chicken over.
**2** Add the wine and herbs. Season, then cover tightly and simmer for 20 minutes. Transfer the chicken to a warmed plate and leave to rest in a warm place.
**3** Mash most of the garlic into the sauce using a potato masher, then bring to the boil, taste and season. Strain the sauce over the chicken or simply pour it over – bits and all! Serve with sugar snaps or mangetout and new potatoes.

## Devilled chicken

A rich and fiery sauce made in minutes with the pan juices and dark balsamic vinegar.

2 tbsp olive oil
4 boneless chicken breasts (with skin)
2 garlic cloves, chopped
2 tbsp balsamic vinegar
6 tbsp dry white wine
4 tbsp well flavoured chicken stock
1 tbsp sun-dried tomato paste
1/2 tsp mild chilli powder
2 tbsp chopped fresh parsley
salt and pepper

**1** Heat the oil in a frying pan, add the chicken, skin side down, and fry gently for 15 minutes, undisturbed.
**2** Turn the chicken over, add the garlic and fry gently for a further 5-10 minutes until cooked through. Transfer to a warmed serving dish and leave to rest in a warm place while making the sauce.
**3** Pour the balsamic vinegar, wine and stock into the pan, scraping up any sediment. Whisk in the tomato paste and chilli powder. Let bubble until reduced and syrupy. Stir in the parsley and any juices from the chicken; taste and season. Pour the devilled sauce over the chicken to serve.

## Chicken with lemon and minted couscous

Simple baked chicken served on a bed of lemon couscous flavoured with mint.

finely grated rind and juice of 2 lemons
2 garlic cloves, crushed
2 tsp ground cumin
8-12 chicken pieces (thighs and drumsticks)
4 tbsp olive oil
salt and pepper
8 spring onions, sliced
350ml/12fl oz chicken stock (approximately)
6 tbsp chopped fresh mint
225g/8oz quick-cook couscous
lemon wedges and mint sprigs, to garnish

1 Preheat oven to 200C/fan oven 180C/Gas 6. Mix the juice and rind of 1 lemon with the garlic and cumin. Rub this mixture all over the chicken pieces.
2 Spoon 2 tbsp of the olive oil over the base of a baking dish and add the chicken. Season, then add 150ml/1/4 pint water. Bake in the oven for 25-30 minutes.
3 Meanwhile, heat the remaining olive oil in a pan, add the spring onions and fry gently for 2-3 minutes until starting to colour. Stir in the remaining lemon rind and juice. Pour in the stock and bring to the boil.
4 Add the mint, then pour in the couscous in a steady stream, stirring briefly to mix. Cover, remove from the heat and leave to swell for 10 minutes. Fork through the grains to break up any lumps; re-cover and keep warm.
5 Transfer the couscous and chicken to warmed plates. If necessary, deglaze the baking dish with a little extra stock or water and drizzle the pan juices over the chicken and couscous. Serve garnished with lemon wedges and mint sprigs.

## Tandoori chicken pieces

For optimum flavour, slash the chicken pieces and leave to marinate in the tandoori mixture overnight.

8-12 skinless chicken pieces (thighs, drumsticks, halved breasts)
juice of 1 lemon
sea salt
*for the marinade*
250ml/9fl oz yogurt
1 onion, cut into chunks
3 garlic cloves, crushed
2.5cm/1in piece fresh root ginger, chopped
2 tbsp turmeric
1 green chilli, seeded
1 tbsp garam masala
*to serve*
lime wedges

1 Cut deep slits in the meatiest parts of the chicken pieces and place in a shallow dish. Sprinkle with lemon juice and salt and let stand for 30 minutes.
2 Meanwhile, whizz all the marinade ingredients together in a food processor or blender to form a smooth paste. Add the chicken pieces and toss to coat. Cover and leave to marinate in a cool place for several hours, or overnight if possible.
3 Preheat a baking sheet in the oven at 250C/fan oven 230C/Gas 9. Lift the chicken out of the marinade and place the drumsticks and thighs on the hot baking sheet. Bake for about 20 minutes, adding the chicken breast pieces after about 5 minutes.
4 Serve with lime wedges and warm naan bread or rice.

NOTE An Indian-style salad of tomato, cucumber and chopped onion, scattered with plenty of chopped fresh coriander is the ideal accompaniment.

## Golden tapenade supremes

Cut into these moist chicken breasts to reveal a soft, savoury stuffing – reminiscent of the flavours of Provence.

4 chicken supremes (see note)
85g/3oz ricotta cheese
4 tbsp black olive tapenade
4 sun-dried tomatoes in oil, chopped
salt and pepper
olive oil, for brushing

1 Preheat oven to 200C/fan oven 180C/Gas 6. Break up the ricotta in a bowl, then beat in the tapenade, sun-dried tomatoes and salt and pepper to taste.
2 Loosen the skin covering each chicken breast and push in as much stuffing as will fit between the skin and the flesh. Gently reform the skin over the stuffing and chicken.
3 Brush the skin with olive oil and season well. Place in a baking dish and bake in the oven for 25 minutes.
4 Allow the chicken to rest for 5 minutes before serving, with roasted peppers and new potatoes or rice.

NOTE Chicken supremes are breast fillets with the wing bone still attached – available ready-prepared from larger supermarkets. Alternatively ask your butcher to prepare them for you.

VARIATION Add a spoonful of chopped capers to the stuffing to cut the richness and add a delicious piquancy.

Rancher's chicken (left);
Spicy chicken korma
with cashews (far left);
Goujons with avocado
mayonnaise (below)

## Goujons with avocado mayonnaise

Poppy seeds, chives and cayenne add a savoury note to these crunchy chicken strips. An avocado dip is the perfect foil.

4 slices softgrain bread
2 tsp poppy seeds
1/4 tsp cayenne pepper
2 tbsp snipped fresh chives
4 skinless chicken breast fillets, thickly sliced
2 eggs, beaten
4 tbsp sunflower oil, for frying
*for the mayonnaise*
1 large avocado, halved and stoned
3 tbsp mayonnaise
2 tbsp French dressing
salt and pepper

**1** First blend the mayonnaise ingredients together in a food processor until creamy; turn into a bowl. Clean the processor.
**2** Break the bread in to the food processor. Add the spices, chives and 1 tsp salt. Process to crumbs; tip on to a plate. Dip the chicken strips in the egg, then into the spicy crumbs to coat.
**3** Heat the oil in a large non-stick frying pan and fry the goujons for 2-3 minutes each side until crisp and golden. Serve hot, with the avocado mayonnaise and a salad.

## Rancher's chicken

This takes minutes to make, yet the smoky sauce adds a special taste. *Serves 2*

2 skinless chicken breast fillets
1 large tomato, finely chopped
2 tbsp hickory barbecue sauce
1 tbsp olive oil
4 rindless smoked streaky bacon rashers
50g/2oz mature Cheddar, grated

**1** Beat the chicken fillets with a rolling pin until flattened to an even thickness. Stir the tomato into the hickory sauce.

**2** Heat the oil in a large cast-iron (or other grillproof) frying pan, add the chicken and bacon and fry for about 1-2 minutes each side. Preheat the grill.
**3** Space the chicken fillets apart in the pan, then spread with the tomato mixture. Sprinkle with the cheese and top with the bacon.
**4** Grill for about 3 minutes until the bacon is turning golden and the cheese has melted. Serve with a salad and jacket potatoes.

## Spicy chicken korma with cashews

Fresh ginger and chillies impart flavour, while ground cashew nuts give this curry an intriguing texture.

2 onions, quartered
4 garlic cloves
7.5cm/3in piece fresh root ginger, chopped
100g/4oz cashew nuts
3 tbsp sunflower oil
2 red chillies, seeded and sliced
1 tsp cumin seeds
1 tsp ground turmeric
1 tsp ground white pepper
700ml/1 1/4 pints chicken stock
4 skinless chicken breast fillets, cubed
150g/5oz carton yogurt
2 bananas, sliced
3 tbsp chopped fresh coriander
coriander sprigs, to garnish

**1** Put the onions, garlic, ginger and nuts in a food processor and blend to a paste.
**2** Heat the oil in a large frying pan, add the onion and cashew mixture with the chilli and cumin and fry for 10 minutes, stirring frequently.
**3** Stir in the turmeric and pepper, then pour in the stock and simmer for 5 minutes.
**4** Add the chicken, cover and simmer gently for 15 minutes.
**5** Stir in the yogurt, bananas and coriander. Garnish with sprigs of coriander and serve with basmati rice or naan bread.

## Pan-fried chicken with shiitake

25g/1oz unsalted butter
4 chicken breast fillets (with skin)
2 garlic cloves, finely chopped
150g/5 1/2oz small shiitake mushrooms
4 tbsp extra dry white vermouth
300ml/1/2 pint carton fresh chicken stock
4 tbsp crème fraîche
salt and pepper
4 spring onions, shredded

**1** Melt the butter in a large frying pan. Add the chicken and cook gently for 5 minutes, turning once. Remove and set aside.
**2** Add the garlic and mushrooms to the pan; stir-fry until the mushrooms start to soften.
**3** Add the vermouth and stock. Increase heat and boil rapidly until the liquid has almost totally evaporated.
**4** Stir in the crème fraîche, season, then return the chicken to the pan. Part cover and simmer for 5 minutes or until the chicken is cooked through. Stir in the onions and heat through. Serve with tagliatelle.

## Maple roast poussins with thyme

4 poussins (baby chicken)
6 tbsp maple syrup
1 tbsp Dijon mustard
3 garlic cloves, crushed
1 1/2 tsp fresh lemon thyme leaves
salt and pepper

**1** Preheat oven to 220C/fan oven 200C/Gas 7. Halve the poussins lengthways along the breast bone, using poultry shears or kitchen scissors, and remove the tips from the wings and knuckles. Place in a large dish.
**2** Mix together the maple syrup, mustard, garlic, lemon thyme and seasoning until well blended. Spoon over the poussins and turn them in the mixture to coat all over.
**3** Arrange the poussins, close together, in a large roasting dish and spoon over the remaining juices. Roast for 25-30 minutes until golden. Serve with vegetables.

## Chicken pies with butternut mash topping

Cubes of chicken, sliced leeks and tart Bramley apple are simmered in cider for these tasty pies. Butternut squash gives a sweet, nutty flavour and light texture to the golden mash topping.

500g/1lb 2oz butternut squash, peeled, seeded and diced

1 kg/2lb 4oz potatoes, peeled and diced

300ml/1/2 pint milk

1 tsp chopped fresh sage

25g/1oz butter

salt and pepper

4 skinless chicken breast fillets, cut into 2.5cm/1in cubes

1 small Bramley apple, peeled, cored and chopped

2 leeks, sliced

150ml/1/4 pint dry cider

1 chicken stock cube, crumbled

50g/2oz mature Cheddar, grated

**1** Put the butternut squash, potatoes, milk, chopped sage and butter in a pan and season with salt and pepper. Bring to the boil, lower the heat, cover the pan tightly and simmer for 20-25 minutes, stirring once, until the potatoes are tender. Mash until the mixture is smooth.

**2** Meanwhile, put the chicken in a pan with the apple, leeks, cider and crumbled stock cube. Season, cover and simmer gently for 25 minutes until the leeks and chicken are tender and the apples are pulpy.

**3** Spoon the chicken mixture over the base of four 350ml/12fl oz pie dishes and top with the mash. Sprinkle with the cheese.

If preparing ahead, cover and keep chilled for up to 2 days.

**4** To serve, preheat oven to 190C/fan oven 170C/Gas 5. Bake the pies for 30 minutes until golden and piping hot. Serve with broccoli or cabbage.

Preparing Mexican enchiladas (above); cooked enchiladas ready to serve (right)

## Coq au vin with thyme and juniper

Juniper berries add an intriguing and subtle fragrance to this version of a classic, which is ideal for entertaining. For added texture, sprinkle with croûtons as you serve.

2-3 tbsp olive oil
8 smoked streaky bacon rashers, halved and rolled up
250g/9oz shallots, peeled (see note)
250g/9oz baby button mushrooms
8 boneless chicken thighs, skinned
2 tbsp seasoned flour
300ml/1/2 pint Beaujolais
2 tbsp brandy
300ml/1/2 pint chicken stock
1 tbsp tomato purée
2 garlic cloves, chopped
4 juniper berries, crushed
1 tbsp fresh thyme leaves
salt and pepper

**1** Preheat oven to 180C/fan oven 160C/Gas 4. Heat 2 tbsp olive oil in a large heavy-based frying pan and fry the bacon rolls for a few minutes until turning golden; transfer to a flameproof casserole, using a slotted spoon.
**2** Fry the shallots and mushrooms in the oil left in the pan for a few minutes, turning, until slightly coloured. Add to the casserole.
**3** Coat the chicken thighs in the seasoned flour, then fry for about 5 minutes until golden, adding more oil to the pan if necessary. Transfer to the casserole.
**4** Pour the wine, brandy and stock into the pan. Stir in the tomato purée, garlic, juniper and thyme. Bring to the boil, then pour over the chicken.
**5** Cover tightly and cook the casserole in the oven for 1 hour or until the chicken and shallots are tender; check the seasoning. If preparing ahead, cool and keep in the fridge for up to 3 days.

**6** When ready to serve, reheat on the hob until bubbling. Serve with green beans and sautéed potatoes.

**NOTE** Before peeling shallots, immerse in boiling water for 5 minutes – you will find the skins come away much more easily.

## Chorizo and chicken gumbo

3 tbsp olive oil
2 tbsp plain flour
2 fresh bay leaves
1 large onion, finely chopped
4 celery sticks, thickly sliced
1 tbsp Cajun seasoning
1 tsp fresh thyme leaves
400g can peeled tomatoes in juice
700ml/1 1/4 pints chicken stock
2 large green peppers, seeded and cubed
140g/5oz okra, trimmed (halved if large)
8 skinless chicken thighs
200g/7oz piece chorizo sausage, skinned and diced
salt and pepper

**1** Heat the oil in a large heavy-based pan or flameproof casserole. Stir in the flour and bay leaves and cook gently for about 5 minutes, stirring frequently until the flour is a nutty brown colour.
**2** Tip in the onion and celery and cook gently for 5 minutes. Stir in the Cajun seasoning and thyme leaves.
**3** Pour in the tomatoes and stock, then stir in all the remaining ingredients, seasoning with salt and pepper to taste. Cover and simmer for 40 minutes until the chicken is tender. If preparing ahead, cool and keep in the fridge for up to 3 days.
**4** When ready to serve, reheat on the hob until piping hot. Serve with mixed basmati and wild rice or bread and a leafy salad.

## Mexican enchiladas

Tortillas and refried beans are important ingredients in Mexican cuisine. They both feature in these delicious spicy pancakes.

2 tbsp olive oil
2 red peppers, seeded and thinly sliced
2 red onions, sliced
3 cloves garlic, crushed
2 red chillies, seeded and sliced
2 tsp ground coriander
2 tsp ground cumin
4 chicken breast fillets, cut into strips
salt and pepper
220g can refried beans
4 tbsp chopped fresh coriander leaves
300ml/1/2 pint soured cream
8 flour tortillas
140g/5oz mature Cheddar, grated

**1** Heat the oil in a large pan, then add the peppers, onions, garlic and three quarters of the chilli. Stir-fry over a high heat for about 8 minutes until softened.
**2** Stir in the ground spices, then add the chicken strips and seasoning. Cover and cook for 5 minutes.
**3** Remove from the heat and stir in the refried beans, three quarters of the fresh coriander and 2 tbsp of the soured cream.
**4** Lay the tortillas on a work surface. Divide the chicken mixture between them and roll up to enclose. Place in a large ovenproof dish and top with the remaining soured cream. Scatter over the cheese, remaining chilli and coriander. If preparing ahead, cover and chill for up to 2 days.
**5** When ready to serve, preheat oven to 190C/fan oven 170C/Gas 5. Cover the tortilla dish with foil and bake for 50 minutes. Remove the foil and bake for a further 10-15 minutes until golden and piping hot. Serve with an avocado and lettuce salad.

Aubergine and chicken 'roulades' (above);
preparing the 'roulades' (main picture)

## Aubergine and chicken 'roulades'

Oven-baked aubergine slices rolled around a tasty minced chicken filling.

450g/1lb skinless chicken breast fillets, or skinned boneless thighs, or a mixture
1 rounded tbsp half fat crème fraîche
2 tbsp finely shredded fresh basil
salt and pepper
2 medium-large aubergines
oil, for brushing
*for the tomato sauce*
2 tsp olive oil
1 small onion or 2 shallots, finely chopped
1 garlic clove, crushed
500ml/18fl oz passata
few basil leaves
1 tbsp red or white wine

**1** Mince the chicken meat or finely chop in a food processor; transfer to a bowl. Mix in the crème fraîche, basil, salt and pepper.
**2** Thinly slice the aubergines lengthwise, to give 10-12 slices from each; discard the outer skin-covered slices. Brush one side of each aubergine slice with a little oil and place, oiled-side down, on a work surface.
**3** Divide the chicken mixture between the aubergine slices and spread evenly, almost to the edges. Roll up the aubergine slices to enclose the filling and thread onto 4 wooden kebab skewers. Place on a non-stick baking sheet. Preheat oven to 190C/fan oven 170C/Gas 5.
**4** To make the sauce, heat the oil in a pan and fry the onion for 3-4 minutes until softened, then add the garlic and cook for 1 minute. Add the passata, basil leaves and wine. Bring to the boil, reduce the heat and simmer gently for about 10 minutes. Season to taste.
**5** Meanwhile, cook the aubergine rolls in the oven for about 20-25 minutes, until the chicken is cooked through, turning halfway through the cooking time. Serve with the tomato sauce and a leafy green salad.

## Skewered rosemary chicken

Grilling meat on herb skewers gives off a wonderful aroma to stimulate the tastebuds.

4 skinless chicken breast fillets, cut into 2.5cm/1in cubes
1 clove garlic, crushed
2 tsp chopped fresh thyme
juice of 1/2 lemon
salt and pepper
8 fresh rosemary stems, at least 23cm/9in long (preferably woody)

**1** Put the chicken in a non-metallic bowl and add the garlic, thyme, lemon juice and seasoning. Toss well and leave to marinate for 30-40 minutes (no longer), turning occasionally.
**2** Strip the rosemary stems of their leaves, except for the 7.5cm/3in at the narrow end. Cut the woody ends obliquely to shape points that will pierce the chicken.
**3** Preheat the grill. Remove the chicken from the marinade, reserving the juice.
**4** Thread the chicken pieces on to the skewers carefully and lay on the grill tray, with the leafy rosemary tips towards you.
**5** Cover the rosemary leaves with a strip of foil to prevent them from scorching. Grill for about 10-15 minutes, turning and basting occasionally with the reserved marinade. Serve with a mixed salad.

## Aromatic chicken parcels

Cooking herb-coated chicken in parcels seals in all of the flavour and moisture. For the parcels you will need 4 sheets of baking parchment, each about 30 x 23cm/12 x 9in.

8 large chicken drumsticks or thighs, skinned
sea salt and pepper
24 large fresh basil leaves, or 2 tbsp chopped fresh basil
a little oil, for brushing

**1** Preheat oven to 200C/fan oven 180C/Gas 6.
**2** Season the chicken generously with salt and pepper, then press 3 basil leaves on to each drumstick or thigh, or roll each chicken piece in chopped basil to coat.
**3** Lightly oil the 4 baking parchment sheets in the centre only. Place 2 chicken pieces on the oiled part of each piece of paper. Fold up the two short sides over the chicken and pleat them together at the top, then fold over the two loose ends and pleat to make a fairly secure parcel.
**4** Place the parcels on a baking tray and bake for about 30 minutes until the chicken is cooked through. Serve with vegetables.

## Lime and ginger grilled chicken

Lean chicken is deeply scored before marinating to encourage the flavours to permeate and ensure quick cooking.

4 skinless chicken breast fillets
1/2 tsp finely grated lime rind
juice of 1/2 large lime
2.5 cm/1in piece fresh root ginger, finely shredded
salt and pepper
2 tsp maple syrup or clear honey
snipped chives, to garnish

**1** Using a very sharp knife, score the chicken deeply in a criss-cross pattern, cutting halfway through the thickness. Place in a shallow dish.
**2** Mix together the lime rind and juice, ginger and seasoning. Brush this over the scored surface of the chicken and leave to marinate for about 20 minutes.
**3** Preheat the grill to high. Brush the chicken with the maple syrup or honey and cook for 7-8 minutes on each side, turning and basting at least twice.
**4** Serve garnished with snipped chives and accompanied by steamed French beans or sugar snap peas.

## Prawn and chicken laksa

1 tbsp vegetable oil
1 onion, finely chopped
2 tsp grated fresh root ginger
2 tsp crushed garlic
3 lemon grass stalks, finely chopped
1 tbsp ground coriander
2 tsp ground cumin
1 red chilli, seeded and thinly sliced
4 boneless chicken thighs, skinned and
cut into bite size pieces
400ml/14fl oz coconut milk
200ml/7fl oz chicken stock
200g/7oz cooked peeled tiger prawns
6 tbsp finely chopped fresh coriander
salt and pepper
200g/7oz packet medium egg noodles

**1** Heat the oil in a large heavy-based pan,
add the onion, ginger, garlic and lemon
grass, and cook gently until the onion is
softened.
**2** Add the spices and stir-fry for 1 minute,
then add the chilli and chicken. Stir-fry for
2-3 minutes, then pour in the coconut milk
and stock. Bring to a simmer and cook
gently for 15-20 minutes. Stir in the prawns
and coriander leaves; season.
**3** Meanwhile cook the noodles according
to the pack instructions; drain well. Divide
between serving bowls and top with the
prawn mixture to serve.

## Tagliatelle with lime chicken

This combination of chilli chicken, noodles
and a creamy lime sauce is a wonderful
fusion of flavours. *Serves 3-4*

2 large skinless chicken breast fillets
2 tsp sesame oil
1 tbsp dark soy sauce
1/2 tsp chilli sauce
300g/10oz dried tagliatelle
4 spring onions, thickly sliced
*for the sauce*
300ml/1/2 pint chicken or vegetable stock
(see note)
200ml carton coconut cream
11/2 tsp Thai fish sauce
6 kaffir lime leaves, shredded
1 garlic clove, sliced
pinch of sugar
salt and pepper
*for the garnish*
coriander leaves

**1** Cut the chicken into strips and toss with
the sesame oil, soy sauce and chilli sauce.
Cover and leave to marinate in a cool place
for 1 hour.
**2** Meanwhile, prepare the sauce. Place all
the ingredients in a saucepan, bring to the
boil and simmer until reduced by half. Pass
through a fine sieve and keep warm.
**3** Bring a large pan of salted water to the
boil. Add the pasta and cook until *al dente*.
**4** Meanwhile, heat a wok or large frying pan
until hot. Add the chicken and stir-fry for 4-5
minutes until browned and cooked thorough.
Add the spring onions, toss well and remove
from the heat.
**5** Drain the pasta and spoon into warmed
bowls. Top with the chicken and spring
onion mixture and drizzle over the lime
sauce. Serve at once, garnished with
coriander leaves.

**NOTE** For the sauce use homemade or
bought fresh stock, available in cartons
from supermarket chilled cabinets.

## Steamed Thai chicken parcels

Banana leaves are the traditional wrappings
for these aromatic parcels. If unobtainable,
lightly oiled baking parchment can be
substituted, but the flavour won't be quite
the same. Trim the leaves or parchment to
20cm/8inch squares.

1 tbsp vegetable oil
4 spring onions, thinly sliced
1 tsp finely grated fresh root ginger
2 lemon grass stalks, thinly sliced
2 skinless chicken breast fillets, cut into
2cm/3/4inch cubes
100g/4oz shiitake mushrooms, sliced
2 tbsp soy sauce
175g/6oz basmati rice, cooked

**1** Heat the oil in a large frying pan and sauté
the spring onions, ginger and lemon grass
for 2-3 minutes. Add the chicken and
mushrooms, and stir-fry for 2 minutes. Add
the soy sauce and cooked rice, and cook,
stirring, for 1 minute.
**2** Divide the mixture between the banana
leaves or parchment and fold over to
enclose the filling; secure the parcels with
bamboo skewers or twine. Place in a
bamboo steamer over a wok, or in a metal
steamer, and steam for 15 minutes.
**3** Serve on warmed plates, allowing guests
to open up their own parcels.

Steamed Thai chicken parcels

## Thai grilled chicken with coriander

Grilled to a crust, these fragrant chicken portions are deliciously moist within.

4 corn-fed chicken breasts (with skin)
2 garlic cloves, chopped
100g/4oz fresh coriander leaves, chopped
25g/1oz fresh mint leaves, chopped
2 tsp ground cumin
2 tsp ground coriander
1 red chilli, sliced
juice and grated rind of 1 lime
2 tsp soft brown sugar
250ml/9fl oz coconut milk
2 tsp sea salt
rocket leaves, to garnish
lime wedges, to serve

**1** Lay the chicken breasts, skin side up, on a board. With a sharp knife, make 3-4 shallow cuts in each one. Place the chicken breasts in a shallow dish, in which they fit snugly.
**2** Put all the remaining ingredients into a food processor, and blend until fairly smooth. Pour this marinade over the chicken and turn each piece to coat thoroughly. Cover and leave to marinate for at least 1 hour.
**3** Preheat the grill to high. Remove the chicken from the marinade and place, skin side up, on a lightly oiled grill pan. Grill for 8-10 minutes or until browned, then turn, baste with the marinade and grill the other side for 6-8 minutes or until cooked through.
**4** Serve hot, garnished with rocket leaves and accompanied by lime wedges, steamed Thai fragrant rice flavoured with coriander, and a green salad.

## Mango and chicken salad

Scented mango, roasted chicken, cashew nuts and crunchy lettuce in a Thai coconut dressing flavoured with fresh mint and lemon grass.

4 cooked chicken breasts (preferably roasted)
2 large mangoes, peeled, halved and stoned
50g/2oz roasted cashew nuts
1/2 head of iceberg lettuce, shredded
*for the dressing*
120ml/4fl oz coconut milk
1/2 tsp ground coriander
1 tbsp Thai fish sauce
1 tbsp soft brown sugar
2 spring onions, finely sliced
1 tbsp finely chopped fresh mint
2 tsp finely chopped fresh lemon grass
salt and pepper

**1** First make the dressing. Put the ingredients in a small pan and heat gently until the sugar is dissolved. Remove from the heat and set aside.
**2** Cut the chicken and mango flesh into cubes or slices and place in a large bowl with the cashew nuts. Toss to mix.
**3** Divide the shredded lettuce between 4 plates and top with the chicken and mango mixture. Stir the dressing and pour over the salad to serve.

**VARIATION** Use paw paw (papayas) instead of mangoes.

## Thai-style risotto

Subtle eastern flavours give this Italian classic an original Thai twist.

2 tbsp sunflower oil
6 spring onions, finely sliced
1 lemon grass stalk, finely sliced
1 tsp crushed garlic
1 tsp finely grated fresh root ginger
350g/12oz arborio (risotto) rice
300g/10oz chicken breast, cut into
2 cm/3/4in cubes
100g/4oz shiitake mushrooms, sliced
1.2 litres/2 pints good quality chicken stock (see note)
4 tbsp chopped fresh coriander
salt and pepper
shredded spring onion, to garnish

**1** Heat the oil in a large heavy-based saucepan. Add the spring onions, lemon grass, garlic and ginger and stir-fry for 1 minute.
**2** Add the rice and cook, stirring, for a few minutes, then add the chicken and mushrooms. Stir-fry for a further 2-3 minutes.
**3** Add a ladleful of the stock and cook gently, stirring frequently, until it is absorbed. Continue adding the stock, a ladleful at a time as each addition is absorbed, until the rice is creamy in texture.
**4** Add the remaining stock and coriander. Season well, and stir over a low heat for a few minutes longer or until the rice is just tender and moist.
**5** Serve immediately, garnished with shredded spring onion.

**NOTE** Use homemade stock or buy a carton of fresh chicken stock.

### Pumpkin and chicken broth

A fragrant soup is an excellent way to start a Thai meal. This broth also makes a good sustaining lunch, served with crusty bread.

1 tbsp oil
4 shallots, finely chopped
1 tsp grated fresh root ginger
2 lemon grass stalks, finely chopped (see note)
2 skinless chicken breast fillets, thinly sliced
400g/14oz pumpkin flesh, cubed
1.2 litres/2 pints good quality chicken stock
4 tbsp chopped fresh basil
salt and pepper
basil leaves, to garnish

**1** Heat the oil in a large heavy-based pan, add the shallots and fry for about 5 minutes until soft. Add the ginger and lemon grass; stir-fry for 1 minute.
**2** Add the chicken and pumpkin flesh. Cook, stirring, for 1 minute.
**3** Pour in the stock. Bring to the boil, cover and simmer for 10-15 minutes or until the chicken is cooked through and the pumpkin is tender.
**4** Stir in the chopped basil and check the seasoning. Pour into warmed bowls and serve garnished with basil leaves.

**NOTE** To prepare lemon grass, remove the tough inedible outer layer, then bruise the stalk with a rolling pin before slicing or chopping to release the aromatic oils.

### Spicy chicken cakes

These tasty morsels are great as an appetiser with drinks. Serve with a fresh tomato, cucumber, coriander and red onion salsa – spiked with lime juice. *Serves 3-4*

350g/12oz minced chicken
2 tbsp Thai red curry paste
1 medium egg, beaten
2 tbsp cornflour
2 kaffir lime leaves (see note), finely shredded
2 tbsp chopped fresh coriander
2 spring onions, finely sliced
1 red chilli, seeded and finely sliced
oil for deep-frying

**1** Put the minced chicken, red curry paste and about half of the egg in a food processor; work until evenly blended. Transfer to a mixing bowl.
**2** Add the cornflour, lime leaves, coriander, spring onions and chilli. Mix well, using your fingers, adding more egg as necessary to bind the mixture.
**3** Divide the mixture into 12 portions and roll each into a ball. Mould and flatten each ball into a 'cake' about 5cm/2in in diameter and 5-7 mm/¼in thick.
**4** Heat a 5cm/2in depth of oil in a wok or deep frying pan. Deep-fry the cakes, a few at a time, for about 5 minutes, until lightly browned and cooked through.
**5** Drain on crumpled kitchen paper and serve hot with a salsa, as an appetiser or with a salad as a starter or light lunch.

**NOTE** Kaffir lime leaves are available in packs of mixed Thai flavourings from some super-markets. If unobtainable, use the grated zest of 2 limes.

### Warm chicken and asparagus salad

An easy, elegant salad enhanced with a warm oriental flavoured dressing.

300g/10oz asparagus, trimmed
4 chicken breast fillets, cut into strips
1 tbsp vegetable oil
salt and pepper
4 tbsp fresh mint leaves
100g/4oz baby spinach leaves
*for the lemon grass dressing*
1 tbsp sesame oil
1 tbsp vegetable oil
1 tsp paprika
2 lemon grass stalks, thinly sliced
3 tbsp lime juice
1 tbsp honey
2 tbsp light soy sauce

**1** Preheat the grill to medium. Blanch the asparagus in boiling water for 3 minutes; drain and pat dry.
**2** Brush the chicken strips and asparagus with oil; season with salt and pepper. Place on the grill rack and grill for 3-4 minutes on each side, or until the chicken is cooked through.
**3** Meanwhile, make the dressing. Gently heat the oils in a small pan. Add the paprika and lemon grass and cook for 1-2 minutes.
**4** Arrange the mint and spinach leaves on plates and top with the asparagus and chicken.
**5** Add the lime juice, honey and soy sauce to the dressing and slowly bring to a simmer. Pour the warm dressing over the salad to serve.

**NOTE** Char-grill the chicken strips and asparagus if you prefer.

## Rosemary and lemon chicken with olives

This is all cooked together in the oven following an effortless preparation. As the flavours are robust, simply serve with a well dressed salad. *Serves 6*

12 skinless boneless chicken thighs
1 unwaxed lemon, halved
6 tbsp olive oil
6 garlic cloves, peeled and halved lengthways
2 onions, halved and sliced
10 fresh rosemary sprigs
950g/2lb 2oz potatoes (preferably organic), peeled
1 tsp ground black pepper
2 tsp Malden salt flakes
18 kalamata olives

1 Trim the chicken thighs of any excess fat and cut in half. Place in a bowl, squeeze the lemon juice over the meat and toss well; leave to stand for 10 minutes. Discard one of the lemon shells; cut the other into slivers and set aside.
2 Preheat oven to 220C/fan oven 200C/Gas 7. Drain the chicken and pat each piece dry. Place in a large shallow roasting tin in a single layer. Mix in the lemon slivers, olive oil, garlic, onions and 5 rosemary sprigs; leave to stand for 20 minutes.
3 Cut the potatoes into 4cm/1½ inch pieces. Add to a pan of boiling water, bring back to the boil and par-cook for 2 minutes only; drain well.
4 Add the potatoes to the chicken and sprinkle with the pepper and half of the salt. Bake in the oven for 50 minutes, turning all the ingredients every 10 minutes. If there is a lot of liquid from the onions 10 minutes before the end, increase the heat to 240C/fan oven 220C/Gas 9.
5 About 5 minutes before the end of the cooking time, replace the rosemary with fresh sprigs and add the olives. Serve sprinkled with the remaining salt flakes.

## Chicken breasts rolled with asparagus and pancetta

These are very easy to prepare, hours in advance. Serve sliced to reveal the pretty asparagus and pancetta. *Serves 6*

150g/5½oz asparagus tips
6 free-range chicken breast fillets, skinned
salt and pepper
18 slices pancetta
2 tbsp olive oil
chervil or parsley sprigs, to garnish

1 Cook the asparagus in boiling water for 2 minutes, then drain and refresh in cold water; drain again and pat dry on kitchen paper.
2 Slice horizontally into each chicken breast without cutting all the way through, then open out. Place, two at a time, between sheets of greaseproof paper and beat with a rolling pin to flatten out slightly.
3 Preheat oven to 190C/fan oven 170C/Gas 5. Season each chicken breast lightly and cover with 1½ slices of pancetta. Place 4 asparagus tips lengthways on top and roll up. Brush the chicken parcels with a little oil and wrap each one in a further 1½ slices of pancetta.
4 Wrap each parcel tightly in foil to seal and hold in the juices. Place on a baking sheet and bake in the oven for 20 minutes.
5 Leave to rest in a warm place for 5-15 minutes, then remove the foil. Slice the chicken parcels into rounds and serve on a bed of rice, with any juices poured over. Garnish with chervil or parsley.

NOTE Packets of thinly sliced pancetta are available from larger supermarkets. Alternatively you can buy pancetta freshly sliced from Italian delicatessens.

## Bronzed paprika chicken

For convenience, prepare the chicken for roasting a few hours ahead. Keep in the fridge, but bring to room temperature before cooking. *Serves 4-6*

1 oven-ready chicken, about 1.6kg/3½lb
salt and pepper
1 unwaxed lemon, halved
small sprig of fresh bay leaves
50g/2oz butter, softened
4 tsp paprika
¼ tsp cayenne pepper
2–3 whole garlic bulbs, halved crosswise
1 tbsp olive oil
450g/1lb cherry tomatoes on the vine
70g/2½oz finely sliced chorizo sausage
bay leaves, to garnish

1 Remove any excess fat from the cavity of the chicken and season. Place the lemon halves and bay leaves inside.
2 Loosen the skin away from the chicken breast and legs, then smear the butter onto the flesh under the skin to keep it moist.
3 Mix the paprika, ¼ tsp salt, ¼ tsp pepper and the cayenne together; rub all over the skin. Tie the legs together. (The chicken can be refrigerated at this stage for several hours. Remove from the fridge 30 minutes before cooking.)
4 Preheat oven to 190C/fan oven 170C/Gas 5 and estimate the cooking time, allowing 20 minutes per 450g/1lb, plus 20 minutes. Place the chicken on a trivet in a large roasting tin. Toss the garlic in a little olive oil and place around the bird. Roast in the oven, basting occasionally.
5 About 10 minutes before the end of the roasting time, toss the cherry tomatoes in the remaining olive oil and add to the roasting tin.
6 Test to ensure the chicken is fully cooked by piercing the thickest part of the leg with a skewer: the juices should be clear and golden; if pink, roast for a little longer.
7 Transfer to a warmed platter and rest for 10-15 minutes. Meanwhile, fry the chorizo slices in a dry pan over a high heat until crisp. Scatter these on top of the chicken and surround with the tomatoes and roasted garlic. Garnish with bay leaves.

## Chicken with caramelised apples

A delicious brew of rich flavours just begging to be piled onto a mound of mashed celeriac and potatoes. *Serves 6*

6 corn-fed chicken breast fillets (with skin)
salt and pepper
50g/2oz unsalted butter
150ml/1/4 pint double cream
3 large cox's apples, about 500g/1lb in total
2 tbsp sunflower oil
400g/14oz shallots, peeled
3 tbsp calvados or brandy

**1** Preheat oven to 190C/fan oven 170C/Gas 5. Season the chicken with salt and pepper.
**2** Melt half the butter in a flameproof casserole. Add the chicken skin side down and fry for about 3 minutes until golden brown. Turn and brown the other side.
**3** Add half the cream, cover and cook in the oven for 20-25 minutes.
**4** Meanwhile quarter, core and slice the apples. Heat the oil in a large heavy-based frying pan and fry the shallots for 8 minutes until browned. Add remaining butter and fry the apples for about 5 minutes, turning, until evenly golden; keep warm.
**5** Remove casserole from oven and place on a high heat. Pour in the remaining cream and let bubble for 1 minute. Add half the apples and shallots. Add the calvados, cover and turn off the heat.
**6** Pile the remaining shallots and apples on top of the chicken and drizzle with the sauce to serve.

## Poussins stuffed with herb butter

Serve these on a mound of buttered saffron couscous. In summer, barbecue rather than grill the poussins. *Serves 6*

6 spatchcocked poussins (see note)
*for the herb butter*
6 garlic cloves (unpeeled)
150g/5 1/2oz unsalted butter, softened
3 tbsp finely chopped fresh tarragon
3 tbsp finely snipped fresh chives
salt and pepper
*for the garnish*
2 tbsp roughly torn flat leaf parsley

**1** Put the garlic cloves in a small pan, add water to cover and simmer for 6 minutes until softened; drain and cool slightly. Snip the root end and squeeze out the garlic flesh into a bowl. Crush and mix in the butter, tarragon, chives and seasoning.
**2** Gently ease up the skin on the breast and upper part of the poussins' legs with your fingers to make a pocket for the herb butter, taking care to avoid puncturing the skin. Spread the butter over the flesh under the skin, then press down the loosened skin.
**3** Thread 2 wooden skewers crosswise through each bird to hold it flat (from wing through to the opposite leg). Set aside until ready to cook.
**4** Preheat the grill to medium and oven to 120C/fan oven 100C/Gas 1/2. Grill the poussins, in 2 batches if necessary, for 20-25 minutes turning occasionally until golden and cooked through. Keep warm in the oven. Scatter with parsley to serve.

**NOTE** To spatchcock a poussin, using sturdy kitchen scissors or poultry shears, cut along each side of the backbone and remove it, then press the poussin firmly to flatten.

## Seared chicken with marsala and sage

This is quick enough to cook between courses. Serve on a large bread croûte with colourful salad leaves. *Serves 6*

4 free-range chicken breast fillets, skinned
salt and pepper
2 tbsp sunflower oil
12 fresh sage leaves
85g/3oz butter
1 tbsp chopped fresh sage
175ml/6fl oz marsala

**1** Cut each chicken fillet lengthways into 6 strips and season lightly. Heat the oil in a frying pan and fry the sage leaves a few at a time for a few seconds; lift out and drain on kitchen paper.
**2** Melt some of the butter in a heavy-based pan and sear the chicken in batches over a high heat to brown all over. Return all chicken to the pan; add the chopped sage.
**3** Pour in a little marsala. As it reduces to a syrup, continue to add marsala a little at a time until only about 2 tbsp remains. Lift the chicken onto warmed plates.
**4** Deglaze the pan with the remaining marsala and pour over the chicken. Top with the fried sage leaves to serve.

## Char-grilled chicken stacks with basil

Serve these with flavoured breads and a leafy salad. *Serves 4*

4 free-range chicken breast fillets, skinned
1 large red pepper
1 large yellow pepper
2 medium-small aubergines
salt and pepper
5 tbsp extra virgin olive oil
*for the basil dressing*
16 fresh basil leaves, roughly torn
2 tbsp cider vinegar
6 tbsp olive oil
1/2 tsp Dijon mustard
*for the garnish*
basil leaves

**1** Holding a sharp knife at an angle, slice each chicken breast into 3 even medallions.
**2** Cut off the tops and a little of the base from the peppers, then cut each one into four, to give even, flat pieces; discard seeds. Cut the aubergine into 12 even slices, about 5mm/1/4in thick.
**3** Put the chicken and vegetables in a large shallow dish, season and pour over the oil. Mix well, cover and leave to marinate in a cool place for at least 30 minutes (or up to 3 hours).

**4** Put the dressing ingredients in a blender, season and pulse until amalgamated but retaining some flecks of basil.
**5** Preheat a chargrill pan (or grill) to high. Sear the chicken and vegetables in batches to obtain a charred effect on both sides; turn down the heat to cook right through.

**6** To assemble, halve the pepper pieces. Place a chicken medallion on each plate and stack the vegetables and remaining chicken medallions on top, alternating the colours and finishing with yellow pepper. Serve hot or cold, drizzled with the dressing and garnished with basil leaves.

**NOTE** The stacks can be assembled ahead in a deep dish, covered and warmed through in the oven to serve.

# aromatic meat

**Enjoy these mouth-watering** meat dishes inspired by flavours from afar. Savour effortless new ideas for **enhancing your Sunday roast**, fast suppers featuring convenient meat cuts, and **easy grills enlivened with fruity salsas** and tasty sauces. Spice up midweek meals with **Caribbean, Mexican and Asian flavours**, or look to prepare ahead casseroles and pies for convenience. Entertain guests in style with our **special occasion main courses**, such as **crusted roast loin of pork**, and seared fillet of beef with roasted onions and physalis fruit. Easy to prepare, these **taste as superb as they look**.

Crisp roast stuffed shoulder of pork

## Horseradish crusted roast beef

*Serves 4-6*

1.3kg/3lb boned, rolled rib of beef
salt and pepper
3 tbsp fresh breadcrumbs
2 tbsp hot horseradish sauce
2 tsp grated horseradish

**1** Preheat oven to 200C/fan oven 180C/Gas 6. Pat the joint dry with kitchen paper if necessary. Season with salt and pepper.
**2** Mix the remaining ingredients together to make a paste, then spread evenly all over the joint.
**3** Put the meat into a roasting tin and roast in the oven for 45 minutes. Reduce oven setting to 180C/fan oven 160C/Gas 4 and roast for a further 45 minutes. Rest in a warm place for 10 minutes before carving.

## Beef studded with bacon, thyme and garlic

*Serves 4-6*

1.3kg/3lb boned, rolled sirloin or rib of beef
85g/3oz smoked bacon lardons
3 garlic cloves, cut lengthwise into wedges
15 small fresh thyme sprigs
salt and pepper
olive oil, for basting

**1** Preheat oven to 200C/fan oven 180C/Gas 6. Cut about 15 slits in the beef with a sharp knife and insert a piece of bacon, a wedge of garlic and a thyme sprig into each one.
**2** Season the joint all over with salt and pepper and rub with a little olive oil.
**3** Roast in the oven for 1½-2 hours until cooked to your preference. Leave to rest in a warm place for 10 minutes before carving.

## Loin of lamb stuffed with mushrooms and nuts

The walnut aperitif, *vin de noix,* adds a subtle flavour to this stuffing which doesn't overpower the sweet taste of the lamb.

700-900g/1½-2lb boned loin of lamb
salt and pepper
1 tbsp olive oil
2 shallots, finely chopped
1 garlic clove, crushed
150g/5½oz chestnut mushrooms, diced
1 small celery stick, finely chopped
100g/4oz cooked, peeled chestnuts (fresh or vacuum packed), roughly chopped
1 tsp paprika
85g/3oz walnuts, finely chopped
25g/1oz fresh breadcrumbs
2 tbsp vin de noix (walnut aperitif) or dry sherry

**1** Cut away any skin and excess fat from the joint, leaving a thin coating. Score this in a criss cross pattern and rub with seasoning.
**2** For the stuffing, heat the oil in a pan and fry the shallots and garlic until transparent. Add the mushrooms and cook gently until softened and all moisture is evaporated.
**3** Add the celery, chestnuts and paprika and cook for 2-3 minutes, then add the walnuts, breadcrumbs, aperitif and 1 tbsp water. Season to taste and let cool slightly. Preheat oven to 190C/fan oven 170C/Gas 5.
**4** Turn the meat flesh side up, and spread with the stuffing. Roll up and tie with string at 2.5cm/1in intervals. Place on a trivet in a roasting tin and roast for 1¼-1½ hours, or 2 hours for well done meat.
**5** Leave the lamb to rest in a warm place for 10 minutes before carving.

## Crisp roast stuffed shoulder of pork

Succulent roast pork flavoured with juicy Agen prunes and a hint of Calvados. To ensure a crisp crackling, make sure the pork rind is deeply scored. *Serves 4-6*

1.3kg/3lb joint boneless shoulder of pork, with scored rind
100g/4oz pitted Agen prunes
4 tbsp Calvados or Marsala
grated rind and juice of 1 orange
sea salt and pepper
1 tsp clear honey

**1** Soak the prunes in the Calvados for 3-4 hours. Drain, reserving the liquor.
**2** Preheat oven to 220C/fan oven 200C/Gas 7. Open out the rolled joint of pork and rub about 2 tsp sea salt into the slits of the scored rind.
**3** Turn the joint over, spoon the prunes on to the flesh and sprinkle with the orange rind.
**4** Roll up the meat to enclose the prune stuffing and secure with string, tied at 2.5cm/1in intervals. Put the meat in a roasting tin and add 4 tbsp water to prevent the fat spluttering. Roast for about 20 minutes until the crackling is formed.
**5** Reduce oven setting to 180C/fan oven 160C/Gas 4. Roast for a further 1½ hours, adding a little more water as needed.
**6** Lift the meat on to a warm serving dish and rest in a warm place for 10 minutes. Skim off the fat from the roasting juices, then add the reserved Calvados, orange juice and honey. Stir to scrape up the sediment and boil to reduce slightly, to a glaze; season.
**7** Carve the pork into thick slices and serve with the meat glaze.

## Chilli pork and cheese burgers

These spicy burgers reveal a hidden pocket of melted blue cheese when cut open.

750g/1lb 10oz minced pork
2 garlic cloves, crushed
2 tbsp sweet chilli sauce
3 spring onions, finely chopped
3 tbsp chopped fresh coriander leaves
salt and pepper
50g/2oz Gorgonzola cheese
oil, for brushing
*to serve*
4 muffins or burger buns, split and toasted

**1** Put the minced pork, garlic, chilli sauce, spring onions and chopped coriander in a bowl. Season with salt and pepper and mix thoroughly until the mixture holds together, Divide into 4 equal portions and shape into flat cakes.
**2** Cut the blue cheese into 4 cubes and mould each portion of pork mixture around a cheese cube to enclose. Flatten to form fat burgers.
**3** Preheat grill to medium. Brush the pork burgers with a little oil. Place on the grill rack and cook under the medium grill for about 7 minutes each side until cooked through. (Alternatively, you can barbecue the burgers over medium hot coals allowing about 6 minutes per side.)
**4** Serve at once, on toasted muffins or burger buns, with chips, ketchup and mustard if you like.

**NOTE** Bring meat to room temperature before grilling, and preheat the grill for at least 10 minutes. Temperature settings of grills vary considerably, so treat suggested cooking times as guidelines only. If you are barbecuing rather than grilling, remember to light the coals well ahead and wait until they are covered with a thin layer of white ash before starting to cook. Always test meat to ensure it is properly cooked to your liking.

## Glazed bacon and mango pockets

Bacon chops are filled with a slice of mango, basted with a tangy citrus glaze during grilling, then served with a mango salsa spiked with chilli.

4 boneless bacon chops, each 175g/6oz
olive oil, for brushing
salt and pepper
*for the glaze*
2 tbsp fine cut orange marmalade
finely grated rind and juice of 1 lime
*for the salsa*
1 large mango, halved, peeled and stoned
finely grated rind and juice of 1 lime
1 small red chilli, seeded and chopped
2 tbsp chopped fresh coriander

**1** For the glaze, warm the marmalade with the lime rind and juice until melted.
**2** Cut 4 thin slices from the mango; chop the rest. Mix the chopped mango with the remaining salsa ingredients and set aside.
**3** Make a horizontal slit in the side of each bacon chop and slip in a slice of mango; secure with a cocktail stick. Brush with olive oil and season well.
**4** Preheat grill to medium. Put the bacon chops on the grill rack and grill for 5 minutes each side, brushing with glaze for the last minute on each side. Serve with the mango salsa.

## Venison steaks with juniper and ginger butter

4 venison steaks, each 175g/6oz
olive oil, for brushing
salt and pepper
*for the butter*
175g/6oz unsalted butter
1 tbsp finely chopped fresh root ginger
3 juniper berries, finely chopped
1 tsp coarse sea salt

**1** For the flavoured butter, beat the butter in a bowl until very soft, then beat in the ginger, juniper berries and salt. Shape into a log, wrap and chill for 1 hour until firm.
**2** Preheat grill to medium. Brush the venison steaks with olive oil and season well. Place on the grill rack and grill for 3-4 minutes on each side.
**3** Serve the venison steaks topped with slices of the flavoured butter.

## Mahogany duck breasts with fruity salsa

Duck breasts are grilled slowly until the skin is mahogany brown, then served with a zesty salsa of apple, pineapple, dried cranberries and lemon.

4 duck breasts, each 175-200g/6-7oz
salt and pepper
*for the salsa*
1 small dessert apple
2 slices fresh pineapple
2 tbsp dried cranberries
finely grated rind and juice of $1/2$ lemon, or to taste

**1** Pat the duck breasts dry with kitchen paper. Score the fat in a criss-cross pattern and rub with plenty of salt. Set aside.
**2** Core and finely dice the apple. Finely dice the pineapple and mix with the cranberries and apple. Add lemon juice and rind to taste, and season with salt and pepper.
**3** Preheat grill to medium. Place the duck breasts, skin side down, on the grill rack and grill for 1 minute to sear the underside.
**4** Turn the duck breasts over and grill under the medium heat for 10 minutes. Reduce the heat to low and continue to cook for a further 10 minutes until the skin is dark brown; the flesh should be just rosy pink.
**5** Slice the duck breasts and serve accompanied by the fruity salsa.

**NOTE** To barbecue, cook the duck breasts flesh side down for 1 minute to seal. Turn over and cook for 10 minutes, dowsing any flames with water as the fat can catch and ignite. Lift the barbecue rack away from the heat source a little and continue to cook for a further 10 minutes.

## Fillet of beef teriyaki

This marinated, grilled fillet of beef is dark on the outside, but remains pink and moist inside. It is served with frazzled pickled ginger, spring onions and garlic.

450g/1lb piece beef fillet (from the tail end)
2 tbsp sesame oil
4 tbsp teriyaki marinade
olive oil, for brushing
vegetable oil, for frying
100g/4oz sliced pickled ginger, drained and dried
4 garlic cloves, peeled and thinly sliced
4-6 spring onions, thinly sliced

**1** Trim the beef of any fat or sinew, then place in a non-metallic dish. Spoon the sesame oil and teriyaki marinade over the meat and turn to coat well. Cover and leave to marinate in the fridge for at least 4 hours, preferably overnight, turning the meat occasionally.
**2** Bring to room temperature, then lift the meat out of the marinade and pat dry.
**3** Preheat grill to high. Brush meat sparingly with olive oil and sear all over under the grill for 2 minutes, turning as necessary. Turn down the heat to medium and grill for a further 20 minutes, turning 3 times.
**4** Transfer the meat to a warm dish, cover with foil and leave to rest in a warm place for 10 minutes.
**5** Meanwhile, heat a 1cm/½in depth of oil in a frying pan until a small piece of bread sizzles instantly as it touches the oil. Add the ginger, sliced garlic and spring onions and fry until golden. Remove with a slotted spoon and drain on kitchen paper.
**6** Serve the meat thinly sliced, drizzled with the meat juices and scattered with the ginger, garlic and spring onions.

## Rump steaks with wilted rocket

Tender, marinated rump steaks served topped with rocket and accompanied by a delicious aioli – made with walnut oil.

4 rump steaks, each 175g/6oz
*for the marinade*
5 tbsp red wine
2 garlic cloves, crushed
3 tbsp olive oil
salt and pepper
*for the aioli*
2 garlic cloves, peeled and crushed
1 egg yolk
3 tbsp walnut oil
100ml/3½fl oz light olive oil
lemon juice, to taste
*to serve*
100g/4oz rocket leaves

**1** In a shallow dish, mix together the wine, garlic, olive oil and seasoning. Add the rump steaks and turn to coat well. Cover and leave to marinate for 30 minutes.
**2** Meanwhile, make the aioli. Pound the garlic with 1 tsp salt in a small bowl. Stir in the egg yolk. Gradually whisk in the oils, a few drops at a time. Once half the oil is incorporated, add a squeeze of lemon juice. Whisk in the remaining oil in a thin, steady stream. Taste and season or add lemon juice as required.
**3** Remove steaks from marinade and pat dry on kitchen paper. Brush with a little olive oil. Preheat grill to medium. Put the steaks on the grill rack and cook for 3 minutes each side, or to taste.
**4** Serve each steak topped with a pile of rocket leaves and accompanied by the aioli.

**NOTE** To barbecue, cook over medium hot coals for 2-3 minutes per side, or to taste.

## Mediterranean veal parcels

Flattened veal escalopes rolled around a tasty stuffing of mozzarella, capsicums, sun-dried aubergine and basil.

2 large veal escalopes, each about 175g/6oz
*for the stuffing*
50g packet sun-dried aubergine slices
2 canned or bottled red peppers (capsicums), drained
olive oil, for brushing
salt and pepper
1 buffalo mozzarella cheese, about 150g/5oz, sliced
handful of fresh basil leaves

**1** For the stuffing, soak the aubergine slices in tepid water for 20 minutes. Drain and pat dry with kitchen paper.
**2** Put the veal escalopes between sheets of greaseproof paper and bat out thinly, without tearing the meat.
**3** Lay the peppers on top of each escalope, followed by the aubergines. Brush with olive oil, season with salt and pepper, then cover with the sliced mozzarella and basil leaves.
**4** Preheat grill to medium. Roll the veal escalopes up from the longest side, enclosing the filling. Secure with cocktail sticks and brush with olive oil. Grill for 20 minutes, gradually turning the parcels to ensure even cooking.
**5** Serve cut into slices, with a salad.

**NOTE** To barbecue, cook the veal parcels over medium coals for 15-20 minutes, turning from time to time.

## Butterflied lamb with a spiced yogurt crust

Ask your butcher to butterfly a leg of lamb for this recipe (ie bone the meat and open out flat). *Serves 6-8*

2kg/4½lb butterfied leg of lamb
1 tbsp dried green peppercorns, crushed
1 tbsp black peppercorns, crushed
3 garlic cloves, crushed
150ml/¼ pint Greek yogurt

**1** Lay the meat, skin side down, and score the thicker parts as necessary to make it an even thickness. Make slits all over the surface.
**2** Mix the crushed peppercorns, garlic and yogurt together and rub this mixture all over the cut surface of the lamb. Lay the meat in a shallow dish, cover and leave to marinate in the fridge for at least 1 hour, preferably overnight.
**3** Lift the lamb on to a foil-lined grill rack and cook under a medium hot grill for 20 minutes each side, until medium.
**4** Leave the meat to rest for 10 minutes before carving into long thin slices. Serve with yogurt flavoured with chopped mint, and grilled naan bread.

**NOTE** To barbecue, cook over medium hot coals for 15-20 minutes, then turn and cook for a further 15-20 minutes.

## Pork and rosemary skewers

Strips of pork fillet are marinated in crushed rosemary, balsamic vinegar and sun-dried tomato paste, then threaded zig-zag fashion on to skewers and grilled.

450g/1lb pork fillet
4 fresh rosemary sprigs, leaves only
3 tbsp balsamic vinegar
2 tbsp sun-dried tomato paste
4 tbsp olive oil
salt and pepper
lime wedges, to serve

**1** Pre-soak 8 wooden kebab skewers in cold water for 20 minutes.
**2** Trim the pork of any membrane, then cut lengthways into 16 thin strips.
**3** Pound the rosemary leaves with the balsamic vinegar, sun-dried tomato paste, olive oil, salt and pepper, using a pestle and mortar. Transfer to a dish. Add the pork strips and turn to coat. Cover and leave to marinate in the fridge for at least 1 hour.
**4** Preheat grill to high. Thread 2 pork strips in a zig-zag fashion on to each of the skewers. Lay on a foil-lined grill pan and grill for 2-3 minutes each side, or until browned on all sides and cooked through.
**5** Serve with lime wedges, and a salad.

**VARIATION** Use stripped rosemary branches for the kebab skewers. Strip the leaves from 8 woody stems, leaving about 2.5cm/1in intact at one end. Thread the pork on to the stems and grill as above.

**NOTE** To barbecue, cook over hot coals for about 2 minutes per side.

## Barbecued rack of lamb with salmoriglio sauce

Racks of lamb are grilled to perfection, then drenched in a Sicilian sauce of lemon, garlic, oregano and olive oil – to bring all the scents of southern Italy to your kitchen. Dried oregano is preferred to fresh here, for its intense, sweet flavour. *Serves 4-6*

2 racks of lamb, each with 6-7 cutlets
salt and pepper
olive oil, for brushing
*for the salmoriglio sauce*
175ml/6fl oz extra virgin olive oil
juice of 1 large or 2 small very ripe lemons
2 tsp dried oregano
2 garlic cloves, finely chopped
2 tbsp chopped fresh parsley

**1** Trim the lamb racks of excess fat, but retain a thin covering to keep the meat moist during cooking. Rub all over with salt and pepper and lightly brush with olive oil.
**2** To make the sauce, whisk all of the ingredients together in a bowl until well combined and thick.
**3** Preheat grill to medium. Lay the racks of lamb down, fat side up, in the grill pan and grill for 15-20 minutes, checking frequently to make sure that the fat doesn't catch.
**4** As soon as the meat is cooked, transfer to a warmed dish and pour over the sauce. Cover and leave to rest in a warm place for 10 minutes. Serve the lamb, cut into double cutlets, with the sauce spooned over.

**NOTE** To barbecue, cook over medium coals for about 15 minutes, then transfer to a dish and pour on the sauce as above.

## Corned beef hash cakes

This unusual, tasty supper also makes a great Sunday brunch. Serve a refreshing leafy salad to follow.

4 tbsp sunflower oil
1 onion, halved and thinly sliced
1 red pepper, quartered, cored, seeded and thinly sliced
2 garlic cloves, sliced
550g/1¼lb potatoes (unpeeled), coarsely grated
6 large eggs
2 tsp Worcestershire sauce
dash of Tabasco sauce
salt and pepper
4 spring onions, finely chopped
200g can corned beef, diced

**1** Heat half of the oil in a large frying pan, add the onion, red pepper, garlic and potatoes and fry, stirring, for 8 minutes until softened.
**2** In a large bowl, beat 2 eggs with the Worcestershire sauce, Tabasco and seasoning. Add the potato mixture, spring onions and corned beef; mix together thoroughly. Divide into 4 portions and shape roughly into round cakes.
**3** Heat the remaining oil in the frying pan. Add the potato cakes, cover and cook for 10 minutes. Turn the potato cakes over and cook for a further 5 minutes.
**4** Meanwhile, poach the remaining 4 eggs in boiling salted water for 3 minutes or until cooked to your liking; lift out with a slotted spoon.
**5** Serve the hash cakes topped with the poached eggs, and an extra few drops of Tabasco if liked.

**NOTE** If you do not have a frying pan large enough to hold all four hash cakes, use two pans rather then cook in batches.

## Duck breasts with berry sauce

Assorted berry fruits in an orange and redcurrant sauce cut the richness of duck to delicious effect.

4 boneless duck breasts, each 175-200g/ 6-7oz
salt and pepper
juice of 1 orange
4 tbsp redcurrant jelly with port
140g/5oz fresh or frozen mixed berries (red and blackcurrants, blackberries, raspberries and cherries)
1/2 tsp white wine vinegar

**1** Preheat oven to 220C/fan oven 200C/Gas 7.
**2** Score the duck breast fat and rub with salt. Preheat a large frying pan over a medium high heat. Add the duck breasts, skin side down, and cook for about 7 minutes until most of the fat is rendered from under the skin.
**3** Turn the duck breasts over and seal briefly on the other side, then transfer to a rack over a roasting tin and roast for 15-20 minutes.
**4** Meanwhile pour off the fat from the frying pan and wipe clean with kitchen paper. Add the orange juice, redcurrant jelly, berry fruits and wine vinegar to the pan. Season with salt and pepper to taste and let bubble until the sauce is syrupy.
**5** Leave the duck to rest for a few minutes before carving into slices. Arrange on warmed serving plates and spoon over the berry sauce. Serve with sauté potatoes and green beans or mangetout.

## French-style bacon steaks

A chunky apple sauce spiked with Calvados, Dijon mustard and green peppercorns is the perfect foil for lightly smoked bacon steaks.

1 1/2 tbsp sunflower oil
4 thick mild cure bacon steak rashers
2 small red apples, cored and cut into wedges
2 tbsp Calvados or brandy
1 tsp green peppercorns in brine, crushed
2 tsp Dijon mustard
200ml carton crème fraîche

**1** Heat the oil in a large frying pan and fry the bacon steaks for about 3 minutes, turning once. Lift from the pan; set aside.
**2** Add the apples to the pan and sauté for 1 minute or until beginning to colour. Add the Calvados, then stir in the peppercorns, mustard and crème fraîche to make a creamy sauce.
**3** Return the bacon steaks to the pan to heat through before serving. Serve with mashed potatoes and stir-fried cabbage.

## Pork steaks with sloe gin

Pork steaks are cooked with a hint of juniper, then served in a rich creamy, sloe gin sauce for a special supper.

4 pork leg steaks, trimmed of fat
2 tbsp well seasoned flour
25g/1oz butter
4 juniper berries, finely chopped
100ml/3 1/2 fl oz sloe gin
150ml/1/4 pint double cream
1 tbsp finely chopped fresh flat leaf parsley
salt and pepper

**1** Toss the pork steaks in the seasoned flour to coat lightly on both sides, shaking off excess.
**2** Melt the butter in a large frying pan and scatter in the juniper berries. Add the pork steaks and fry for about 3 minutes each side until just cooked through and turning golden.
**3** Pour in the sloe gin and allow to bubble until reduced by half.
**4** Lift out the pork steaks and transfer to hot serving plates; keep warm. Add the cream to the pan juices with the chopped parsley and stir to make a sauce, scraping up any sediment from the base of the pan. Season with salt and pepper to taste. Bring to a simmer, stirring.
**5** Pour this sauce over the pork steaks and serve at once with new potatoes, broccoli and sugar snaps.

**NOTE** Sole gin is available from selected supermarkets and off licences. Alternatively you can, of course, make your own in the autumn by macerating sloes, picked from the hedgerows, with gin and sugar.

## Lamb chops with lemon, garlic and sweet potatoes

Sweet potatoes are sautéed with lemon, red onions and fresh thyme, then topped with lamb chops and quick roasted.

4 lean chump chops or 8 lamb cutlets
4 tbsp olive oil
1kg/2 1/4lb sweet potatoes, peeled and cubed
2 red onions, cut into wedges
8 garlic cloves (unpeeled)
1 tbsp light muscovado sugar
juice of 1 lemon
1 small lemon, halved and thinly sliced
1 tbsp fresh thyme leaves
salt and pepper
thyme sprigs, to garnish

**1** Trim the lamb of any excess fat. Preheat oven to 220C/fan oven 200C/Gas 7.
**2** Heat the olive oil in a large frying pan. Add the sweet potato cubes, onion wedges, garlic and sugar and fry, stirring, over a high heat for about 5 minutes until the vegetables start to soften and caramelise. Transfer to a roasting tin.
**3** Add the lemon juice, lemon slices, thyme leaves and seasoning, then top with the lamb chops and thyme sprigs.
**4** Roast in the oven for 25-30 minutes until the lamb is cooked and the sweet potatoes are tender. Serve garnished with thyme and accompanied by spinach.

## Bean casserole with chorizo

Molasses and spicy chorizo sausages give this rustic dish a wonderful depth of flavour. Serve with garlic bread and a salad.

250g/9oz dried pinto beans
100g/4oz dried butter beans
1 tbsp olive oil
450g/1lb pickling onions, peeled
225g/8oz thick smoked gammon steak, cubed
200g/7oz chorizo sausage, skinned and cut into chunks
1 each green and orange pepper, cored, seeded and cut into chunks
700g bottle or carton passata
425ml/³/4 pint chicken stock
3 tbsp molasses
2 tbsp wholegrain mustard
4 fresh bay leaves
1 tbsp fresh thyme leaves
1 tsp paprika

**1** Soak the pinto and butter beans separately in plenty of cold water overnight.
**2** The next day, rinse the beans and place in separate large pans. Add fresh cold water to cover and bring to the boil. Fast boil the butter beans for 10 minutes; pinto beans for 20 minutes. Drain.
**3** Heat the oil in a large pan. Add the whole onions and fry over a medium heat for about 5 minutes, stirring frequently.
**4** Add the gammon, chorizo and peppers and cook, stirring, for a few minutes. Pour in the passata and stock, then stir in the beans, molasses, mustard, herbs and paprika. Cover and simmer gently, stirring frequently, for 45 minutes or until the beans are tender.
**5** If preparing ahead, cool, then cover and refrigerate for up to 2 days, or freeze.
**6** To serve, defrost at cool room temperature overnight (if frozen). Reheat in a pan until piping hot.

## Lamb with Chinese spices

Rich soy sauce, honey and the star anise in Chinese five spice powder add intriguing flavours to this casserole.

2 tsp sunflower oil
500g/1lb 2oz lean lamb fillet, cut into chunks
1 tbsp fresh root ginger julienne (fine sticks)
1 tsp Chinese five spice powder
4 tbsp Chinese rice wine or dry sherry
4 tbsp dark soy sauce
3 tbsp clear honey
227g can water chestnuts, drained
2 leeks, sliced on the diagonal
1 large red pepper, cored, seeded and cut into diamonds
shredded spring onion, to garnish (optional)

**1** Heat the oil in a large heavy-based pan or flameproof casserole. Add the lamb and ginger and stir-fry until the meat is evenly coloured. Sprinkle with the five spice powder, then stir in the wine or sherry, soy sauce, honey and water chestnuts. Bring to a simmer.
**2** Cover the pan with a tight fitting lid and simmer over a gentle heat for 20 minutes.
**3** Stir in the leeks and red pepper, then cover and cook for a further 40 minutes until the meat and vegetables are tender.
**4** If preparing ahead, cool, then cover and refrigerate for up to 2 days, or freeze.
**5** To serve, defrost at cool room temperature overnight (if frozen). Reheat in a pan until piping hot.
**6** Serve topped with shredded spring onion if wished. Accompany with rice, or noodles tossed with bean sprouts and steamed shredded sugar snaps.

**VARIATION** Replace the water chestnuts with a 227g can sliced bamboo shoots. Serve sprinkled with toasted cashew nuts.

## Whisky braised beef with pecans

Braising steaks are cooked with a tot of whisky, whole shallots and smoky bacon, then served topped with a buttery mix of toasted pecans and crisp fried bacon.

4 lean, thick braising steaks, about 800g/1³/4lb in total
3-4 tbsp seasoned flour
1 tbsp olive oil
25g/1oz butter
2 garlic cloves, thinly sliced
250g/9oz shallots, peeled
2 fresh bay leaves, crushed
200g/7oz smoked bacon lardons
4 tbsp whisky
425ml/³/4 pint beef stock
50g/2oz pecan nuts
3 tbsp chopped fresh parsley

**1** Preheat oven to 180C/fan oven 160C/Gas 4. Coat the steaks with the seasoned flour.
**2** Heat the oil and half the butter in a large frying pan and fry the steaks until sealed on both sides. Transfer to a shallow casserole.
**3** Add the garlic, shallots, bay leaves and half of the lardons to the frying pan; stir-fry until browned. Add the whisky, bubble to reduce, then stir in the stock, scraping up any sediment from the base of the pan. Pour over the beef.
**4** Cover and braise in the oven for 2 hours until tender. If preparing ahead, cool, then cover and chill for up to 3 days, or freeze.
**5** To serve, defrost at cool room temperature overnight (if frozen). Reheat in a pan until piping hot. Fry the rest of the lardons in the remaining butter until golden. Add the pecans and cook for a few minutes. Stir in the parsley.
**6** Serve the beef casserole topped with the pecan mix. Accompany with creamy mashed potato and a green vegetable, such as braised cabbage.

## Hickory'n'maple ribs

Smoky hickory sauce and maple syrup make an excellent coating for meaty pork spare ribs. Serve them accompanied by jacket potatoes topped with garlic butter and a chunky homemade coleslaw.

8 meaty pork ribs, about 1.3kg/3lb in total
*for the marinade*
125ml/4fl oz maple syrup
3 tbsp hickory barbecue sauce
juice of 1 small lemon
1 tbsp sweet chilli sauce
2 garlic cloves, crushed

**1** Put the pork ribs in a shallow non-metallic dish. Mix all the marinade ingredients together in a bowl, then pour the mixture over the ribs and turn to coat well. Cover and leave to marinate in the fridge for up to 2 days.
**2** Preheat oven to 190C/fan oven 170C/Gas 5. Transfer the ribs to a large, shallow roasting tin and baste with the marinade. Cover the tin loosely with foil and bake for 40 minutes, then uncover and bake for a further 40 minutes, basting occasionally, until the meat is tender.
**3** Serve the pork ribs accompanied by jacket potatoes and coleslaw or warm bread and a leafy green salad.

**VARIATION** Replace the marinade with a hot, spicy sauce. Mix together 6 tbsp tomato ketchup, 4 tbsp Worcestershire sauce, 2 tbsp Dijon mustard, 4 tbsp muscovado sugar and a dash of Tabasco sauce. Marinate the ribs in the mixture and cook as above. Serve with garlic bread and a salad.

## Sausage and apple pie with potato crust

This potato pastry has a lovely light, buttery texture. For best results, use low fat rather than traditional sausages for the filling.

*for the pastry*
225g/8oz self-raising flour
1/4 tsp salt
1/4 tsp pepper
175g/6oz butter, diced
225g/8oz cold mashed potato
*for the filling*
1 tbsp olive oil
2 onions, chopped
2 cooking apples, about 350g/12oz, peeled, cored and chopped
900g/2lb low fat pork sausages, skinned
195g can sweetcorn, drained
1/4 tsp grated fresh nutmeg
1/2 tsp ground black pepper
1/2 tsp salt
1 large egg, beaten

**1** For the pastry, sift the flour and seasoning into a bowl, then rub in the butter until the mixture resembles breadcrumbs. Add the potato and work to a soft dough. Wrap in plastic film and leave to rest in the fridge while making the filling.
**2** Heat the oil in a pan, add the onions and fry gently for about 5 minutes until beginning to soften. Add the apples and cook for 2-3 minutes until starting to soften, then turn into a bowl.
**3** Add the sausagemeat, sweetcorn, nutmeg, seasoning and beaten egg. Mix thoroughly with clean hands, then transfer to a shallow 1.4 litre/2½ pint pie dish.
**4** Lightly press out the pastry with your hands on a lightly floured surface until large enough to cover the pie. Carefully lift over the filling, trim the edges and make a slit in the top of the pie. Chill for up to 24 hours until ready to bake.
**5** Preheat a baking tray in the oven at 190C/fan oven 170C/Gas 5. Place the pie on the baking tray and bake for 1-1¼ hours, covering lightly with foil if the pastry appears to be overbrowning. Serve hot, with seasonal vegetables.

## Penne with venison and ceps

Available from selected large supermarkets and butchers, venison mince is a good low fat alternative to beef, although extra lean minced beef can be used here if preferred.

15g/1/2oz dried ceps, rinsed and chopped
150ml/1/4 pint boiling water
2 tbsp olive oil
2 large onions, halved and sliced
700g/11/2lb venison mince
150ml/1/4 pint red wine
3 tbsp sun-dried tomato paste
1 tbsp chopped fresh marjoram
salt and pepper
*for the pasta and sauce*
175g/6oz penne or other pasta shapes
50g/2oz butter
50g/2oz plain flour
600ml/1 pint milk
1 egg, beaten
175g/6oz mature Cheddar, grated
1 slice of bread, diced

**1** Soak the dried ceps in the boiling water for about 15 minutes.
**2** Heat the oil in a large pan and gently fry the onions for 8-10 minutes, until golden. Add the venison and stir-fry until browned.
**3** Pour in the wine and add the mushrooms with their soaking liquid. Stir in the tomato paste, marjoram and seasoning, then cover and simmer for 10 minutes.
**4** Cook the pasta in a large pan of boiling water for 10 minutes or until *al dente*; drain.
**5** Meanwhile put the butter, flour and milk in a pan and whisk over a low heat until smooth and thickened. Stir in the pasta, season and let cool slightly, then beat in the egg and two thirds of the cheese.
**6** Spread the venison mixture in a large ovenproof dish. Spoon over the pasta and sauce, then top with the bread and the rest of the cheese. If preparing ahead, cover and chill for up to 2 days, or freeze.
**7** To serve, preheat oven to 190C/fan oven 170C/Gas 5. Bake the pasta dish in the oven for 40 minutes until bubbling and golden. Serve with a crisp leafy salad.

## Rabbit in wine with olives and oregano

Make this delicious wine-enriched casserole in advance to allow time for the flavours to fully develop.

800g/13/4lb boneless rabbit portions, cut into large chunks
4 tbsp seasoned flour
2-3 tbsp olive oil
250g/9oz large shallots, peeled and quartered
2 large garlic cloves, crushed
250g/9oz large button mushrooms, halved
300ml/1/2 pint dry white wine
150ml/1/4 pint chicken stock
100g/4oz green olives
2 tbsp chopped fresh oregano
salt and pepper

**1** Coat the rabbit pieces in the seasoned flour. Heat the oil in a flameproof casserole and fry the rabbit in batches until golden on all sides; remove with a slotted spoon. Add the shallots, garlic and mushrooms to the pan; stir-fry for 3 minutes.
**2** Pour in the wine and stock, return the rabbit pieces and stir in the olives and oregano. Cover tightly and simmer for about 30 minutes until the rabbit is tender. Taste and adjust the seasoning.
**3** If preparing ahead, cool, then cover and refrigerate for up to 2 days, or freeze.
**4** To serve, defrost at cool room temperature overnight (if frozen). Reheat in a flameproof casserole or heavy-based pan until piping hot. Serve with creamy mashed potatoes and a green vegetable.

## Spiced pork escalopes with apricots

Tender pork fillet, beaten thin, cooks very quickly without losing its juiciness. Fresh apricots spiced with cloves are the perfect foil, though plums or apple slices can be used as an alternative. *Serves 2-3*

450g/1lb pork fillet (tenderloin), cut into 1cm/1/2in slices
1 tsp powdered cloves
salt and pepper
6 fresh apricots, stoned and quartered
3 whole cloves
6 tbsp water
2 tsp clear honey

**1** Lay the pork slices between sheets of greaseproof paper and beat with a rolling pin to flatten. Sprinkle with the ground cloves, salt and pepper.
**2** Heat a large non-stick frying pan until very hot. Cook the pork in batches for about 1 minute each side until tender; transfer to a warmed dish, cover and keep warm in a low oven while cooking the sauce.
**3** Add the apricots and whole cloves to the pan and cook, shaking the pan, for 2-3 minutes until they are lightly singed. Add the water and honey, scraping up the sediment. Continue to cook until the apricots are softened but still hold their shape, adding a little more water if needed.
**4** Serve the meat topped with the apricots and pan juices. Accompany with French beans or steamed courgettes.

## Mustard steaks on mushrooms

A highly seasoned juicy steak cooked without extra fat and served with a crunchy julienne of vegetables. *Serves 2*

2 fillet steaks, each 175g/6oz
salt and pepper
2 tsp wholegrain mustard
2 tsp black olive paste
2 large flat mushrooms, about 10cm/4in across
*for the vegetable julienne*
1/2 each red and yellow pepper, seeded and cut into fine strips
50g/2oz celeriac, cut into very fine strips

**1** Preheat oven to 240C/fan oven 220C/Gas 9. Using a sharp knife, score the steaks in a criss cross pattern at 1cm/1/2in intervals, cutting just less than halfway through depth.
**2** Mix together the mustard and olive paste and spread over the meat and into the cuts. Place the steaks, mustard side down, on a foil lined baking tray. Cook under a preheated high grill for about 3 minutes.
**3** Put the mushrooms, flat side up, on the baking tray. Turn the steaks over and carefully place on top of the mushrooms. Bake in the oven for 10 minutes or until the mushrooms are cooked through; the steaks should still be pink in the middle. (For well done steaks cook for 2 to 3 minutes longer.)
**4** Quickly toss together the vegetable julienne and pile on top of the steaks. Serve at once, with a salad.

## Baked aubergines with minted lamb

Tasty aubergines are slit and filled with slices of lean lamb fillet and aromatic flavourings, then baked to create a delicious, healthy meal. Minted, garlicky yogurt is the perfect complement.

4 aubergines, each about 225g/8oz
280g/10oz thin cut lean lamb fillet
salt and pepper
1 red onion, thinly sliced
2 tbsp shredded fresh mint leaves
a little oil, for brushing (optional)
*for the minted yogurt*
200ml/7fl oz low fat yogurt
1-2 tbsp finely shredded fresh mint
1 garlic clove, crushed (optional)

**1** Preheat a baking tray in the oven at 200C/fan oven 180C/Gas 6. Cut each aubergine lengthwise into 5 slices, but not quite right through.
**2** Season the lamb with salt and pepper and insert a slice into each aubergine slit, with some onion and shredded mint. Brush sparingly with oil and loosely wrap each aubergine in foil.
**3** Place the parcels on the baking tray and bake for 45 minutes to 1 hour until the aubergine is tender through to the centre.
**4** Meanwhile, mix the yogurt with the mint, salt, and garlic if using. Chill until required.
**5** Serve the baked aubergines hot, accompanied by the minted yogurt and basmati rice or steamed couscous.

## Savoy cabbage and veal parcels

Serve with a fresh tomato sauce. *Serves 2*

6 medium green Savoy cabbage leaves
2 tsp olive oil
2 shallots, finely chopped
1 garlic clove, crushed
280g/10oz lean minced veal
1 tsp finely chopped fresh rosemary leaves
4 juniper berries, crushed
150ml/¼ pint well flavoured chicken stock
50g/2oz fresh breadcrumbs
salt and pepper

**1** Blanch the cabbage leaves in boiling water for 1-2 minutes. Drain and refresh in cold water, then drain and leave to dry on kitchen paper while preparing the filling.
**2** Heat the oil in a pan and fry the shallots and garlic for 5 minutes or until soft and translucent. Add the minced veal with the rosemary and crushed juniper berries; fry for 5-6 minutes until opaque. Add the stock and continue cooking for 2-3 minutes.
**3** Remove from the heat and add the breadcrumbs. Mix thoroughly, seasoning with pepper and a little salt if required.

**4** Divide the veal mixture between the cabbage leaves. Fold in the sides of the leaves, then roll up loosely from the stem end. Secure each parcel with a wooden cocktail stick.
**5** Put the cabbage parcels in a steamer and steam for 8-10 minutes until the cabbage is tender and the filling is piping hot. Serve with a fresh tomato sauce.

**VARIATION** Use pork instead of veal for the filling but, to ensure a low fat dish, buy lean pork fillet and mince it yourself.

## Mexican beef stew with lime and chilli

Known as *picadillo* in Mexico, this unusual stew is flavoured with fresh chilli, lime juice, apples and cumin. It is served on a bed of fried potatoes and topped with cheese.

3 tbsp vegetable oil
700g/1½lb lean minced beef
1 large onion, finely chopped
1 green chilli, thinly sliced
4 tbsp lime juice
400g can chopped tomatoes
2 Granny Smith's apples, peeled, cored and roughly chopped
2 tbsp capers
salt and pepper
3 large potatoes, peeled and cut into 2cm/¾in cubes
1 garlic clove, finely chopped
2 tsp ground cumin
grated Cheddar, to garnish

**1** Heat 2 tbsp oil in a large heavy-based frying pan. Add the beef and onion and fry, stirring, until the meat is browned.
**2** Add the chilli, lime juice, tomatoes, apples and capers. Lower the heat, cover with a tight fitting lid and simmer for 25 minutes or until the meat is tender. Season to taste.
**3** Meanwhile, par-boil the potatoes in salted water for 10 minutes; drain thoroughly.
**4** Heat the remaining oil in a large, non-stick frying pan. Add the potatoes, garlic and cumin and fry, stirring, until golden brown.
**5** Divide the spiced potatoes between warmed plates and top with the stew. Sprinkle with grated cheese and serve with tortillas or crusty bread and a salad.

## Creole meatballs

Tender lamb meatballs cooked in a mildly spiced creole sauce with fresh pineapple and red peppers.

600g/1lb 5oz lean minced lamb
1 onion, finely chopped
3 tbsp plain flour
1 tsp hot paprika
salt and pepper
oil for shallow-frying
*for the creole sauce*
1 tbsp vegetable oil
1 onion, finely chopped
2 red peppers, cored, seeded and chopped
3 garlic cloves, finely chopped
400g can chopped tomatoes
1 bay leaf
200g/8oz fresh pineapple, roughly cubed
200ml/7fl oz water

**1** For the meatballs, put the minced lamb, onion, flour, paprika and seasoning in a bowl and mix thoroughly. With wet hands, divide the mixture equally into 16 pieces and shape into balls.
**2** Heat the oil in a large frying pan and carefully fry the meatballs, turning until evenly browned. Drain on crumpled kitchen paper and set aside. Preheat oven to 200C/fan oven 180C/Gas 6.
**3** To make the creole sauce, heat the oil in a frying pan and gently fry the onion until softened. Add the red peppers and garlic; stir-fry for 1 minute. Add the remaining ingredients, season well and bring to the boil, stirring.
**4** Put the meatballs in a shallow ovenproof dish. Pour over the sauce and bake in the oven for 20-25 minutes. Serve with plain boiled rice and a crisp green salad.

## Jamaican jerk pork chops

This traditional Jamaican recipe, usually made with chicken-on-the-bone, works well with pork chops too. It is also a great recipe for a barbecue.

4 spring onions, finely chopped
2 red chillies, seeded and chopped
3 tbsp vegetable oil
1 tsp allspice
2 tbsp light muscovado sugar
2 tbsp vinegar
2 tsp fresh thyme leaves
salt and pepper
4 pork loin chops, each about 200g/7oz

**1** Put the spring onions, chillies, oil, allspice, sugar, vinegar and thyme leaves in a food processor. Season well and process until well blended.
**2** Make 3-4 shallow slashes on both sides of each pork chop and lay in a shallow, non-metallic dish. Pour the jerk mixture over the chops and turn them to coat thoroughly. Cover and leave to marinate in a cool place for 1 hour.
**3** Preheat the grill to medium high. Transfer the chops to the grill rack and grill for 5-7 minutes on each side or until the meat is tender, basting occasionally.
**4** Serve the grilled chops accompanied by baked sweet potatoes and an avocado, tomato and red onion salad.

## Duck kebabs with honey, ginger and orange

These tangy duck and sweet pepper kebabs are best served with Thai jasmine rice and a leafy salad.

6 duck breast fillets, each about 175g/6oz
grated rind and juice of 1 orange
4 tbsp clear honey
1 tbsp dark soy sauce
1 tsp ground ginger
1 tsp chilli powder
1 red pepper, halved, cored and seeded
1 yellow pepper, halved, cored and seeded
*for the garnish*
toasted sesame seeds
shredded spring onion

**1** Remove the skin and fat from the duck breasts. Cut the meat into 4cm/1½in pieces and put into a shallow, non-metallic dish.
**2** Mix together the orange rind and juice, honey, soy sauce, ginger and chilli powder. Drizzle the mixture over the meat and turn to coat well.
**3** Cut the peppers into 4cm/1½in squares and add to the meat. Toss well and leave to marinate for 30 minutes.
**4** Preheat the grill to high. Thread the duck and pepper pieces alternately on to 8 metal skewers.
**5** Place the kebabs on the grill rack and baste with the marinade. Grill for about 10 minutes, turning and basting from time to time, until the peppers are charred and the duck is evenly browned and cooked through.
**6** Transfer the kebabs to warmed serving plates, allowing two per person. Sprinkle over toasted sesame seeds and garnish with shredded spring onion. Serve at once, accompanied by rice and a salad.

## Bobotie

Serve this spicy Cape Malay meatloaf with yogurt, naan bread and a salad. *Serves 6-8*

1 tbsp vegetable oil
1 large onion, finely chopped
2 garlic cloves, finely chopped
1 kg/2¼lb lean minced lamb
2 tsp ground coriander
1 tsp ground cumin
1 tsp paprika
85g/3oz fresh white breadcrumbs
2 tbsp white wine vinegar
2 eggs, beaten
4 tbsp sultanas
4 tbsp apricot jam
salt and pepper
*for the topping*
2 eggs
200ml/7fl oz double cream
2 tbsp chopped fresh coriander leaves
coriander sprigs, to garnish

**1** Line a 23cm/9in loose bottomed cake tin with non-stick baking parchment. Preheat oven to 180C/fan oven 160C/Gas 4.
**2** Heat the oil in a large non-stick frying pan, add the onion and garlic and fry gently until lightly browned. Add the meat and fry, stirring, until browned.
**3** Take off the heat and mix in the spices, breadcrumbs, vinegar, beaten eggs, sultanas, apricot jam and salt to taste. Turn the mixture into the prepared tin and spread evenly.
**4** For the topping, beat the eggs and cream together in a bowl; season well, then pour the mixture over the meat. Scatter the coriander over the surface. Stand the cake tin on a baking sheet and bake for 1 hour.
**5** Carefully unmould the bobotie. Serve cut into wedges, garnished with coriander.

## Lamb tagine

A wonderful Moroccan stew of lamb and dried fruit, enriched with saffron, ginger, cinnamon and honey.

2 tbsp vegetable oil
1 large onion, finely chopped
2 garlic cloves, finely chopped
1kg/2¼lb boned shoulder of lamb, cut into 5cm/2in cubes
1 tsp saffron threads
1 tsp ground ginger
850ml/1½ pints lamb stock or water
250g/9oz ready-to-eat dried prunes
250g/9oz ready-to-eat dried apricots
2 tsp ground cinnamon
2 tbsp clear honey
salt and pepper

**1** Heat the oil in a heavy-based pan or flameproof casserole and sauté the onion and garlic until soft. Add the meat and fry, turning, until evenly browned.
**2** Add the saffron, ginger and stock or water and stir well. Cover and simmer gently for 1½ hours or until the meat is tender, adding a little hot water if the stew appears to be a little too dry.
**3** Add the prunes, apricots, cinnamon and honey. Season with salt and pepper to taste, re-cover and simmer for a further 15 minutes.
**4** Taste and adjust the seasoning. Serve with steamed couscous or rice, and a salad or green vegetable.

## Thai-style lamb shanks

These succulent shanks of lamb are subtly flavoured with coconut milk and Thai spices and baked until meltingly tender.

4 lamb shanks
1 tbsp vegetable oil
2 large onions, finely chopped
2 tbsp Thai green curry paste
2 tbsp lemon grass, finely chopped
1 tsp ground cumin
1 tsp ground coriander
400ml can coconut milk
500ml/18fl oz vegetable stock
3 tbsp chopped fresh coriander leaves
salt and pepper
*to garnish*
coriander leaves or finely sliced chilli

**1** Preheat oven to 220C/fan oven 200C/Gas 7. Place the lamb shanks in a roasting tin and roast for 40 minutes, turning them halfway through cooking.
**2** Lift out the lamb shanks, drain off all of the fat, then transfer to a casserole in which they fit snugly. Lower the oven setting to 190C/fan oven 170C/Gas 5.
**3** Heat the oil in another pan, add the onions and sauté until light golden. Add the curry paste, lemon grass, cumin and coriander and stir-fry for 1 minute. Add the coconut milk, stock and chopped coriander.
**4** Pour this mixture over the lamb shanks, cover and cook in the oven for 2¹/2 hours until the meat is very tender. Check the seasoning of the sauce.
**5** To serve, place each lamb shank in a warmed shallow serving bowl. Spoon over some of the sauce and scatter with fresh coriander or sliced chilli. Serve with Thai jasmine rice and a steamed green vegetable, such as bok choi.

### Spiced crisp belly pork

This is perfect with steamed bok choi and sticky rice. Buy organic belly pork if you can – its thick skin is easier to score. *Serves 4-6*

1.25kg-1.3kg/2¾-3lb piece belly pork, boned
salt
1 tsp Thai 7 spice mix
300g/10oz shallots, finely sliced
6 garlic cloves, finely chopped
2 fat red chillies, seeded and finely chopped
2 tbsp sunflower oil
4 tbsp clear honey
100ml/3½fl oz white wine
3 tbsp dark soy sauce
coriander sprigs, to garnish

**1** Using a very sharp knife, deeply score the pork skin through to the fat at 1cm/½in intervals. Rub in plenty of salt and leave to draw out moisture for 1-1½ hours.
**2** Preheat oven to 200C/fan oven 180C/Gas 6. Dry the pork skin well with kitchen paper and rub in the spice mix. Place in a shallow roasting tin and roast for 25 minutes. Mix the shallots, garlic and chillies with the oil.
**3** Spoon the shallot mixture under the pork and roast for 50 minutes or until the skin is very crisp.
**4** Brush with 2 tbsp honey and return to the oven for 10 minutes. Brush with another 1 tbsp honey; roast for a final 10 minutes.
**5** Transfer the pork and shallots to a serving plate and rest in a warm place until the sauce is ready. Pour off the fat from the tin, place on the hob and add the wine, soy and remaining honey, stirring to deglaze.
**6** Cut the meat into squares. Serve on a bed of rice, with the sauce and shallots. Garnish with coriander sprigs.

### Maple and mustard glazed ham

Ask your butcher for the knuckle end to get a traditional ham shape. Unless it is mild cure or pre-soaked, you will need to soak it for 24 hours before cooking otherwise the meat will be too salty. *Serves 6-8*

1 bone-in ham, smoked or unsmoked, about 3kg/6½lb
150ml/¼ pint maple syrup
25g/1oz caster sugar
2 tsp Dijon or honey mustard
15 cloves

**1** Preheat oven to 160C/fan oven 140C/Gas 3. Line a large roasting tin with a sheet of extra wide foil, allowing plenty of overhang at each end. Lay another sheet of foil cross-wise on top, to overhang the sides of the tin generously. Put the ham in the centre and bring the ends of the foil up over the top. Fold together to seal well and make a roomy tent over the ham. Bake in the oven, allowing 15 minutes per 450g/1lb.
**2** Put the maple syrup and sugar in a small heavy-based pan and heat gently until the sugar is dissolved. Add the mustard and simmer until syrupy.
**3** Drain off the juices from the ham. Increase oven setting to 220C/fan oven 200C/Gas 7. Cut a zig zag pattern in the skin at the narrow end of the joint, to about 7.5cm/3in from the end. Remove the skin from the rest of the ham, leaving a thick layer of fat. Score the fat in a lattice pattern, at 2.5cm/1in intervals.
**4** Brush the whole joint with half of the syrup. Roast, uncovered, for 5 minutes per 450g/1lb until glazed and golden, brushing with the remaining syrup and studding each lattice with a clove halfway through this time. Serve hot or cold.

### Duck with Campari, rosemary and caramelised orange

1 Gressingham duck, about 1.8kg/4lb
200g/7oz sugar
juice of 1 orange
3 tbsp Campari
1 small onion, peeled
5 large fresh rosemary sprigs
salt
1 small orange, cut into slices
150ml/¼ pint well flavoured duck or chicken stock

**1** Sit the duck on a rack in the sink and pour over 2 kettlefuls of boiling water. Drain and let dry on kitchen paper in a cool place for 30 minutes, or hang the duck so air can circulate around it. (This firms up the skin.)
**2** Preheat oven to 220C/fan oven 200C/Gas 7. Put the sugar, orange juice and 2 tbsp Campari in a heavy-based pan on a low heat until the sugar is dissolved. Bring to the boil and simmer for 5 minutes or until syrupy.
**3** Prick the duck skin all over. Put the onion and 1 rosemary sprig into the cavity. Sit the duck on a rack in a roasting tin containing 150ml/¼ pint water. Roast for 20 minutes.
**4** Brush the duck with some of the syrup and sprinkle with salt. Roast for a further 30 minutes. Brush with more syrup and roast for another 30 minutes, lowering setting to 200C/fan oven 180C/Gas 6 if overbrowning.
**5** Dip orange slices in remaining syrup and lay on the duck breast with the rosemary. Brush all over with syrup and roast for a final 30 minutes or until the duck is cooked.
**6** Transfer to a platter, cover loosely and rest in a warm place for 15 minutes. Pour off fat from roasting tin, then place over a medium heat. Add stock and remaining Campari, stirring to deglaze. Add any remaining syrup and heat through. Serve with the duck.

## Lamb stuffed with dates and spices

8 tbsp olive oil
2 onions, 1 chopped, 1 finely sliced
2 plump garlic cloves, 1 crushed, 1 cut
into slivers
large pinch of saffron strands
¹/₄ tsp ground cinnamon
1 tsp ground cumin
salt and pepper
2 pieces preserved lemon, rinsed and finely
chopped, or finely grated rind of 2 lemons
8 medjool dates, stoned and finely chopped
3-4 tbsp chopped fresh coriander leaves
1.3kg/3lb leg of lamb, part boned (see note)
2 cinnamon sticks, broken

**1** Heat 4 tbsp oil in a heavy-based frying
pan and fry the chopped onion and
crushed garlic until soft and golden.
Add the saffron, cinnamon, cumin and
seasoning; stir well. Take off the heat and
add the lemon and dates. Stir to mix and
set aside until cold.
**2** Mix the fresh coriander into the stuffing
and use to stuff the lamb. Secure with
skewers or sew up the stuffed pocket.
**3** Preheat oven to 200C/fan oven 180C/Gas 6.
Make small incisions in the skin of the lamb
and insert the garlic slivers. Put in a roasting
tin and brush with 2 tbsp oil. Season well
and surround with the cinnamon sticks.
**4** Roast for 1 hour 20 minutes, basting from
time to time. Transfer to a warm platter,
cover loosely and rest in a warm place for
15 minutes. Meanwhile, fry the sliced onion
in the remaining oil until golden and crisp.
**5** Serve the lamb topped with the fried onion
and cinnamon sticks.

**NOTE** Part boning leg of lamb to give a
pocket for the stuffing is not difficult. Given
notice, your butcher should do it for you.

## Seared fillet of beef with roasted onions and physalis fruit

Serve this tender beef, crowned with the
physalis fruit in their papery husks, on a
mound of potato and celeriac mash with the
sweet roast onions and rich meat juices.

400g/14oz baby onions, peeled
3 tbsp olive oil
1kg/2¹/₄lb piece beef fillet
salt and pepper
70g/2¹/₂oz physalis fruit
200ml/7fl oz Muscat de Beaume de Venise,
or Sauternes

**1** Preheat oven to 230C/fan oven 210C/Gas 8.
Put the onions in a roasting tin, add 1 tbsp
of the oil and toss to coat. Roast for
10 minutes.
**2** Meanwhile, pat the beef fillet dry with
kitchen paper, rub with 1 tbsp of oil and
season well.
**3** Preheat a heavy-based frying pan, add
the beef and brown on all sides over a high
heat for about 5 minutes. Transfer the beef
to the roasting tin and roast with the onions
for 15 minutes.
**4** Toss the physalis fruit in the remaining
1 tbsp oil. Add to the meat and roast for a
further 7 minutes. Transfer the beef, onions
and physalis to a warm serving dish and
leave to rest in a warm place for about
15 minutes.
**5** Meanwhile, add the wine to the roasting
tin, stirring to deglaze and bubble over a
high heat for about 1 minute. Pour any meat
juices that have collected in the serving
dish into the roasting tin and heat through.
**6** Carve the beef into medium thick slices.
Serve with the physalis fruit and roast
onions on a bed of celeriac and potato
mash, drizzled with the meat juices.

## Venison in coppa with chestnuts

Venison is marinated overnight with juniper
and mustard, then wrapped in coppa and
roasted with chestnuts. *Serves 4-6*

1 tsp black mustard seeds
1 tsp juniper berries
1 tsp black peppercorns
600g/1lb 5oz piece venison fillet
salt
350g/12oz shelled fresh chestnuts (in skins)
1 tbsp oil
115g/4oz coppa (20 thin slices), or pancetta
100ml/3¹/₂fl oz fruity red wine
knob of unsalted butter

**1** Coarsely grind the mustard seeds, juniper
and peppercorns, with a pestle and mortar.
Rub the mixture all over the venison. Wrap
tightly in cling film; refrigerate for 24 hours.
**2** Bring meat to room temperature 1 hour
before cooking and season lightly with salt.
Preheat oven to 220C/fan oven 200C/Gas 7.
**3** Pierce the skin of each chestnut, then put
in a shallow roasting dish and toss with the
oil. Season with salt and roast for 5 minutes.
**4** Lay the coppa slices overlapping on
greaseproof paper to form a rectangle,
large enough to wrap around the venison.
Lay the venison on the long edge and, with
the aid of the paper, roll the coppa around it
to enclose. Wrap in oiled foil and roast with
the chestnuts for 15 minutes.
**5** Unwrap the venison, pour the juices into a
small pan, then roast for a further 5 minutes
until the coppa is slightly crisp. Transfer to
a serving dish, cover loosely and rest in a
warm place for 15 minutes; continue to
roast the chestnuts during this time.
**6** Add the wine to the meat juices and boil
for 1 minute. Stir in the butter. Carve the meat
and serve with the chestnuts and glaze.

## Crusted roast loin of pork

Buy a whole pork loin with 6-8 chops and ask your butcher to remove all skin, fat and connecting bone, leaving the thin individual bone attached to each chop. *Serves 6-8*

1.3kg/3lb loin of pork, with 6-8 bones
1 tbsp balsamic vinegar
4 tsp caraway seeds, roughly crushed
2 tsp white peppercorns, roughly crushed
3 tsp Malden salt
9 sprigs of fresh bay leaves
2 tbsp olive oil

**1** Tie the meat with string to ensure the bones stand upright. Rub well with balsamic vinegar and leave to stand for 20 minutes. Preheat oven to 200C/fan oven 180C/Gas 6.

**2** Mix the caraway, white pepper and 2 tsp salt together and press all over the meat. Lay 1 bay sprig in a shallow roasting tin. Stand the pork loin on top and drizzle with the oil. Roast for 15 minutes, basting with the pan juices occasionally.

**3** Push the rest of the bay leaf sprigs under the string and roast for a further 20 minutes.

**4** Lower oven setting to 180C/fan oven 160C/Gas 4. Cover the meat loosely with foil and roast for a further 30 minutes or until cooked through. To test, insert a skewer into the middle: the juices should run clear.

**5** Lift meat on to a dish, cover loosely and rest in a warm place for 15 minutes. Meanwhile, pour off the fat from the tin, then add 3 tbsp water, stirring to deglaze.

**6** Scatter the loin with the remaining salt and serve cut into thick slices with the bone attached, and the pan juices spooned over. Serve with baked baby beets and potatoes.

# vibrant **vegetables**
# & **salads**

**Turn over a new leaf** with these refreshing ideas for vegetables and salads. Maximise the **flavour of succulent vegetables** and crisp colourful salad leaves with **aromatic herbs**, sublime sauces and **decadent dressings**. For optimum flavour, **choose organic produce** - most supermarkets now stock a good range. Discover how to make the most of **exotic vegetables** with exciting recipes from the Far East and South Asia. Try our **imaginative healthy salads**, featuring nuts, seeds and fruit. And if you are short of ideas for **vegetarian entertaining**, you will find **plenty of inspiration** in this chapter.

## Spiced roast potatoes with garlic

1.1kg/2¹/₂lb potatoes, peeled and cut into
5cm/2in chunks
2 tbsp plain flour
1 tbsp smoked paprika or mustard powder
1 tsp salt
4 tbsp vegetable oil
2 garlic bulbs, cloves separated (unpeeled)

**1** Preheat oven to 220C/fan oven 200C/Gas 7.
Put the potatoes in a large pan and add
cold water to cover. Bring to the boil and
boil steadily for 5 minutes. Immediately
drain and leave, uncovered, to cool slightly.
**2** Mix together the flour, paprika or mustard
and salt. Put the oil in a roasting tin and
heat in the oven for a minute or two.
**3** Meanwhile, toss the potato chunks in the
spice mix to coat well. Carefully add to the
hot oil, with the garlic cloves. Roast in the
oven for 40-50 minutes until the potatoes
are crunchy and browned, turning halfway
through cooking. Serve piping hot.

## Potato and celeriac rösti

700g/1¹/₂lb floury potatoes (King Edward or
Romano)
salt and pepper
350g/12oz celeriac, peeled
1-2 tsp fennel seeds (optional)
2 tbsp olive oil
50g/2oz butter

**1** Put the unpeeled potatoes in a large
pan of cold salted water with the celeriac.
Bring to the boil and par-cook for about
8-10 minutes. Drain and leave until cool
enough to handle, then peel the potatoes.
**2** Coarsely grate the potatoes and celeriac
into a large bowl and toss in the fennel
seeds if using; mix well. Season with salt
and pepper to taste.

**3** Heat 1 tbsp of the oil in a 23cm/9in sauté
pan and add half of the butter. When melted
and foaming, tip in the potato mixture and
spread evenly; don't press down too firmly.
Cook over a moderate heat for about
15 minutes, shaking the pan from time to
time to prevent the rösti from sticking.
**4** Invert a plate over the pan, then turn the
rösti out on to the plate. Add the remaining
oil and butter to pan and heat until foaming.
Slide the rösti back into the pan and fry the
uncooked side for 15-20 minutes, shaking
the pan occasionally. Serve cut into wedges.

**VARIATION** Add 85g/3oz finely sliced
pastrami or smoked ham at stage 2.

## Hassleback potatoes

These thyme scented, fanned roast potatoes
are excellent with poultry and game.

8 even sized, slightly oval potatoes, each
about 140g/5oz
2 tbsp truffle oil, or extra virgin olive oil
1 small bunch (or packet) fresh thyme
sea salt

**1** Preheat oven to 220C/fan oven 200C/Gas 7.
Slice each potato vertically across its width
at 3mm/¹/₈in intervals, without cutting right
through. Rinse, then put the potatoes in a
bowl of chilled water for 15 minutes; they
will open out slightly. Drain and dry well.
**2** Brush the oil between the potato slices
and all over the skin. Push a small thyme
sprig into each slit. Season with salt.
**3** Place each potato on a 20cm/8in square
of foil, pull up the corners and twist loosely.
Put the parcels on a baking sheet and bake
in the oven for 40 minutes. Fold back the foil
slightly and bake for a further 30-40 minutes
until the potatoes are cooked.

## Caramelised new potatoes with orange

New potatoes with a sweet hint of marmalade
to partner duck, chicken and pork.

900g/2lb new potatoes, scrubbed
salt and pepper
2 fresh mint sprigs
50g/2oz butter
2 tbsp fine cut Seville orange marmalade
1 tbsp finely chopped fresh mint

**1** Add the potatoes to a large pan of boiling
salted water with the mint sprigs and cook
for 7-10 minutes, depending on size, until
almost tender. Drain well; discard the mint.
**2** Melt the butter in a wide based pan, add
the potatoes and shake the pan to coat the
potatoes in the butter.
**3** Add the marmalade and heat gently to
melt it, turning the potatoes to coat well.
Cook for about 15 minutes, stirring regularly,
until golden brown and caramelised.
**4** Toss in the chopped mint and serve.

## Mashed potatoes with horseradish

900g/2lb floury potatoes, peeled and cut
into chunks
salt and pepper
200ml/7fl oz soured cream
2 tbsp grated hot horseradish
1 tbsp olive oil or butter

**1** Add the potatoes to a large pan of cold
salted water, bring to the boil and boil for
15-20 minutes until very tender.
**2** Drain well, then shake the potatoes in the
covered pan to drive off moisture. Let rest
in the pan with the lid ajar for a few minutes.
**3** Meanwhile warm the cream, horseradish
and oil or butter together in a small pan.
**4** Mash the potatoes with the horseradish
cream until smooth. Season and serve.

## Baby beets with orange and walnuts

Young beetroot – bought in bunches – are best baked to retain all their earthy flavour. Combined with orange, walnuts and their leafy tops, they make a heart-warming dish.

16 baby beetroot with leaves (2 bunches)
4 oranges
4 tbsp olive oil
salt and pepper
85g/3oz walnut halves

**1** Preheat oven to 190C/fan oven 170C/Gas 5. Cut the tops from the beetroot; set aside. Scrub the beetroot and put in a baking dish.
**2** Finely grate the rind from 2 oranges and squeeze the juice. Add this rind and juice to the beetroot with half the olive oil, and seasoning; toss to coat. Cover with foil and bake for 45 minutes or until tender.
**3** Meanwhile, peel and segment the remaining oranges, discarding all of the membrane and pips.
**4** Heat the remaining oil in a frying pan and add the beetroot tops. Sauté for 2-3 minutes until wilted and tender. Stir in the orange segments and walnuts. Season generously with salt and pepper.
**5** Add the baked beetroot to the wilted beet tops and toss to mix. Serve immediately.

## Courgette, chilli and sugar snap sauté

A fast stir-fry of green vegetables with a hint of chilli, enriched with a little soured cream.

3 tbsp olive oil
4 medium courgettes, cut into broad strips
175g/6oz sugar snap peas
1 plump green chilli, halved, seeded and finely chopped
2 tbsp soured cream
3 tbsp chopped fresh coriander
salt and pepper

**1** Heat the oil in a frying pan or sauté pan and add the courgettes and sugar snaps. Stir-fry for 3 minutes, then add the chilli and stir for 1 minute. Remove from the heat.
**2** Stir in the soured cream and coriander. Season and serve at once.

## Roasted squash with shallots

Sweet butternut squash enriched with caramelised shallots and earthy roast garlic. Serve with roast pork, turkey or duck.

2 butternut squash, each about 450g/1lb
50g/2oz butter
3 tbsp maple syrup
12 shallots, peeled
12 garlic cloves (unpeeled)
2 tbsp raisins
salt and pepper

**1** Preheat oven to 200C/fan oven 180C/Gas 6. Halve the squash, scoop out the seeds, then peel. Cut the flesh into large chunks.
**2** Melt the butter with the maple syrup in a roasting dish. Add the shallots and squash, toss to coat and bake for 20 minutes.
**3** Add the garlic cloves and raisins and bake for a further 20 minutes or until the squash and garlic are tender and beginning to caramelise. Season generously and serve.

## Moroccan spiced cauliflower with mint

Cauliflower is lightly steamed until tender, then tossed in a Moroccan spiced melted butter with fresh mint leaves. *Serves 4-6*

1 medium cauliflower, divided into florets
85g/3oz butter
1 tsp sweet paprika
1/2 tsp ground cumin
1/2 tsp ground coriander
salt and pepper
handful of fresh mint leaves

**1** Steam the cauliflower over boiling water for 10-12 minutes until just tender. Remove and allow to dry a little.
**2** Melt the butter in a frying pan. When sizzling, add the spices and fry, stirring, for 30 seconds. Add the cauliflower florets and stir to coat with the buttery spices. Season well with salt and pepper.
**3** Add the mint leaves and cook gently until wilted. Serve immediately.

## Peas with cherry tomatoes and spinach

This is a sort of quick vegetable stew – very colourful and full of goodness! Serve with grilled or roast meat or poultry.

225g/8oz shelled fresh or frozen peas
150ml/1/4 pint dry white wine
2 tbsp olive oil
1-2 fresh bay leaves
175g/6oz whole ripe cherry tomatoes
225g/8oz fresh leaf spinach, stalks removed (see note)
salt and pepper

**1** Place the peas in a large pan with the wine, olive oil and bay leaves. Bring to the boil, then lower the heat and simmer gently for 5 minutes.
**2** Add the cherry tomatoes and simmer for a further 5 minutes until tender and the liquid is well reduced.
**3** Finally, stir in the spinach and cook for a few minutes, turning occasionally, until the leaves just wilt.
**4** Season with salt and pepper to taste. Serve immediately.

**NOTE** For convenience, buy bags of ready prepared spinach from supermarkets. Otherwise, choose small, tender spinach leaves and wash thoroughly in several changes of water to remove all traces of grit. Drain thoroughly before cooking.

## Baked root layer cake

This layered 'cake' of carrot, parsnip and celeriac is perfect with roast meat or game.

350g/12oz carrots
350g/12oz parsnip
350g/12oz celeriac
2 tbsp clear honey
2 tbsp lemon juice
85g/3oz butter
salt and pepper
thyme sprigs, to garnish

**1** Preheat oven to 200C/fan oven 180C/Gas 6. Peel and coarsely grate the carrots, parsnip and celeriac, using a hand grater or food processor fitted with a coarse grating disc, keeping each vegetable separate. Place in individual bowls.
**2** Warm the honey, lemon juice and butter in a small pan over a low heat until melted. Season with salt and pepper. Pour a third of this mixture over each vegetable and mix well to coat.
**3** Line a shallow 20cm/8in springform cake tin with non-stick baking parchment. Spoon the carrot into the tin, spread evenly and press down gently. Repeat with the parsnip. Finish with the celeriac, pressing down gently as before.
**4** Cover with buttered foil and bake for 35 minutes, removing the foil for the final 10 minutes to brown the top.
**5** Leave to stand for 10 minutes, then turn out on to a serving plate and remove the lining paper. Garnish with thyme and serve cut into wedges.

## Roasted tomato and pepper salad

A gutsy, colourful cooked salad inspired by the flavours of the Mediterranean. Serve as an accompaniment to grilled meat or poultry.

2 red peppers, halved, cored and seeded
2 yellow peppers, halved, cored and seeded
6 tbsp olive oil
6 ripe plum tomatoes, quartered and cored
12 large garlic cloves (unpeeled)
2 tbsp balsamic vinegar
salt and pepper

**1** Preheat oven to 200C/fan oven 180C/Gas 6. Cut each pepper half into 3 or 4 thick strips. Toss with the olive oil and place in a baking tin. Bake for 15 minutes.
**2** Stir in the tomatoes and unpeeled garlic cloves and roast for a further 15-20 minutes or until the garlic cloves are soft and the peppers begin to colour.
**3** Lift out the roasted vegetables and garlic with a slotted spoon and place in a warm serving dish. Swirl the balsamic vinegar into the pan juices. Bring to the boil and let bubble for 30 seconds, then pour over the tomatoes and peppers.
**4** Season with salt and pepper to taste and serve immediately or allow to cool to room temperature; do not refrigerate.

## Chicory, radish and red onion salad

A crunchy salad with a vivid green, peppery dressing of puréed watercress.

4 heads of chicory, cut into chunks
1 bunch red salad radishes, quartered
1 red onion, very finely sliced
*for the dressing*
1 bunch watercress, stalks removed
4 tbsp extra virgin olive oil
1 tbsp white wine vinegar
1 tsp black peppercorns
salt

**1** Put the salad ingredients in a bowl of iced water while making the dressing.
**2** Whizz the watercress leaves, oil, vinegar and black peppercorns in a blender or food processor until almost smooth. Taste and season with salt – it should be quite peppery.
**3** Drain and dry vegetables. Toss with half of the dressing and place in a salad bowl. Drizzle with remaining dressing to serve.

## Courgette, cucumber and rocket salad

4 medium courgettes
175g/6oz piece cucumber, diced
100g/4oz rocket leaves
salt and pepper
extra virgin olive oil, for drizzling

**1** Coarsely grate the courgettes, using a hand grater or a food processor fitted with a coarse grating disc. Turn into a bowl.
**2** Add the cucumber to the courgette and toss to mix. Add the rocket leaves and toss carefully. Season with salt and pepper.
**3** Arrange the salad in a shallow bowl and drizzle with olive oil to serve.

## Fennel, endive and lime salad

Wafer-thin slices of fennel are marinated in a tangy citrus dressing to soften, then combined with crisp curly endive to make a refreshing side salad.

2 Florence fennel bulbs (with fronds)
100g/4oz curly endive
*for the dressing*
finely grated rind and juice of 2 limes
6 tbsp extra virgin olive oil
2 tbsp finely shredded fresh basil
2 tbsp finely diced pitted Greek black olives
2 sun-dried tomatoes in oil, drained and finely chopped
salt and pepper

**1** Mix the dressing ingredients together in a large bowl and set aside.
**2** Trim the fennel, discarding the stalks but reserving the feathery fronds. Halve and core the bulbs, then finely slice, using a mandolin or very sharp knife. Immediately toss the fennel slices in the dressing and leave to marinate for 15 minutes.
**3** Add the curly endive and reserved fennel fronds to the marinated fennel, toss gently to mix, then transfer to a clean salad bowl. Serve immediately.

**NOTE** To prevent discoloration, toss the fennel in the dressing as soon as it is sliced and do not marinate the salad for longer than stated in the recipe.

## Vegetable and goat's cheese salad

A delicious warm salad of asparagus, leeks and sugar snaps, topped with goat's cheese and toasted pumpkin seeds.

200g/7oz small, young leeks
140g/5oz sugar snap peas
280g/10oz asparagus
50g/2oz pumpkin seeds
140g/5oz firm goat's cheese, cubed
pepper
a little walnut or olive oil (optional)

**1** Cut the leeks into 2.5cm/1in lengths, put into a steamer and steam for 2 minutes. Add the sugar snaps and cook for a further 5 minutes. Transfer both vegetables to a warm bowl; set aside.
**2** Cut the asparagus into 5cm/2in lengths and steam for 5 minutes or until just tender. Add to the other vegetables.
**3** Preheat a heavy-based frying pan and dry fry the pumpkin seeds for 2 minutes until they begin to pop and brown slightly.
**4** Arrange the vegetables in a serving dish. Top with the goat's cheese, pumpkin seeds and pepper. Drizzle with a little walnut or olive oil to serve if wished.

## Avocado and red chilli salad

An unusual medley of flavours makes this a lively, nutritious salad. *Serves 3-4*

2 large or 3 small ripe avocados
2 bananas
2 tbsp lemon juice
1 tsp very finely chopped red chilli
50g/2oz walnuts, roughly chopped
salt and pepper
1 tbsp finely shredded coriander leaves

**1** Peel the avocados and bananas, then cut into bite size pieces, discarding the avocado stone. Place in a bowl.
**2** Immediately toss with the lemon juice, chilli, walnuts, seasoning and coriander. Serve at once, with wholemeal bread.

## Shredded cabbage salad with fruit and pistachios

A wonderfully refreshing, juicy salad – colourful enough to tempt even the most jaded of palates. *Serves 4-6*

600g/1lb 5oz white cabbage, cored and finely shredded
1 yellow grapefruit
1 pink grapefruit
1 orange
100g/4oz raisins (preferably large semi-dried raisins)
1 small bunch fresh chives, snipped
1 tbsp walnut oil
salt and pepper
50g/2oz shelled roasted salted pistachio nuts, roughly chopped (100g/4oz weight in shells)

**1** Put the shredded cabbage in a large bowl.
**2** Cut away all the skin and white pith from the grapefruit and orange then, with a sharp knife, carefully cut the flesh from between the membranes. Do this over the bowl of cabbage, to catch the fruit and citrus juices.
**3** Add the raisins, chives, oil and seasoning; toss gently together.
**4** Just before serving, toss in the chopped pistachio nuts.

## Roasted aubergine and red rice salad

A rustic dish of intriguing flavours and muted colours – delicious warm or cold.

2 medium aubergines, 500g/1lb 2oz in total
2 tbsp tahini paste
salt and pepper
1 tbsp sesame seeds
2 red onions, cut into wedges
1 tbsp olive oil
200g/7oz red Camargue rice
200g/7oz radicchio, torn
handful of rocket leaves
a little walnut oil and lemon juice (optional)

**1** Preheat oven to 220C/fan oven 200C/Gas 7. Cut the aubergines into 4cm/1½in cubes, brush with tahini paste and place in a non-stick roasting tin. Season and sprinkle with sesame seeds.
**2** Put the onion wedges in another roasting tin and sprinkle with the olive oil.
**3** Put both tins in the oven and roast for about 40 minutes or until tender, swapping shelves halfway through cooking.
**4** Meanwhile, put the rice in a pan with 600ml/1 pint cold water. Bring to the boil, reduce heat, cover and simmer for about 40 minutes until tender. Drain if necessary.
**5** Allow the vegetables and rice to cool slightly, then gently toss together while still warm. Set aside to cool further.
**6** Serve warm or cold on the radicchio and rocket, dressed with a little walnut oil and lemon juice if liked.

## Warm mushroom salad with sweet potato and ham

A substantial warm salad, topped with sweet potato croûtons. *Serves 2*

25g/1oz butter
1 small sweet potato, peeled and diced
100g/4oz small chestnut mushrooms, halved
80g packet Black Forest ham, each
slice halved
50g/2oz baby spinach leaves
25g/1oz watercress sprigs
*for the dressing*
3 tbsp extra virgin olive oil
1 tbsp tarragon or red wine vinegar
1 garlic clove, crushed
1 tsp chopped fresh tarragon
1 tbsp chopped fresh basil
salt and pepper
*to garnish*
basil sprigs

**1** Melt the butter in a frying pan, add the sweet potato and fry, stirring frequently, for 8-10 minutes until tender and golden.
**2** Meanwhile, mix the dressing ingredients together in a bowl, seasoning with salt and pepper to taste.
**3** Remove sweet potato from the pan; keep warm. Add the mushrooms to the pan and fry for 3-4 minutes until softened. Add the ham and cook for 1-2 minutes.
**4** Put the spinach and watercress on to serving plates. Scatter with the mushrooms, ham and sweet potato croûtons. Drizzle with the dressing and serve garnished with basil.

**NOTE** If Black Forest ham is unobtainable, use Parma ham instead.

## Pan-fried feta cheese salad

Hot slices of feta with a crisp spicy coating, served on a tomato and avocado salad.

6 tbsp instant polenta
1 tsp ground cumin
450g/1lb feta cheese, cut into 12 slices
2 eggs, beaten
8 tbsp olive oil
2 Little Gem lettuce, separated into leaves
1 large avocado, peeled, stoned and sliced
4 vine ripened tomatoes, sliced
2 shallots, thinly sliced
*for the dressing*
1 large garlic clove, finely chopped
juice of 2 limes
4 tbsp clear honey (preferably acacia)
2 tbsp chopped fresh mint

**1** Mix polenta with cumin. Dip the feta slices in the egg, then coat in the spiced polenta.
**2** Heat half the oil in a large frying pan and fry the feta in batches on both sides until crisp.
**3** Meanwhile, mix the dressing ingredients with the remaining oil and 2 tbsp water.
**4** Pile the lettuce, avocado, tomatoes and shallot into bowls and top with the fried feta.
**5** Wipe any polenta from the pan, then pour in the dressing and heat until bubbling. Pour over the salad and serve, with warm pittas.

## Charred pepper and steak tacos

4 tbsp olive oil
4 tsp Cajun spice seasoning
2 sirloin steaks, each 175g/6oz, cut into strips
2 garlic cloves, crushed
4 yellow peppers, seeded and thinly sliced
3 red onions, sliced
12 small taco shells
two 220g cans refried beans
4 tbsp fresh coriander leaves, chopped
300ml/1/2 pint soured cream

**1** Mix half the oil with the spice in a shallow dish. Add the steak and toss well; set aside.
**2** Heat remaining oil in a wok and stir-fry the garlic, peppers and onions over a high heat for 8-10 minutes until lightly charred. Add the steak and stir-fry for 4-5 minutes.
**3** Meanwhile warm the tacos and beans according to the packet instructions. Stir the chopped coriander into the soured cream.
**4** Spoon the beans into the taco shells. Top with the pepper mixture and cream.

## Butternut risotto with rocket

4 tbsp pumpkin seeds
50g/2oz butter
2 onions, finely chopped
3 garlic cloves, thinly sliced
350g/12oz arborio or other risotto rice
1.2 litres/2 pints chicken or vegetable stock
1 butternut squash, about 550g/1lb 4oz, peeled, seeded and cubed
150ml/1/4 pint extra dry vermouth
100g/4oz pecorino or Parmesan shavings
25g/1oz rocket leaves
salt and pepper

**1** Dry fry the pumpkin seeds in a large frying pan for 1 minute until they start to pop. Remove and set aside.
**2** Melt the butter in the pan and fry the onions and garlic for 5 minutes to soften. Add the rice and stir to coat in the butter.
**3** Pour in the boiling stock and boil rapidly for 5 minutes, stirring frequently.
**4** Add the squash, vermouth and 300ml/1/2 pint boiling water. Return to the boil, lower heat and cook, stirring often, for 10 minutes until the rice and squash are just tender.
**5** Add two thirds of the cheese, half the rocket and the pumpkin seeds. Season to taste. Serve topped with the remaining rocket and cheese shavings.

## Red pepper tagine with kidney beans and harissa

Serve on a mound of fluffy couscous as a sustaining meal, with extra harissa for added spice if you like.

4 tbsp olive oil
4 red peppers, cored, seeded and roughly chopped
3 red onions, chopped
4 garlic cloves, crushed
1/2 tsp ground cumin
1/2 tsp ground coriander
1/2 tsp paprika
two 400g cans chopped tomatoes
two 420g cans red kidney beans
4 celery sticks, sliced
1 tbsp harissa (see note)
1 tsp salt
3-4 tbsp chopped fresh coriander
3-4 tbsp chopped fresh mint
mint or coriander sprigs, to garnish

**1** Heat the oil in a large pan. Add the red peppers, onions and garlic, and fry, stirring, over a high heat until softened. Stir in the spices and cook, stirring, for about 30 seconds to release their flavour.
**2** Pour in the tomatoes. Drain the liquid from the kidney beans into the pan, then stir in the celery, harissa and salt. Cover and simmer for 15 minutes or until the celery is just tender.
**3** Stir in the kidney beans and heat through until simmering. If preparing ahead, allow to cool, then cover and chill for up to 2 days, or freeze.
**4** To serve, defrost at cool room temperature overnight (if frozen). Reheat the tagine in a large pan until bubbling and stir in the chopped coriander and mint. Serve on a bed of steamed couscous, garnished with mint or coriander.

**NOTE** Harissa is a fiery hot North African spice paste made from ground red peppers, chillies, onions and spices. It is available in jars from selected supermarkets and delicatessens.

## Goat's cheese and bacon gougère

4 rindless smoked streaky bacon rashers
115g/4oz butter
150ml/¼ pint water
115g/4oz strong plain flour
1 tsp English mustard
4 large eggs, beaten
salt and pepper
115g/4oz soft goat's cheese, in pieces
*for the filling*
3 tbsp olive oil
3 garlic cloves, crushed
450g/1lb courgettes, thickly sliced
1 large aubergine, cubed
400g can chopped tomatoes
1 tbsp chopped fresh oregano
1 tsp sugar
50g/2oz pitted green olives

**1** Preheat oven to 220C/fan oven 200C/Gas 7. Grease 4 individual 300ml/½ pint soufflé dishes. Dry fry the bacon in a pan until crisp, then snip into small pieces.
**2** To make the choux pastry, put the butter and water in a heavy-based pan and heat until the butter is melted and the mixture boils. Add the flour all at once and beat vigorously over the heat for about 1 minute until the mixture leaves the side of the pan. Take off the heat and stir until lukewarm.
**3** Add the mustard, then gradually beat in the eggs, until smooth. Stir in the bacon and season. Carefully fold in the cheese, so that it forms pockets through the mixture.
**4** Divide the mixture between the soufflé dishes and bake for 25 minutes until well risen and golden.
**5** Meanwhile, prepare the filling. Heat the oil in a pan and fry the garlic, courgettes and aubergine until beginning to soften. Stir in tomatoes, oregano, sugar and seasoning, Cover and simmer for 15 minutes.
**6** Add the olives to the vegetables. Spoon some on top of the gougère; serve the remainder separately.

**NOTE** If preparing ahead, at stage 5, cool and chill (up to 24 hours) or freeze gougère and filling separately. To use, defrost filling. To reheat gougère, bake from frozen (if appropriate) at 190C/fan oven 170C/Gas 5 for 20-25 minutes; if chilled, allow 15 minutes. Reheat sauce and complete stage 6.

Goat's cheese and bacon gougère (above); Bubble and squeak chorizo cake (right)

## Vegetable pie with Parmesan crust

Pesto enriched vegetables topped with a savoury crumbly pie crust.

*for the vegetable filling*
300ml/½ pint vegetable stock
1 fennel bulb, halved and sliced
3 leeks, sliced
3 carrots, sliced
3 courgettes, thickly sliced
3 tbsp pesto
salt and pepper
*for the Parmesan topping*
175g/6oz self-raising flour
85g/3oz butter, in pieces
50g/2oz fresh breadcrumbs
100g/4oz Parmesan, freshly grated
4 tbsp buttermilk (or half yogurt/half milk)

**1** Preheat oven to 200C/fan oven 180C/Gas 6. Bring the stock to the boil in a pan. Add the fennel, leeks and carrots, cover and simmer for 10 minutes. Stir in the courgettes, pesto and seasoning to taste; cook for 5 minutes.
**2** For the topping, tip the flour into a food processor, add the butter with a little seasoning and process until incorporated.
**3** Add the breadcrumbs and Parmesan to the processor and pulse until evenly mixed, then add the buttermilk (or yogurt and milk) and process briefly until the mixture forms small clumps.
**4** Spoon the vegetables into a 2.3 litre/4 pint ovenproof dish and cover with the topping.
**5** Bake for 20-25 minutes until the topping is firm and golden. Serve with a leafy salad.

**NOTE** If preparing ahead, at stage 4, let the vegetables cool completely before adding the Parmesan topping. Cover and chill for up to 24 hours, or freeze. If frozen, defrost at room temperature. To serve, bake as above allowing an extra 5-10 minutes.

## Bubble and squeak chorizo cake

Spanish chorizo adds a unique flavour to this traditional favourite. Serve with grilled tomatoes. *Serves 2-4*

1kg/2¼lb potatoes, peeled and cubed
450g/1lb green cabbage, cored and shredded
2 leeks, thinly sliced
1 tsp salt
1 tsp coarsely ground black pepper
50g/2oz butter
200ml/7fl oz milk
140g/5oz chorizo sausage, skinned and chopped
2 tbsp sunflower oil
chopped parsley, to garnish

**1** Add the potatoes to a large pan of boiling salted water, bring to the boil and position a steamer on top. Put the cabbage and leeks in the steamer and cook for 20 minutes.
**2** Drain the potatoes and mash with the seasoning, butter and milk until smooth and creamy. Stir in the cabbage, leeks and chorizo sausage. Allow to cool. If preparing ahead, cover and chill for up to 2 days.
**3** To serve, heat 1 tbsp oil in a large heavy-based frying pan. Add the potato mixture and press down to make a cake. Fry over a medium heat for 10 minutes.
**4** Turn the cake out on to a large plate. Heat the remaining oil in the frying pan, then slide the potato cake back into the pan and fry the other side for 5-10 minutes until golden and heated through. Serve at once, scattered with plenty of chopped parsley.

## Sri Lankan vegetable curry

500g/1lb 2oz pumpkin, peeled and seeded
225g/8oz potato, peeled
2 tbsp vegetable oil
1 onion, finely chopped
1-2 cinnamon sticks
2 garlic cloves, finely chopped
2 green chillies, seeded and finely sliced
1/4 tsp turmeric
1 tsp fenugreek seeds
100g/4oz green beans, trimmed and halved
8-10 fresh curry leaves
400ml can coconut milk
salt and pepper

**1** Cut pumpkin and potato into 2.5cm/1in cubes. Heat the oil in a large pan and gently fry the onion with the cinnamon until soft.
**2** Add the garlic, chillies, turmeric and fenugreek seeds. Cook, stirring, for 1 minute.
**3** Add the pumpkin, potato and green beans and fry, stirring, for 1-2 minutes. Add curry leaves, coconut milk and 150ml/1/4 pint water.
**4** Bring to the boil and simmer, covered, for 15 minutes. Season and serve with rice.

## Vietnamese salad

A light, crisp Vietnamese-style coleslaw.

4 tbsp lime juice
3 tbsp caster sugar
salt and pepper
1 red onion, halved and finely sliced
250g/9oz white or Savoy cabbage, very finely shredded
1 large carrot, roughly grated
2 cooked boneless chicken breasts, skinned
2 tbsp vegetable oil
3 tbsp fresh mint leaves, roughly torn
2 tbsp fresh coriander leaves, roughly torn
1 tbsp roasted peanuts, roughly chopped

**1** Mix the lime juice, sugar, 1/2 tsp salt and 1/2 tsp pepper in a bowl. Add the onion and leave to marinate for 30 minutes.
**2** In a large, shallow serving bowl, toss the cabbage and carrot together.
**3** Cut the chicken into strips, and add to the salad with the onion, marinade and oil. Toss well to mix.
**4** Just before serving, fold in the mint and coriander and scatter over the peanuts.

## Spiced okra and potato stew

A delicious, spicy stew flavoured with ginger, cumin, chilli and coriander.

500g/1lb 2oz potatoes, peeled
2 tbsp vegetable oil
1 onion, halved and thinly sliced
2 garlic cloves, finely chopped
2.5cm/1in piece fresh root ginger, finely chopped
1 red chilli, halved and finely sliced
2 tsp cumin seeds
1/2 tsp turmeric
2 tsp ground coriander
300ml/1/2 pint vegetable stock or water
400g can chopped tomatoes
450g/1lb small okra, tips trimmed (see note)
salt and pepper
3 tbsp chopped fresh coriander leaves

**1** Cut the potatoes into 2.5cm/1in cubes. Heat the oil in a large pan, add the onion and cook gently for 10-15 minutes until soft and golden. Add the garlic, ginger, chilli and spices; fry, stirring, for 1 minute. Add the potatoes and mix well.
**2** Pour in the stock and bring to the boil. Lower the heat, cover and simmer for 5 minutes.
**3** Stir in the tomatoes and cook briskly for 5 minutes, then add the okra. Season well with salt and pepper, cover and simmer gently for 15 minutes, stirring occasionally. Off the heat, stir in the chopped coriander. Serve with warm naan bread.

**NOTE** To trim okra, remove a small piece from each end. Do not cut right into the pods or you will release the sticky juices inside and the stew will acquire an unpleasant glutinous texture during cooking.

## Gado gado

This classic Indonesian salad is served with a creamy coconut and peanut dressing, spiked with garlic and chilli.

250g/9oz potatoes, halved if large
3 carrots, cut into 5mm/1/4in slices
225g/8oz green beans, halved
250g/9oz white or Savoy cabbage, cored and thinly shredded
1 small cucumber, thickly sliced
200g/7oz bean sprouts
4 hard-boiled eggs, quartered
50g/2oz roasted peanuts, roughly chopped
*for the dressing*
1 tbsp vegetable oil
1 small onion, finely chopped
2 garlic cloves, finely chopped
1 red chilli, finely chopped
200g/7oz crunchy peanut butter
200ml/7fl oz coconut milk
150ml/1/4 pint water
1 tbsp soy sauce
1 tbsp tomato ketchup

**1** Cook the potatoes in lightly salted water until just tender. Drain and leave until cool enough to handle, then peel and cut into 5mm/1/4in slices.
**2** Add the carrots to a pan of boiling salted water and blanch for 5 minutes; drain and refresh in cold water; drain thoroughly. Repeat with the green beans and cabbage, allowing 3-5 minutes blanching time for the beans, 3 minutes for the cabbage.
**3** To make the dressing, heat the oil in a heavy-based pan. Add the onion, garlic and chilli and cook gently for 5 minutes. Add the peanut butter, coconut milk and water. Bring to the boil, stirring constantly. Lower the heat, then add the soy sauce and tomato ketchup. Remove from the heat, stir well and leave to cool.
**4** Arrange all of the vegetables and the hard-boiled eggs on a large serving platter in separate piles. Scatter over the roasted peanuts.
**5** To serve, spoon some of the dressing over the eggs and vegetables. Serve the remainder separately.

## Bok choi with shiitake mushrooms

A quick and easy Chinese stir-fry, best served with rice or egg noodles.

600g/1lb 5oz bok choi or pak choi, stems removed
2 tbsp vegetable oil
3 large garlic cloves, finely sliced
6 spring onions, finely sliced
350g/12oz shiitake mushrooms, thickly sliced
1/2 tsp coarsely ground black pepper
1 1/2 tbsp caster sugar
1 tsp sesame oil
1 tbsp rice wine or rice wine vinegar
3 tbsp dark soy sauce
*to serve*
sesame oil, for drizzling (optional)

**1** Separate and roughly chop the bok choi leaves. Add to a large pan of boiling water and cook for 2 minutes; drain thoroughly and set aside.
**2** Heat the oil in a large wok. Add the garlic, spring onions, mushrooms and pepper, and stir-fry for 4-5 minutes.
**3** Add the sugar, sesame oil, rice wine and soy sauce. Stir-fry for 2 minutes, then add the blanched bok choi, toss well and heat through.
**4** Serve at once in warmed bowls, drizzled with a little sesame oil if wished and accompanied by rice or noodles.

## Indian potato and sweetcorn salad

Paprika, cumin and lemon juice give this unusual salad a piquant flavour.

700g/1lb 9oz potatoes (preferably Desiree), peeled and cut into 2.5cm/1in cubes
2 tbsp vegetable oil
6 spring onions, finely sliced
2 tsp cumin seeds
1 tsp hot paprika
two 340g cans sweetcorn niblets, drained
juice of 1 lemon
1/2 tsp garam masala
3 tbsp chopped fresh coriander leaves
salt

**1** Cook the potatoes in lightly salted water until tender. Drain and set aside.
**2** Heat the oil in a large frying pan and stir-fry the onions for 1-2 minutes. Add the cumin seeds; fry, stirring, for 30 seconds.
**3** Add the paprika, potatoes and sweetcorn. Heat through, then stir in the lemon juice and garam masala. Take off the heat and gently stir in the coriander. Season with salt and serve warm, or at room temperature.

## Thai mushroom and mangetout salad

A delicious salad fragrantly flavoured with lemon grass, chilli and lime juice.

300g/10oz mangetout, halved
3 tbsp vegetable oil
2 garlic cloves, finely chopped
4 shallots, finely chopped
500g/1lb 2oz portobello mushrooms, stalks removed, thickly sliced
2 tsp clear honey
juice of 2 limes
2 tsp lemon grass, very finely chopped
2 tsp Thai fish sauce
1 hot red chilli (eg bird's eye), finely sliced
3 tbsp fresh basil leaves, roughly torn
3 tbsp fresh coriander leaves, roughly torn
salt and pepper

**1** Cook the mangetout in boiling water for 2 minutes until just tender. Drain and set aside.
**2** Heat oil in a wok and stir-fry the garlic and shallots for 2 minutes. Add the mushrooms and stir-fry for 5 minutes. Add the mangetout and stir-fry for 1 minute. Turn into a bowl.
**3** Mix the honey, lime juice, lemon grass and fish sauce together, then add to the salad with the chilli and herbs. Toss well and check the seasoning. Serve the salad at room temperature.

**NOTE** Large flat mushrooms can be used instead of portobello mushrooms.

## Sabzi pulao

Serve this one pot meal with hot pickles, yogurt, and a cucumber and tomato salsa.

400g/14oz basmati rice
2 tbsp vegetable oil
1 onion, halved and thinly sliced
6 cardamom pods
6 cloves
1 cinnamon stick
225g/8oz mushrooms, roughly chopped
2 carrots, cut into cubes
1 red pepper, cored, seeded and roughly chopped
225g/8oz frozen peas
1 tsp saffron threads, soaked in 2 tsp hot water
salt and pepper
crisp fried onion slices, to garnish

**1** Rinse the rice in a large sieve under cold running water until the water is clear; drain thoroughly.
**2** Heat the oil in a large heavy-based pan and sauté the onion over a medium heat until lightly browned.
**3** Add the cardamom pods, cloves and cinnamon. Stir-fry for 1 minute, then add the rice and fry, stirring, for a further 1 minute. Add the vegetables and stir well.
**4** Stir in 750ml/1 1/2 pints boiling water, the infused saffron and seasoning. Cover tightly. Simmer on a very low heat for 15 minutes.
**5** Leave to stand, covered, for 10 minutes then fluff up the rice with a fork. Serve garnished with crisp fried onions.

## Caramelised leeks and shallots on sweet potato rösti

1kg/2¹/₄lb sweet potatoes
1 egg, beaten
salt and pepper
4 tbsp olive oil
25g/1oz butter
300g/10oz shallots, peeled and split
250g/9oz baby leeks, halved
1 tsp finely chopped fresh sage leaves
1¹/₂ tsp sugar
1 tbsp marsala (optional)
sage leaves, to garnish

**1** Preheat oven to 190C/fan oven 170C/Gas 5. Coarsely grate the sweet potatoes, mix with the beaten egg and season well. Shape the grated potato into 12 heaped spoonfuls on 2 oiled baking sheets, spacing apart. Flatten slightly and bake for 5-8 minutes until golden. Turn over and bake for a further 5 minutes.
**2** Heat 2 tbsp oil and half of the butter in a heavy-based pan over a high heat until sizzling. Add the shallots, lower the heat, cover and cook for about 8 minutes until soft and evenly browned. Remove with a slotted spoon and place in a warm dish.
**3** Heat the remaining oil and butter in the pan over a high heat until sizzling. Add the leeks with the chopped sage and cook in the same way, for about 5 minutes.
**4** Increase heat and return shallots to the pan. Add the sugar, seasoning and marsala if using and cook, stirring, until caramelised. Arrange the röstis and vegetables on warmed plates, allowing 3 röstis per person. Serve at once, garnished with sage.

**NOTE** For convenience, prepare the röstis in advance. Reheat in oven at 200C/fan oven 180C/Gas 6 for 10 minutes to serve.

## Cracked wheat pilaf with chestnuts and fennel

A simple dish to prepare which can be varied to taste. Try using a mixture of herbs, scatter with toasted pine nuts or add a drained can of aduki beans. Alternatively serve the pilaf cold, with a herb vinaigrette folded through.

4 red onions, peeled with root end intact
4 small fennel bulbs, trimmed with root end intact
6 tbsp olive oil
salt and pepper
250g/9oz cracked wheat (bulgar wheat)
700ml/1¹/₄ pints well flavoured vegetable stock (preferably homemade)
200g/7oz cooked peeled chestnuts
3 tbsp chopped flat leaf parsley

**1** Preheat oven to 220C/fan oven 200C/Gas 7. Cut each onion and fennel bulb lengthways into 6-8 pieces. Place on a baking tray and drizzle with half of the oil. Season with salt and pepper and turn well to coat the vegetables with the oil.
**2** Rinse the cracked wheat and drain well. Heat 2 tbsp oil in a heavy-based flameproof casserole. Add the cracked wheat and stir to coat with the oil. Pour in the stock and bring to the boil. Lower the heat, cover and simmer gently for 15-20 minutes.
**3** Meanwhile, roast the vegetables in the oven for 20 minutes.
**4** When the cracked wheat is ready, turn off the heat, remove the lid and cover with a clean tea-towel or muslin.
**5** Add the chestnuts to the vegetables, turn to coat with oil and return to the oven for a further 5 minutes. Fold the vegetables into the cracked wheat with the remaining 1 tbsp oil and the chopped parsley to serve.

## Polenta with thyme scented vegetables

1.3 litres/2¹/₄ pints water
salt and pepper
125g/4¹/₂oz butter, cut into cubes
375g/12oz quick cook polenta
2 egg yolks, beaten
100g/4oz pecorino cheese or Parmesan
8 tbsp extra virgin olive oil
1 onion, finely chopped
4 garlic cloves, crushed
1 red pepper, cored, seeded and chopped
4 fresh thyme sprigs
175g/6oz small okra, tips trimmed
250g/9oz patty pans or courgettes, halved
2 large tomatoes, skinned and chopped
thyme sprigs, to garnish

**1** To make the polenta, bring the water to the boil in a pan. Add salt and half of the butter. Take off the heat and pour in the polenta, whisking constantly. Continue to whisk over a low heat until thick. Off the heat, whisk in the egg yolks and two thirds of the cheese. Tip on to a dampened baking tray and spread to an even thickness, about 1.5cm/⁵/₈in. Leave to cool. Melt remaining butter.
**2** Heat 4 tbsp oil in a large pan and fry the onion and garlic until softened. Add the red pepper and thyme sprigs; cook for 5 minutes. Lift out the vegetables with a slotted spoon.
**3** Heat remaining oil in the pan and stir-fry the okra over a high heat for 2 minutes. Add patty pans and cook, stirring, for 2 minutes. Add the onion mixture, tomatoes and seasoning. Lower heat and cook for about 4 minutes; the vegetables should retain a bite.
**4** Preheat oven to 200C/fan oven 180C/Gas 6. Cut polenta into triangles; arrange overlapping on baking sheets. Brush with melted butter, scatter with remaining cheese and bake for 10-20 minutes until golden. Serve topped with the vegetables and fresh thyme.

## Grilled aubergine terrine

Serve this elegant terrine as a stylish vegetarian lunch with toasted olive ciabatta.

2 large aubergines, about 700g/1lb 9oz in total
6-8 tbsp extra virgin olive oil
salt and pepper
4 plum tomatoes, cored and cut into 3mm/⅛in slices
135g jar black olive tapenade
18 fresh large basil leaves (about 20g/¾oz), stalks removed
*for the vinaigrette dressing*
2 tsp cider vinegar
2 tbsp olive oil
½ tsp Dijon mustard

**1** Cut the aubergines into 3mm/⅛in slices. Preheat the grill to high. Brush the aubergine slices with oil and season with salt and pepper. Grill in batches for 3-4 minutes each side or until golden, turning once. Drain on kitchen paper.
**2** Line the base and sides of a 450g/1lb non stick loaf tin with overlapping slices of aubergine. (Alternatively use an ordinary loaf tin lined with cling film.)
**3** Arrange a layer of tomato slices in the tin. Spread a third of the tapenade over the tomato, then scatter over a third of the basil leaves. Cover with a layer of aubergine slices. Repeat these layers twice more, finishing with a layer of aubergine. Cover the terrine with cling film and chill in the refrigerator for 2-4 hours.
**4** For the dressing, put the ingredients in a screw topped jar, season with salt and pepper and shake well to emulsify.
**5** To serve, unmould the terrine on to a board or plate and cut into thick slices. Serve drizzled with the dressing.

## Char-griddled radicchio and asparagus with black beans

This wonderful combination of flavours is quite delicious. Serve warm or cold, with char-grilled flat bread if you like.

500g/1lb 2oz thin asparagus, trimmed to 13cm/5in lengths
2 radicchio, each cut into 6 wedges
4 garlic cloves, crushed
½ tsp dried chilli flakes
8 tbsp extra virgin olive oil
salt and pepper
200g/7oz cooked black beans (see note), or canned black, aduki or red kidney beans
4 tsp balsamic vinegar

**1** Put the asparagus and radicchio in a large shallow dish. Add the garlic, chilli flakes, 4 tbsp oil and seasoning. Turn the vegetables to coat well.
**2** Preheat a ridged griddle pan or heavy-based frying pan over a medium heat, then cook the asparagus for 2 minutes on each side. Return to the dish.
**3** Add the radicchio to the pan and cook for 1 minute each side; add to the asparagus.
**4** Put the black beans in a pan with some of their liquid. Warm through, then drain and add to the vegetables. Toss to mix and check the seasoning.
**5** Serve warm or cold, drizzled with the balsamic vinegar and remaining oil.

**NOTE** To obtain this weight of cooked beans, soak 100g/4oz dried black beans in cold water overnight. Drain, put into a pan and cover with fresh water. Bring to the boil and boil fast for 10 minutes, then lower the heat and simmer for 1½ hours or until tender.

## Spinach, ricotta and pistachio filo pie

Serve this unusual coiled filo pie hot or cold, with a leafy salad. *Serves 6*

8 large sheets filo pastry
*for the filling*
450g/1lb small, young spinach leaves
250g/9oz ricotta cheese, drained
100g/4oz shelled pistachio nuts, finely chopped
50g/2oz sun-dried tomatoes, finely chopped
2 tbsp finely chopped fresh marjoram (optional)
salt and pepper
1 egg yolk, beaten
*to assemble*
1 egg white, beaten
85g/3oz butter, melted

**1** Grease a 25cm/10in springform cake tin or pizza tin.
**2** For the filling, blanch the spinach in boiling water for 30 seconds. Drain, refresh in cold water and drain well, squeezing out as much moisture as possible. Chop the spinach finely and place in a bowl.
**3** Add the ricotta, pistachio nuts, sun-dried tomatoes, and marjoram if using. Mix well and season generously, then stir in the egg yolk to bind the mixture.
**4** Preheat oven to 220C/fan oven 200C/Gas 7. Lay one sheet of filo on a clean surface; keep the rest wrapped to prevent them drying. Take an eighth of the filling and lay it along one long edge of the filo. Roll up to within 1cm/½in from the edge, to form a lip (for the next roll to sit on).
**5** Curl the roll into a coil and place in the centre of the tin. Brush the lip with egg white, then brush the top of the filo roll with melted butter.
**6** Repeat with the rest of the filo and filling, positioning the rolls in the tin as you make them to form a continuous spiral. (The final roll won't need a lip.)
**7** Brush the top of the filo pie with the remaining butter and bake for 20-30 minutes until golden and crisp. Carefully unmould the pie on to a flat plate and serve hot or cold, with a salad.

## Beetroot soufflés with chives

Serve as a sophisticated light lunch, with melba toast and a side salad.

125g/4¹/₂oz butter
25g/1oz pecorino cheese, finely grated
70g/2¹/₂oz plain flour
450ml/16fl oz milk
salt and white pepper
250g/9oz cooked beetroot, drained
200g/7oz Welsh soft goat's cheese, finely crumbled
4 medium egg yolks
3 tbsp finely snipped fresh chives
6 medium egg whites

**1** Preheat oven to 190C/fan oven 170C/Gas 5. Melt 50g/2oz butter; dice the rest and set aside. Brush 4 individual 350ml/12fl oz soufflé dishes with melted butter and chill for 10 minutes. Brush with butter again and dust with the grated cheese.
**2** Put the diced butter, flour and milk in a pan and whisk on a medium heat until smooth, thickened and bubbling; season very generously (see note). Remove from the heat.
**3** Dice 1 small beetroot and divide between the soufflé dishes, scattering over a quarter of the crumbled goat's cheese.
**4** Put the remaining beetroot in a blender or food processor with the sauce and work to a purée. Add the egg yolks with the remaining goat's cheese and process briefly until incorporated. Transfer to a bowl and fold in the chives.
**5** Whisk the egg whites in a clean bowl until they form peaks. Fold into the beetroot mixture, a little at a time.
**6** Spoon the mixture into the soufflé dishes to within 1cm/¹/₂in of the rim. Stand on a baking sheet and cook for 20-30 minutes until risen. Serve immediately.

**NOTE** It is important to season the soufflé mixture generously as the addition of whisked egg whites will dilute the flavour significantly.

# delectable **desserts & bakes**

**A host of seductive ideas**, from **tantalising tarts and pastries**, through **refreshing fruity desserts** to irresistible, **gooey traybakes** and melt-in-the-mouth, **crumbly cookies**. Reflecting today's flexible style of eating, many of the recipes double up as **scrumptious puddings** and teatime treats. **For convenience**, most of the desserts - as well as the bakes - can be prepared well in advance. **Entertain friends and family** to fabulous **new flavour combinations**, such as rich chocolate cake with star anise and coffee syrup, **heavenly coconut and mango meringue pie**, or poached tamarillos with pink panna cotta.

Amaretti and apricot tart

## Treacle and orange tart

*Serves 8*

*for the filling*
2 small whole oranges
500g/1lb 2oz golden syrup
85g/3oz hazelnuts, finely chopped
85g/3oz white breadcrumbs
2 tbsp lemon juice
2 large eggs, beaten
*for the pastry*
225g/8oz plain flour
140g/5oz unsalted butter, diced
1 egg yolk
1 tbsp caster sugar
2 tbsp cold water

**1** Put the oranges in a small pan, just cover with boiling water and simmer gently for 30 minutes or until the skins are soft. Drain; leave to cool.
**2** To make the pastry, blend the flour and butter in a food processor until the mixture resembles breadcrumbs. Add the egg yolk, sugar and water. Mix briefly to a smooth dough. Wrap and chill for 30 minutes.
**3** Preheat oven to 200C/fan oven 180C/Gas 6. Roll out the pastry on a lightly floured surface and use to line a 25cm/10in loose-bottomed flan tin, 4cm/1½in deep. Line with greaseproof paper and baking beans and bake blind for 15 minutes. Remove paper and beans; bake for a further 5 minutes.
**4** Halve the cooked oranges, discard any pips and blend to a purée. Warm the golden syrup in a pan until slightly thinned. Stir in the nuts, breadcrumbs, orange purée and lemon juice, then the eggs.
**5** Turn into the pastry case and bake for about 30 minutes until the filling is pale golden but not firmly set. Cool slightly before serving.

## Amaretti and apricot tart

Crushed amaretti biscuits and apricots set in a deep creamy custard within a rich pastry case. A saffron and almond syrup is the perfect complement. *Serves 8*

*for the pastry*
175g/6oz plain flour
85g/3oz unsalted butter
3 large egg yolks
50g/2oz caster sugar
*for the filling*
200g/7oz ready-to-eat dried apricots, sliced
3 tbsp Grand Marnier or Cointreau
140g/5oz amaretti biscuits, halved
2 large eggs, plus 1 egg yolk
40g/1½oz caster sugar
50g/2oz unsalted butter, melted
300ml/½ pint double cream
300ml/½ pint milk
*for the syrup*
½ tsp saffron strands, soaked in 1 tbsp boiling water
85g/3oz caster sugar
250ml/9fl oz water
*to finish*
icing sugar, for dusting

**1** To make the pastry, put the flour and butter in a food processor and process until the mixture resembles fine breadcrumbs. Add the egg yolks and sugar and work briefly to a firm dough. Wrap and chill for 30 minutes.
**2** Preheat oven to 200C/fan oven 180C/Gas 6. Roll out the pastry on a lightly floured surface and use to line a 24cm/9½in flan tin, 4cm/1½in deep. Line with greaseproof paper and baking beans and bake blind for 15 minutes. Remove paper and beans; bake for a further 5 minutes. Reduce setting to 170C/fan oven 150C/Gas 3.
**3** Soak apricots in the liqueur for 15 minutes. Scatter the biscuits in the pastry case.
**4** Beat the eggs, yolk, sugar and butter together in a bowl. Bring the cream and milk to the boil, then whisk into the egg mixture. Strain the custard into the pastry case, scatter over half of the apricots and bake for 25-30 minutes until lightly set.
**5** For the syrup, dissolve sugar in the water in a pan on a low heat, then boil for 5 minutes until syrupy. Stir in the saffron, remaining apricots and liqueur. Dust the tart with icing sugar and serve with the saffron syrup.

## Walnut beignet with coffee cream

A sweet layer of walnut paste makes a delicious filling for crisp, light choux pastry. The beignet is best served warm, but can be prepared up to 4 hours in advance for convenience if preferred. *Serves 6*

*for the walnut paste*
200g/7oz walnut pieces
50g/2oz caster sugar
1 large egg
*for the choux pastry*
65g/2½oz plain flour
50g/2oz unsalted butter
150ml/¼ pint water
2 tbsp caster sugar
2 large eggs, lightly beaten
*for the coffee cream*
1 tbsp espresso coffee powder
25g/1oz light muscovado sugar
75ml/2½fl oz water
300ml/½ pint double cream
2 tbsp Tia Maria (optional)
*to finish*
icing sugar, for dusting

**1** Preheat oven to 220C/fan oven 200C/Gas 7. Lightly grease a 20cm/8in spring-release cake tin. Set aside 50g/2oz walnuts. Process the rest of the nuts in a food processor until finely ground. Add the sugar and egg and blend to a soft paste.
**2** For the choux pastry, sift the flour on to a sheet of greaseproof paper. Heat the butter, water and sugar in a pan until melted, then bring to the boil. Take off the heat, tip in the flour and beat well until the mixture leaves the side of the pan. Cool for 2 minutes.
**3** Gradually beat in the eggs, a little at a time, until smooth and glossy. Spread half the mixture in the prepared tin and dot with the walnut paste. Spread the remaining mixture over the top and scatter with the reserved walnuts, pressing them in gently.
**4** Bake for 20 minutes until well risen, then reduce setting to 190C/fan oven 170C/Gas 5 and bake for a further 10 minutes until crisp and golden.
**5** Meanwhile, for the coffee cream, gently heat the coffee, sugar and water in a small pan for 5 minutes. Strain through a fine sieve into a clean pan. Add the cream and cook for 3 minutes until slightly thickened.
**6** Dust the pastry with icing sugar and serve warm, with the coffee cream.

## Coconut and mango meringue pie

*Serves 8*

175g/6oz plain flour
85g/3oz unsalted butter
3 large egg yolks
25g/1oz caster sugar
*for the filling and topping*
2 medium, ripe mangoes, peeled
2 tbsp cornflour
150ml/¼ pint orange juice
200g/7oz caster sugar
3 large eggs, separated
85g/3oz creamed coconut, finely grated
toasted coconut shavings (optional)

**1** Make pastry as for Amaretti and apricot tart (page 136); chill for 30 minutes.
**2** Preheat oven to 200C/fan oven 180C/Gas 6. Roll out the pastry thinly on a lightly floured surface and use to line a 20cm/8in loose-bottomed flan tin, about 4cm/1½in deep. Bake blind for 20 minutes, then remove paper and beans and bake for a further 5 minutes. Increase setting to 220C/fan oven 200C/Gas 7.
**3** Slice 1 mango, discarding stone; arrange in the pastry case. Purée the flesh from the other mango in a blender until smooth.
**4** In a pan, mix the cornflour with 2 tbsp orange juice. Add remaining orange juice, mango purée and 25g/1oz sugar. Bring to the boil, stirring until thickened. Beat in the egg yolks. Turn into the pastry case.
**5** For the meringue, whisk egg whites in a clean bowl until stiff. Gradually whisk in the remaining sugar, a spoonful at a time, until the meringue is stiff and glossy. Fold in the grated coconut, then spoon over the filling. Bake for 5-10 minutes until the meringue is golden. Cool before serving, topped with coconut shavings if liked.

## Pear, pine nut and lemon strudel

*Serves 4*

2 ripe pears
finely grated rind of 1 lemon
2 tbsp lemon juice
50g/2oz unsalted butter
85g/3oz pine nuts
50g/2oz white breadcrumbs
25g/1oz light muscovado sugar
70g/2½oz clear honey, such as
orange blossom
100g/3½oz filo pastry
icing sugar, for dusting

**1** Preheat oven to 200C/fan oven 180C/Gas 6. Peel, core and thinly slice the pears crossways. Immerse in a bowl of cold water with 1 tbsp of the lemon juice added.
**2** Melt 15g/½oz butter in a frying pan and fry the pine nuts until pale golden. Add the breadcrumbs and fry gently until golden.
**3** Drain the pears, dry on kitchen paper and put in a bowl with the breadcrumb and pine nut mixture, sugar and lemon rind.
**4** Melt another 25g/1oz butter. Keep one sheet of filo pastry for the topping, well wrapped to prevent it drying out. Layer the remaining filo sheets on a clean surface, brushing each with a little melted butter.
**5** Spoon the filling on top to within 2.5cm/1in of the edges. Drizzle with the honey and lemon juice; dot with remaining firm butter. Fold the short ends over the filling, then roll up, starting at a long side. Lift on to a lightly greased baking sheet, join uppermost.
**6** Brush with any remaining melted butter, then crumple the reserved filo sheet around the strudel. Bake for about 25 minutes until golden. Cool slightly, then dust with icing sugar. Serve warm, cut into slices, with Greek yogurt or crème fraîche.

## Plum and almond butter puffs

*Makes 6*

50g/2oz unsalted butter, softened
25g/1oz caster sugar
50g/2oz ground almonds
½ tsp almond extract
340g/12oz ready-made puff pastry
500g/1lb 2oz red plums, halved and stoned
beaten egg, to glaze
1 tbsp slivered or flaked almonds
2 tbsp icing sugar

**1** Put 25g/1oz butter in a bowl with the sugar, ground almonds and almond extract and beat to a stiff paste.
**2** Roll out half the pastry on a lightly floured surface and cut out six 10cm/4in rounds; lay on a lightly greased baking sheet. Spread to 1cm/½in from the edges with the almond paste. Roll out the remaining pastry and cut out rounds, as above. Position over the filling. With the tip of a sharp knife, cut a shallow rim, 1cm/½in from the edge of each round. Chill for 30 minutes.
**3** Preheat oven to 210C/fan oven 190C/Gas 7. Cut the plums into thick wedges and scatter over the pastry rounds, within the cut rim.
**4** Brush the pastry edges with beaten egg, then scatter with the almonds. Bake for 10 minutes until risen and golden.
**5** Dot the plums with the remaining butter, dust with icing sugar and bake for a further 10-12 minutes until the pastry is deep golden. Serve with pouring cream.

## Caramelised rice tartlets

Serve these with berry fruits. *Makes 8*

*for the pastry*
225g/8oz plain flour
140g/5oz unsalted butter
4-5 tsp cold water
*for the filling*
40g/1¹/₂oz flaked rice
450ml/16fl oz milk
1 vanilla pod
100g/3¹/₂oz caster sugar
150ml/¹/₄ pint double cream
2 large eggs, beaten

**1** To make the pastry, blend the flour and butter in a food processor until the mixture resembles fine breadcrumbs. Add the water and process briefly to a firm dough. Chill for 30 minutes.

**2** Preheat oven to 200C/fan oven 180C/Gas 6. Roll out the pastry thinly on a lightly floured surface and use to line eight 9cm/3¹/₂in loose-bottomed tartlet tins. Line the pastry cases with greaseproof paper and baking beans and bake blind for 15 minutes. Remove the paper and beans; bake for a further 5 minutes. Reduce oven setting to 180C/fan oven 160C/Gas 4.

**3** Put the rice, milk, vanilla pod and 40g/1¹/₂oz sugar in a heavy-based pan. Bring to the boil, reduce the heat and simmer gently for about 8 minutes until the rice is tender and the mixture is thickened. Leave to cool slightly. Remove the vanilla pod, then beat in the cream and eggs.

**4** Pour the filling into the tartlet cases and bake for 5-8 minutes until very lightly set. Preheat grill to moderate. Sprinkle the remaining sugar in an even layer over the tartlets and grill for about 4 minutes until lightly caramelised. Serve warm or cold, with sugared raspberries or strawberries.

## White chocolate and berry creams

Tart summer berries under a contrasting blanket of smooth, creamy white chocolate are an irresistible combination.

500g bag frozen mixed summer fruits (raspberries, blackberries, redcurrants, cherries etc)
3 tbsp icing sugar
4 tsp cassis, framboise or kirsch
200g/7oz white chocolate, in pieces
150g carton whole milk raspberry yogurt
500g carton fromage frais with added cream
white chocolate curls or grated chocolate, to decorate

**1** Tip the frozen fruits into a bowl, stir in the icing sugar, then spoon into 4 wide stemmed glasses and drizzle over the liqueur.
**2** Put the chocolate in a large heatproof bowl over a pan of gently simmering water and leave until just melted. Remove from the heat, then beat in the yogurt and fromage frais until smooth.
**3** Spoon the chocolate mixture over the fruit and leave in a cool place to allow the fruits to thaw slowly.
**4** Serve topped with chocolate curls or grated chocolate.

## Lime and papaya posset

Papaya's special affinity with lime works beautifully in this dessert, although the papaya must be completely ripe to fully appreciate its true fragrance. *Serves 6*

600ml/1 pint double cream
175g/6oz caster sugar
finely grated rind of 1 lime
juice of 2 limes
2 papayas, peeled, seeded and chopped

**1** Put the cream and sugar in a pan, heat gently until the sugar is dissolved, then boil for 3 minutes. Add half of the lime rind and all of the lime juice; stir well. Leave to cool for about 10 minutes.
**2** Set aside 6 pieces of papaya; divide the rest between 6 individual glass bowls, then pour the lime mixture on top. Top with the lime rind and reserved papaya. Chill until ready to serve.

## Caramelised apples on brioche toasts

Butter enriched brioche makes a delicious base for serving pan-fried apple slices.

3 tbsp caster sugar
3 Cox's apples, peeled, cored and thickly sliced
25g/1oz butter
large pinch of ground cinnamon
3 tbsp raisins
juice of 1 lemon
4 thick slices of brioche (from a large cottage brioche)
250g carton Greek yogurt

**1** Sprinkle the sugar over the base of a large frying pan and heat gently until it melts and begins to caramelise – don't allow to darken.
**2** Add the apples and toss to coat, then add the butter, cinnamon, raisins, lemon juice and 1 tbsp water. Cook, turning frequently, for 1-2 minutes.
**3** Meanwhile, toast the brioche slices under a hot grill until golden on both sides. Place on serving plates.
**4** Spoon the yogurt on to the brioche and top with the caramelised apples and pan juices to serve.

## Pan-fried bananas with orange and cardamom

Cardamom adds an exotic flavour to this hot dessert. Vanilla ice cream is the perfect accompaniment.

50g/2oz unsalted butter
50g/2oz light muscovado sugar
5 cardamom pods, lightly crushed
4 bananas, peeled and halved lengthways
grated rind and juice of 1 large orange

**1** Melt the butter in a large frying pan, then add the sugar with the cardamom and stir until the sugar is dissolved.
**2** Add the bananas and cook for 1-2 minutes, turning them in the juices, until softened. Add the orange juice and rind and let bubble until reduced and syrupy. Discard the cardamon pods.
**3** Serve hot, with vanilla ice cream.

## Amaretto and blueberry syllabubs

Blueberries have a delicate flavour, which is enhanced when the berries are very lightly poached. Topped with a white wine and almond liqueur syllabub they make an elegant, quick dessert – ideal for mid-week entertaining.

*for the blueberry layer*
2 x 170g punnets blueberries
1 tbsp amaretto liqueur
1 tbsp caster sugar
*for the syllabub*
284ml carton double cream
2 tbsp caster sugar
90ml/3fl oz medium white wine, such as Riesling
3 tbsp amaretto liqueur
8 amaretti biscuits, broken into small pieces
*to decorate*
mint leaves

**1** Tip the blueberries into a large pan. Add the liqueur and sugar and poach gently for 1-2 minutes until the berries have softened, but not burst. Allow to cool.
**2** To make the syllabub, pour the cream into a bowl. Add the sugar, wine and liqueur, and whisk until the mixture holds its shape.
**3** Toss the blueberries with the amaretti biscuits, then layer with the creamy syllabub in 4 stemmed glasses. Chill until required.
**4** Serve the chilled syllabubs decorated with mint leaves.

**NOTE** Fresh gooseberries, apricots and plums all make excellent alternatives to blueberries. Stone and quarter plums or apricots. Adjust the sugar accordingly and poach until the fruit is tender, but still retaining shape.

## Passion fruit brûlées

Passion fruit adds a refreshing contrast to the irresistible creaminess of a classic crème brûlée.

4 large egg yolks
1/4 tsp vanilla extract
1 tbsp cornflour
2 tbsp caster sugar
284ml carton double cream
2 passion fruit, halved
*for the caramel topping*
8 tbsp caster sugar

**1** Whisk the egg yolks, vanilla extract, cornflour and sugar together in a bowl until evenly blended.
**2** Heat the cream in a heavy-based pan to just below the boil. Pour on to the egg yolk mixture, whisking all the time. Return to the pan and cook, whisking constantly, until the custard thickens; do not boil. If the custard starts to become lumpy, quickly take off the heat and whisk briskly until smooth, then continue.
**3** Scoop the seeds and pulp from the passion fruit into a sieve over a bowl; rub to separate the juice from the seeds. Stir the passion fruit juice into the custard with 1/2 tsp of the seeds. Pour into 4 small ramekins or other grillproof dishes. Chill for 2-3 hours until set, or up to 24 hours if preparing ahead.
**4** To make the caramel topping, sprinkle 2 tbsp sugar evenly over each custard and put under a preheated hot grill until the sugar melts and caramelises.
**5** Chill for 2-3 hours until the caramel is set hard before serving.

**NOTE** If you have a blow-torch, use to caramelise the topping, rather than grill.

## Meringue roulade with melba fruits

A luscious mallowy meringue rolled around a peach and raspberry filling. *Serves 8*

*for the meringue*
3 large egg whites
175g/6oz caster sugar
1 tbsp cornflour
2 tsp vanilla extract
1 tsp white wine vinegar
*for the melba filling*
284ml carton double cream
2 tbsp icing sugar, plus extra for rolling
2 tbsp peach schnapps or dessert wine
1 large peach, peeled, stoned and diced
100g/4oz raspberries

**1** Preheat oven to 140C/fan oven 120C/Gas 1. Line a 28x23cm/11x9in Swiss roll tin with baking parchment.
**2** Whisk the egg whites in a clean bowl until stiff, then gradually whisk in the sugar, a tablespoonful at a time, until stiff and glossy.
**3** Quickly and carefully fold in the cornflour, vanilla and vinegar. Spoon into the prepared tin and spread very gently to the edges.
**4** Bake for 35 minutes until set. On removing from the oven, cover the meringue with a slightly damp tea-towel and leave to cool.
**5** To serve, lightly whip the cream with the sugar and schnapps or wine. Dust a sheet of non-stick baking parchment with icing sugar. Turn the meringue on to the paper, then spread with the cream and scatter over the fruit. Roll up carefully and place on a plate. If preparing ahead, refrigerate for up to 4 hours until required. Dust with icing sugar to serve.

## Rum punch trifle with exotic fruits

Tropical fruits and plenty of rum give this trifle a Caribbean twist. *Serves 6-8*

250g/9oz bought Madeira cake
1 small pineapple, peeled, cored and chopped
1 mango, peeled, stoned and chopped
2 bananas, peeled and thickly sliced
juice and grated rind of 1 lime
juice of 1 orange
3 tbsp icing sugar
90ml/3fl oz dark rum
50g/2oz custard powder
900ml/1 1/2 pints milk
4 tbsp caster sugar
284ml carton double cream, lightly whipped
mint sprigs, to decorate

**1** Slice the Madeira cake and use to cover the base of a large glass serving bowl. Toss the fruits with the lime juice and orange juice, icing sugar and rum, then scatter over the cake.
**2** Blend the custard powder with 4 tbsp milk until smooth. Heat the remaining milk in a heavy-based pan until boiling, then whisk into the custard mix. Pour back into the pan, add the sugar and stir over the heat until thickened. Cook, stirring, for 1 minute.
**3** Pour the custard evenly over the fruit and leave to cool completely. Cover with the whipped cream and chill for 2-3 hours, or up to 2 days if preparing ahead.
**4** Serve topped with the lime rind and mint.

## Rosewater pashka

Rosewater adds a floral note to this delectable Russian dessert. *Serves 6*

2 x 250g cartons curd cheese
2 large egg yolks
6 tbsp crème fraîche
2 tsp rosewater essence
50g/2oz butter, softened
50g/2oz caster sugar
85g/3oz chopped mixed candied and glacé fruits, such as pineapple, cherries and candied citrus peel
25g/1oz raisins
15g/1/2oz chopped pistachio nuts
*to serve*
few chopped pistachio nuts
orange slices (optional)

**1** Line a 900ml/1 1/2 pint pudding basin with muslin, allowing plenty to overhang the rim. Tip the curd cheese into a sieve to drain off any whey, then turn into a bowl. Beat in the egg yolks, crème fraîche and rosewater.
**2** Cream the butter and sugar together in another bowl, then add to the cheese mixture and beat thoroughly until smooth. Stir in the fruits, raisins and pistachios.
**3** Spoon the mixture into the lined basin. Cover the surface with the overhanging muslin, then invert the basin and place muslin side down on a wire rack over a tray.
**4** Refrigerate overnight, or for up to 3 days if preparing ahead. As the mixture chills, excess whey drains from the pashka and the texture becomes firmer.
**5** To serve, remove the pudding basin and muslin. Spoon the pashka on to serving plates and scatter with pistachios. Serve with orange slices if liked, and dessert biscuits.

## Wild berry roulade with pastise

A light, airy fatless sponge rolled around flavoured summer berries. *Serves 6*

*for the sponge*
3 large eggs
85g/3oz caster sugar
70g/2¹/₂oz plain flour
15g/¹/₂oz cornflour
2 tsp orange flower water
*for the filling*
500g/1lb 2oz mixed soft fruit, such as raspberries, sliced strawberries, blackberries and redcurrants
3 tbsp pastise, such as Ricard or Pernod
1 tbsp clear honey
2 tbsp low fat crème fraîche
2 tbsp yogurt

**1** Preheat oven to 220C/fan oven 200C/Gas 7. Grease and line a 33x23cm/13x9in Swiss roll tin. Put the fruit in a bowl, add the pastise and honey and toss gently to mix. Set aside to macerate for about 1 hour.
**2** To make the sponge, whisk the eggs and sugar together in a bowl, using an electric whisk, for about 5 minutes until the mixture is pale, foamy and doubled in volume.
**3** Sift the flour and cornflour together over the mixture, add the orange flower water and fold in carefully.
**4** Turn the mixture into the prepared tin and spread gently and evenly with a palette knife. Bake for 8-10 minutes until well risen and just springy to the touch; do not overcook.
**5** Invert the sponge on to a wire rack, peel off lining paper, then trim the edges. Lay a clean tea-towel on top and carefully roll up the warm sponge with the cloth inside; leave to cool.
**6** For the filling, combine the crème fraîche and yogurt in a bowl. Drain the macerated fruit, reserving the juice, then fold into the yogurt mixture.
**7** Carefully unroll the sponge and remove the tea-towel. Spoon two thirds of the filling evenly over the surface and carefully roll up again. Place on a serving dish, with the join underneath. Chill for 1-2 hours before serving.
**8** Mix the remaining fruit with the reserved juice to make a sauce. Serve the roulade, cut into slices, with the berry sauce.

## Melon, mint and ginger salad

A refreshing, healthy fruit salad with the zing of freshly pressed ginger. Make sure the melons are perfectly ripe. *Serves 8*

1 medium Galia melon
1 Charantais or Cantaloupe melon
¹/₄ small watermelon
2.5cm/1in piece fresh root ginger, peeled and roughly chopped
1 tbsp freshly torn mint leaves
rosemary flowers or mint sprigs, to decorate

**1** Halve the whole melons. Scoop out the seeds from all 3 melons, then cut the flesh into chunks and place in a large bowl, adding any juices.
**2** Put the ginger in a clean garlic press, hold over the melon bowl and press firmly, to extract the ginger juice. Add the mint leaves and toss gently. Chill until required.
**3** Just before serving, toss lightly and scatter with rosemary flowers or mint sprigs.

## Peaches in elderflower Champagne

Luxuriously steeped in Champagne with a little sweetness offered by the elderflower cordial, these peaches make a deliciously refreshing dessert. *Serves 6-8*

6-8 peaches, ripe but firm
100ml/3¹/₂fl oz elderflower cordial
375ml/13fl oz (¹/₂ bottle) dry Champagne or good quality sparkling white wine

**1** Preheat oven to 200C/fan oven 180C/Gas 6. Arrange the peaches closely in a deep ovenproof dish (just large enough to hold them in a single layer).
**2** Measure the elderflower cordial into a jug, add the Champagne or sparkling wine, then pour the mixture over the peaches. Cover the dish with a lid, or with greaseproof paper then a layer of foil to seal.
**3** Bake for 40-50 minutes or until the peaches are tender right through. If they are not fully submerged in the liquid, turn them over halfway through the cooking time.
**4** Leave the peaches to cool in the syrup. If preferred, lift out and peel off the skins, then return the peaches to the elderflower Champagne to serve.

## Raspberry yogurt ice

A wonderfully fresh-tasting ice. *Serves 4-6*

500g/1lb 2oz raspberries
2 tbsp light muscovado sugar
6 tbsp maple syrup
500ml/18fl oz organic yogurt

**1** Put the raspberries and sugar in a blender or food processor and work to a purée, then pass through a sieve into a bowl to remove the seeds.
**2** Stir the maple syrup and yogurt into the raspberry purée.
**3** Freeze in an ice cream maker if you have one, according to the manufacturer's instructions. Alternatively, pour the fruit mixture into a freezerproof container and place in the coldest part of the freezer until partially frozen. As the ice crystals begin to form around the edges, remove the container from the freezer and whisk the raspberry mixture to break up the ice crystals. Return to the freezer. Repeat this process once more, then freeze until firm.
**4** If necessary, transfer the yogurt ice to the fridge 30 minutes before serving to soften.

## Strawberry yogurt ice

Make this refreshing ice during the summer when flavourful homegrown strawberries are available. *Serves 4-6*

150g/5oz caster sugar
175ml/6fl oz water
500g/1lb 2oz strawberries
500ml/18fl oz organic yogurt

**1** Dissolve the caster sugar in the water in a small pan over a low heat. Increase the heat, bring to the boil and boil steadily until the syrup registers 107C on a sugar thermometer. Allow to cool.
**2** Put the strawberries in a blender or food processor and work to a purée, then pass through a sieve into a bowl to remove the seeds. Stir in the sugar syrup, followed by the yogurt. Freeze as for Raspberry yogurt ice (above).
**3** If necessary, transfer the strawberry yogurt ice to the fridge approximately 30 minutes before serving to soften.

## Iced pear parfait

These delicate parfaits, wafer-thin pear crisps and butterscotch sauce can all be made well in advance. *Serves 6*

225g/8oz caster sugar
225ml/8fl oz water
6 ripe flavourful pears, such as Comice
4 tbsp poire williams liqueur
300ml/1/2 pint double cream
1 small egg white

**1** Put the sugar and water in a heavy-based pan and dissolve over a low heat, then increase the heat and boil until syrupy.
**2** Using a mandolin or very sharp knife, cut 6-12 very thin slices lengthways from the central part of 2 pears, keeping the peel, core and stalk intact. Lay them in the syrup.
**3** Peel and core the rest of these 2 pears, and the other 4 pears. Roughly chop the flesh and put into a heavy-based pan with the poire williams. Cover and cook over a low heat for about 8 minutes until soft, checking to make sure they don't stick. Transfer the pears and liquor to a blender and purée. Turn into a large bowl and cool.
**4** Preheat oven to 110C/fan oven 100C/Gas 1/4. Carefully drain the pear slices and lay on a silicone lined baking tray, reserving excess syrup. Put in the oven for 2 hours until crisp, but not coloured. Peel off the paper. Store in an airtight container between sheets of kitchen paper for up to 2 days.
**5** Whip half the cream in a bowl to soft peaks, then fold into the cooled pear purée. In a clean bowl, whisk the egg white until stiff, then add 3 tbsp of the reserved syrup and whisk until glossy. Gently fold into the pear purée.
**6** Spoon the parfait mixture into six 125-150ml/4-5fl oz timbales or dariole moulds, level the tops and freeze for at least 8 hours.

**7** To make the butterscotch sauce, boil the remaining sugar syrup to a golden caramel colour. Take off the heat and pour in the rest of the cream, taking care as it will splutter; stir well to dissolve the caramel.
**8** To unmould the parfaits, stand moulds in cold water for about 30 seconds, then invert on to a fish slice and transfer to a tray. Return to the freezer until ready to serve.
**9** To serve, warm the butterscotch sauce. Place a parfait on each serving plate and surround with a drizzle of butterscotch sauce. Decorate with the pear crisps.

## Mocha fudge torte

An irresistible, gooey dessert enhanced with a rich coffee syrup – best served with pouring cream. Make the torte a day ahead and keep chilled until required. *Serves 6-8*

140g/5oz plain chocolate, in pieces
85g/3oz butter, cut into cubes
85g/3oz ground almonds
3 medium eggs, separated
85g/3oz caster sugar
1 tbsp coffee powder
*for the syrup*
24 coffee beans
85g/3oz caster sugar
100ml/31/2fl oz water
4 tbsp kalhúa or other coffee liqueur

**1** Preheat oven to 180C/fan oven 160C/Gas 4. Line the base of a loose-bottomed 20cm/8in cake tin with greaseproof paper. Melt the chocolate in a heatproof bowl over a pan of simmering water. Add the butter and leave until melted. Remove from the heat and stir in the ground almonds.
**2** Whisk the egg yolks, sugar and coffee powder together in a large bowl, using an electric whisk, until thickened. Add the chocolate mixture and fold in.
**3** Whisk the egg whites in a clean bowl until stiff, then gently fold into the mixture. Pour into the prepared cake tin and bake for 30-40 minutes until crusty on top; it should still be slightly soft in the middle. Leave to cool in the tin, then remove.

**4** For the syrup, put the coffee beans, sugar and water in a heavy-based pan over a low heat until the sugar is dissolved, then increase the heat and boil for 5 minutes until syrupy. Add the liqueur and pour into a bowl; cool. Cover and chill until required.
**5** Serve the torte, cut into wedges and drizzled with the coffee syrup.

## Glazed filo mille feuilles

This impressive dessert is deceptively easy. Prepare ahead to the end of stage 4; assemble 2 hours before serving.

8 small sheets filo pastry (each about 21x19cm/121/2x71/2in)
50g/2oz butter, melted
8 tbsp icing sugar, sifted
115g/4oz mascarpone
4 tsp rosewater essence
150ml/1/4 pint double cream
400g/14oz mixed soft fruit, such as raspberries, strawberries, redcurrants, blueberries and blackcurrants
mint leaves, to decorate (optional)

**1** Preheat oven to 200C/fan oven 180C/Gas 6. Lay a sheet of filo on a clean surface (keep the rest covered). Brush with melted butter, then layer 3 more sheets on top, brushing all except the top sheet with butter. Repeat to make another stack with remaining filo.
**2** Cut each stack into 6 triangles, it won't matter if they are a little uneven. Place on baking sheets and dust with approximately 2 tbsp of the icing sugar. Bake for 10-12 minutes until crisp and golden.
**3** Pop under a hot grill (not too close to the element) for 15-30 seconds to glaze. Transfer to a wire rack to cool.
**4** For the filling, beat the mascarpone with 4 tbsp icing sugar and the rosewater until smooth. Lightly whip the cream in another bowl, then gently fold into the mascarpone.
**5** To assemble, layer 3 filo triangles per serving with mascarpone cream and fruit. Top with a sprig of redcurrants, and mint leaves if using. Just before serving, dust with the remaining icing sugar.

## Poached tamarillos with pink panna cotta

Teamed with panna cotta, tamarillos make a stylish prepare-ahead dessert.

250g/9oz caster sugar

4 star anise

100ml/3½fl oz grenadine

150ml/¼ pint water

4 tamarillos, stalks intact

450ml/¾ pint double cream

2 tsp vanilla extract

50g/2oz white chocolate

1 tsp powdered gelatine

1 Put the sugar, star anise, grenadine and water in a heavy-based pan over a low heat until the sugar is dissolved. Increase the heat and bring to a simmer.

2 Cut a cross in the skin at the pointed end of each tamarillo. Add to the sugar syrup, cover and poach gently, turning occasionally, for 10-15 minutes until just soft; test with a skewer. Leave in the syrup for 24 hours.

3 Meanwhile, make the panna cotta. Slowly heat the cream in a heavy-based pan over a very low heat until bubbles start to appear around the edge; this should take 10-15

minutes. Take off the heat and add the vanilla and chocolate, stir until melted.

4 Measure 150ml/¼ pint of the poaching syrup into a small heatproof dish. Sprinkle over the gelatine, leave to soften for a few minutes, then stand over a pan of simmering water until dissolved. Stir into the cream.

5 Pour into four 150ml/¼ pint oval darioles or other moulds and chill for 24 hours until set.

6 To unmould the panna cotta, dip the moulds briefly into hot water, then invert on to plates. Place a tamarillo on each plate and spoon over some of the syrup to serve.

### Sicilian cassata

This elegant frozen ricotta cake is richly flavoured with exotic dried fruit, cherries, dark chocolate and pistachios. It can be prepared well ahead. *Serves 10-12*

350g/12oz bought all-butter Madeira cake
150ml/¼ pint cassis or framboise
750g/1lb 10oz ricotta cheese
175g/6oz icing sugar, sifted
150ml/¼ pint whipping cream
250g/9oz ready-to-eat exotic dried fruit mix (papaya, pineapple, mango and melon), finely diced
100g/4oz glacé cherries, finely diced
100g/4oz dark, bitter chocolate, chopped
50g/2oz shelled pistachio nuts, chopped
3 tbsp strega liqueur or Marsala
candied or fresh cherries on stalks to decorate (optional)

**1** Cut the cake into 1cm/½in thick, long slices and brush one side with cassis. Use to line the side and base of a 23cm/9in spring-release cake tin, placing the brushed sides outwards and trimming to fit the tin as necessary, so there are no gaps. Brush the inside of the case with cassis, then chill.
**2** In a large bowl, whisk the ricotta with the icing sugar until smooth. Whip the cream in another bowl until it forms soft peaks, then fold into the ricotta mixture.
**3** Fold in the dried fruits, cherries, chocolate and pistachios, then the liqueur. Spoon the mixture into the prepared tin and freeze for at least 10 hours until firm and easy to slice.
**4** Unmould the cassata on to a plate. Cut into wedges and serve each portion topped with a cherry on a stalk if wished.

**NOTE** If the cassata has been frozen for longer than 10 hours, transfer to the fridge 30 minutes before serving to soften slightly.

### Trio of mango

This is a perfect finale to a special dinner. Matching fresh rose petals lend a fragrant finishing touch. *Serves 4-6*

300g/10oz caster sugar
juice of 3 lemons
4 large or 6 medium ripe mangoes
300ml/½ pint double cream
425g can lychees in syrup

**1** Put the sugar, lemon juice and 4 tbsp water in a heavy-based pan over a low heat until the sugar is dissolved. Increase the heat and boil until syrupy. Allow to cool.
**2** Peel the mangoes, cut the flesh from the stones and put in a blender with the sugar syrup. Whizz to a purée. Transfer 6 tbsp purée to a bowl and reserve for the sauce.
**3** Transfer two thirds of the remaining mango purée to an ice cream maker (if you have one); mix in the double cream and churn according to the manufacturer's instructions. Or pour the purée and cream into a freezerproof container, stir well and freeze for 1½ hours until partially frozen, then turn into a food processor and whizz until smooth. Refreeze, repeat once more, then freeze until required.
**4** For the sorbet, drain lychees over a bowl to catch the syrup. Add the lychees with 150ml/¼ pint of their syrup to the mango purée in the blender and purée. Freeze following instructions for freezing ice cream.
**5** Add the remaining lychee syrup to the mango purée reserved for the sauce. Mix well, cover and chill.
**6** If necessary, soften the ice cream and sorbet in the fridge for 20 minutes before serving. Serve the sorbet in a separate little dish set on a large plate with a scoop of ice cream and a swirl of mango sauce. Scatter with rose petals to decorate, if wished.

### Date and pistachio wontons

Fried wontons filled with a scented paste, bathed in a saffron and rosewater syrup, then dusted with crushed pistachios.

large pinch of saffron strands
250g/9oz caster sugar
100ml/3½fl oz water
100g/4oz shelled pistachio nuts
12 medjool dates, stoned and chopped
4 tbsp rosewater essence
12 wonton wrappers
vegetable oil for deep-frying

**1** Put the saffron, sugar and water in a heavy-based pan over a low heat to dissolve the sugar. Increase heat and boil for 3 minutes until syrupy.
**2** Put the pistachio nuts in a food processor and process until roughly ground. Remove about one third and reserve for dusting.
**3** Add the dates, 2 tbsp rosewater and 3 tbsp syrup to the processor and work to a paste. Add the remaining rosewater to the syrup.
**4** Put a spoonful of paste in the centre of each wonton wrapper, brush the edges with water and draw up over the filling; press together to seal. Cover with plastic film until ready to cook.
**5** Heat the oil in a deep fryer to 170C. Fry the wontons in batches for 30 seconds until golden; drain on kitchen paper. Shortly before serving, reheat the syrup. Bathe the wontons in the hot syrup just before serving.
**6** To serve, put 3 wontons on each plate, drizzle with some of the hot syrup and dust with the reserved crushed pistachios. Serve with crème fraîche.

### Lemon polenta cake

Polenta colours this cake a pretty shade of yellow, and adds a subtle crunch. Fresh strawberries and crème fraîche are the perfect complement. *8-10 slices*

115g/4oz polenta (ordinary or quick-cook), plus extra for dusting
115g/4oz plain flour
1½ tsp baking powder
2 large eggs, plus 3 egg whites
175g/6oz caster sugar
grated rind of 2 lemons
125ml/4fl oz lemon juice (juice of 2-3 lemons)
1 vanilla pod, seeds extracted
100ml/3½fl oz vegetable oil
150ml/¼ pint buttermilk
*to serve (optional)*
crème fraîche
strawberries

**1** Preheat oven to 180C/fan oven 160C/Gas 4. Grease and base line a 25cm/10in spring release cake tin. Dust the tin out with a little polenta.
**2** Sift the flour and baking powder together into a bowl, then stir in the polenta.
**3** In a separate bowl, whisk the whole eggs, egg whites and sugar together until pale and thick.
**4** Add the polenta mixture, lemon rind and juice, vanilla seeds, oil and buttermilk. Carefully fold into the whisked mixture, using a large metal spoon.
**5** Spoon the mixture into the prepared tin and bake for 30 minutes, or until a skewer inserted into the centre comes out clean. Transfer to a wire rack and leave to cool completely.
**6** Cut into slices and serve with crème fraîche and strawberries if you like.

### Orange almond cake with rosewater cream

A lovely light almond sponge with a hint of orange, accompanied by an exotic rosewater and cardamom cream. *8-10 slices*

6 large eggs, separated
175g/6oz caster sugar
grated rind of 2 oranges
juice of 1 orange
225g/8oz ground almonds
*for the rosewater cream*
2 cardamom pods, seeds extracted
2 tbsp rosewater essence
1 tbsp caster sugar
300ml/½ pint double cream

**1** Preheat oven to 180C/fan oven 160C/Gas 4. Grease and base line a 23cm/9in spring release cake tin.
**2** In a bowl, whisk the egg yolks, sugar and orange rind together until pale and thick. Stir in the orange juice, then fold in the ground almonds.
**3** In a clean bowl, whisk the egg whites until just peaking, then fold into the cake mixture.
**4** Spoon into the prepared tin and bake for 45-50 minutes until risen and firm to touch, covering loosely with foil after 20 minutes, if the cake appears to be overbrowning.
**5** Meanwhile, for the cream, lightly crush the cardamom seeds and put in a small pan with the rosewater and sugar. Warm gently to dissolve the sugar. Allow to cool, then strain.
**6** Whip the cream in a bowl, slowly adding the cooled syrup, until it forms soft peaks.
**7** Serve the cake cut into wedges, accompanied by the rosewater cream.

### Saffron rum babas

Divine saffron babas, flavoured with a pomegranate and rum syrup. *Serves 6*

2 tbsp milk
½ tsp saffron strands
225g/8oz plain flour, sifted
pinch of salt
2 tbsp caster sugar
1 tsp fast action dried yeast
2 large eggs, lightly beaten
50g/2oz butter, melted
*for the syrup*
100g/3½oz granulated sugar
6 tbsp rum
1 tsp pomegranate syrup
*to serve*
lightly whipped cream
1 pomegranate, seeds extracted

**1** Grease 6 small timbales or baba tins. Heat the milk with the saffron almost to the boil, then set aside to infuse until tepid.
**2** Mix the flour, salt, sugar and yeast in a bowl. Make a well in the centre and add the milk, eggs and butter. Mix to a soft, sticky dough, then beat thoroughly for 5 minutes.
**3** Spoon into the tins, cover loosely with oiled plastic film and leave in a warm place for 1 hour or until the dough is risen almost to the tops of the tins; remove plastic film.
**4** Preheat oven to 200C/fan oven 180C/Gas 6. Bake for 15 minutes until risen and golden.
**5** For the syrup, dissolve the sugar in 200ml/7fl oz water in a pan over a low heat, then boil for 3 minutes until syrupy. Cool, then stir in the rum and pomegranate syrup.
**6** Unmould babas, cool slightly, then stand in a shallow dish. Pour on two thirds of the syrup and leave to soak for 30 minutes.
**7** Serve the babas drizzled with syrup and topped with cream and pomegranate seeds.

## Chocolate star anise cake with coffee syrup

A superb chocolate cake, flavoured with star anise and soaked in a coffee syrup as it cools. For optimum appreciation, serve still slightly warm, with crème fraîche. *12 slices*

225g/8oz good quality plain dark chocolate
115g/4oz unsalted butter
4 large eggs, plus 2 egg yolks
115g/4oz caster sugar
50g/2oz plain flour, sifted
2 tsp ground star anise
50g/2oz fresh white breadcrumbs
*for the syrup*
300ml/1/2 pint strong black coffee
115g/4oz caster sugar
2 tbsp kahlúa or other coffee liqueur
1 star anise

**1** Preheat oven to 190C/fan oven 170C/Gas 5. Grease and base line a deep 20cm/8in round cake tin. Melt the chocolate and butter together in a bowl set over a pan of gently simmering water. Let cool slightly.
**2** Put the eggs, egg yolks and sugar in a bowl and whisk until pale and thickened. Sift the flour and star anise over the mixture. Add the breadcrumbs and melted chocolate, and fold in carefully using a large metal spoon.
**3** Spoon the mixture into the prepared tin and level the surface. Bake for 35 minutes or until a skewer inserted into the centre comes out clean.
**4** Meanwhile, make the syrup. Put the coffee and sugar in a heavy-based pan and heat gently until the sugar is dissolved. Increase heat and boil for 5 minutes until reduced and thickened slightly. Stir in the coffee liqueur and star anise; keep warm.
**5** Pierce the surface of the cake with a skewer, then drizzle over half of the coffee syrup. Set aside to cool. Serve cut into wedges, with the remaining coffee syrup and crème fraîche.

**VARIATION** Replace the star anise with the crushed seeds from 3 cardamom pods.

**NOTE** Ground star anise is available from selected supermarkets and Asian food stores. Alternatively, buy whole star anise and grind them yourself, using a coffee or spice grinder, or pestle and mortar.

## Gingerbread with figs

This cake improves with keeping. Wrap and store in a tin for up to 1 week. *16-20 slices*

450g/1lb self-raising flour
1/2 tsp salt
1/2 tsp bicarbonate of soda
2 tsp ground ginger
115g/4oz dried figs, chopped
50g/2oz crystallised ginger, diced
225g/8oz light muscovado sugar
175g/6oz butter
175g/6oz treacle
175g/6oz golden syrup
300ml/1/2 pint milk
2 medium eggs, beaten

**1** Preheat oven to 180C/fan oven 160C/ Gas 4. Grease and line a 25cm/10in square cake tin.
**2** Sift the flour, salt, bicarbonate of soda and ground ginger into a bowl. Stir in the figs and diced ginger. Make a well in the centre.
**3** Put the sugar, butter, treacle, syrup and milk in a pan and heat gently until melted. Pour into the well and add the eggs. Stir to mix, then beat for 1 minute.
**4** Turn the mixture into the prepared tin and bake for 1-1¼ hours until a skewer inserted in the centre comes out clean.
**5** Leave in tin for 10 minutes, then transfer to a wire rack to cool. Serve cut into fingers.

## Coconut and blueberry cakes

Deliciously moist, fruity buns. *Makes 8*

115g/4oz unsalted butter, at room temperature
115g/4oz caster sugar
2 tbsp milk
2 large eggs, lightly beaten
85g/3oz self-raising flour
1/2 tsp baking powder
85g/3oz desiccated coconut
140g/5oz blueberries

**1** Preheat oven to 180C/fan oven 160C/Gas 4. Line a muffin tray with 8 paper muffin cases.
**2** Cream the butter and sugar together in a bowl until pale and fluffy, then stir in the milk. Beat in the eggs, a little at a time.
**3** Sift the flour and baking powder together over the mixture, add the coconut and fold in carefully. Gently fold in most of the blueberries and spoon into the paper cases.
**4** Scatter the remaining blueberries on top and bake for 20-25 minutes until firm to the touch. Cool on a wire rack.

Coconut and blueberry cakes

## Upside down cider apple cake

This is excellent served warm as a pudding, with ice cream or cream. *Serves 8*

2 Granny Smith's apples
25g/1oz unsalted butter
50g/2oz granulated sugar
115g/4oz butter, softened
115g/4oz light muscovado sugar
grated rind of 1 lemon
2 large eggs, beaten
3 tbsp dry cider
175g/6oz self-raising flour
1 tsp ground mixed spice
50g/2oz sultanas

**1** Preheat oven to 180C/fan oven 160C/Gas 4. Grease the side of a deep 20cm/8in round cake tin (not a loose-bottomed one).
**2** Peel, core and thickly slice the apples. Heat the unsalted butter and granulated sugar in a large, heavy-based frying pan until the butter is melted and the sugar starts to brown. Add the apple slices and fry for 1-2 minutes each side until golden. Cool slightly.
**3** Cream the softened butter, muscavado sugar and lemon rind together in a bowl until fluffy, then beat in the eggs, cider, flour, and spice until smooth. Fold in the sultanas.
**4** Arrange the apples over the base of the cake tin, adding any pan juices. Spoon the cake mixture on top and spread evenly. Bake for 30-35 minutes until a skewer inserted in the middle comes out clean.
**5** Leave in the tin for 10 minutes, then invert on to a wire rack to cool. Serve warm.

## Plum and hazelnut crumble cake

A delicious hazelnut sponge base, covered with fresh plum halves and topped with a rich nutty crumble. *8-10 slices*

225g/8oz self-raising flour
1½ tsp baking powder
1 tsp ground cinnamon
140g/5oz unsalted butter, softened
140g/5oz caster sugar
3 large eggs, beaten
115g/4oz ground hazelnuts
6-8 plums, halved and stoned
*for the crumble topping*
25g/1oz plain flour
25g/1oz rolled oats
25g/1oz chilled butter, finely diced
50g/2oz light muscovado sugar
50g/2oz hazelnuts, roughly chopped

**1** Preheat oven to 180C/fan oven 160C/Gas 4. Grease and base line a 25x20cm/10x8in baking tin. Sift the flour with the baking powder and cinnamon.
**2** Cream the butter and sugar together in a bowl until pale and fluffy, then gradually beat in the eggs, adding a little of the flour with the last of the egg, to prevent curdling.
**3** Fold in the remaining flour mixture and ground nuts. Spoon into the prepared tin and level the surface.
**4** Arrange the plums cut side up over the cake, pressing down gently. Mix the crumble ingredients together and scatter over the top.
**5** Bake for 45-50 minutes until risen, lightly golden, and a skewer inserted into the centre comes out hot. Leave in tin for 10 minutes, then transfer to a wire rack to cool.

**VARIATION** Use ground almonds instead of hazelnuts, and apricots in place of plums.

Cinnamon chocolate chip cookies; Lavender and ginger cookies

## Cinnamon chocolate chip cookies

Giant cookies – crisp on the outside, yet soft within. Shape smaller ones if you prefer, reducing the cooking time slightly. *Makes 24*

140g/5oz butter or margarine, softened
200g/7oz soft brown sugar
50g/2oz caster sugar
2 medium eggs, beaten
350g/12oz plain flour
1 tsp bicarbonate of soda
1/2 tsp salt
1 tsp ground cinnamon
115g/4oz chopped peanuts
2 x 115g packets plain chocolate drops

**1** Preheat oven to 190C/fan oven 170C/Gas 5. Cream the butter and sugars together in a bowl until soft and fluffy. Beat in the eggs.
**2** Sift the flour, bicarbonate of soda, salt and cinnamon together over the mixture. Beat well, then stir in the peanuts and chocolate.
**3** Drop tablespoonfuls of the mixture well apart on to baking sheets lined with non-stick baking parchment and flatten slightly. Bake for 15-17 minutes until golden.
**4** Leave on baking sheets for 10 minutes, then transfer cookies to a wire rack to cool.

## Lavender and ginger cookies

Exquisite fragrant cookies. *Makes about 36*

115g/4oz butter, softened
85g/3oz caster sugar
1 medium egg, beaten
1 tsp vanilla extract
1 tbsp fresh or dried lavender flowers
1 tbsp chopped preserved stem ginger
225g/8oz plain flour
1/4 tsp bicarbonate of soda
1/2 tsp each baking powder and salt
1/2 tsp ground ginger
50ml/2fl oz soured cream or crème fraîche

**1** Cream the butter and sugar together in a bowl until soft. Beat in the egg, vanilla and lavender, then fold in the chopped ginger.
**2** Sift the flour with the bicarbonate of soda, baking powder, salt and ground ginger. Beat into the mixture, alternately with the soured cream; the dough will be quite soft.
**3** Tip the dough on to a sheet of grease-proof paper and gently roll into a cylinder, about 5cm/2in thick. Wrap tightly in plastic film and refrigerate for at least 6 hours, preferably overnight.
**4** To bake, preheat oven to 190C/fan oven 170C/Gas 5. Slice off thin rounds from the dough. Place on baking sheets lined with non-stick baking parchment. Bake for 8-10 minutes until pale golden and set.
**5** Cool slightly on the baking sheets, then transfer to a wire rack to cool completely.

## Carrot and raisin cookies

These lightly spiced drop cookies are perfect for lunch boxes. *Makes about 36*

225g/8oz freshly cooked carrots, drained
115g/4oz butter or margarine, softened
140g/5oz light muscovado sugar
1 large egg, beaten
400g/14oz plain flour
1 1/2 tsp baking powder
1/2 tsp ground cinnamon
1/4 tsp ground nutmeg
1/4 tsp ground ginger
1/4 tsp salt
85g/3oz seedless raisins
50g/2oz pecan nuts or walnuts, chopped

**1** Preheat oven to 190C/fan oven 170C/Gas 5. Line two baking sheets with non-stick baking parchment. Dry the carrots on kitchen paper, then mash thoroughly until smooth.
**2** Cream the butter and sugar together in a bowl. Add the mashed carrot and egg.

**3** Sift the flour, baking powder, spices and salt over the mixture, then beat together thoroughly. Stir in the raisins and nuts.
**4** Drop teaspoonfuls of the mixture on to the baking sheets, spacing well apart. Bake for 12-15 minutes until light golden brown.
**5** Leave on the baking sheet for 10 minutes, then transfer to a wire rack to cool.

## Vanilla thins

Serve with coffee or ice cream. *Makes 36*

300g/10oz plain flour
1 tsp baking powder
1/2 tsp salt
2 vanilla pods, split
225g/8oz butter, cubed and softened
225g/8oz caster sugar
1 large egg, beaten

**1** Sift the flour with the baking powder and salt on to a sheet of greaseproof paper.
**2** Scrape the seeds from the vanilla pods into the food processor. Add the butter and sugar and process until pale and fluffy. Add the egg and mix until incorporated.
**3** Add the sifted flour and process briefly to a soft dough; do not overwork.
**4** Turn on to a floured surface and knead lightly. Lift on to greaseproof paper and roll the dough into a cylinder, 5cm/2in thick. Wrap tightly in plastic film and refrigerate for at least 6 hours, preferably overnight.
**5** To bake, preheat oven to 190C/fan oven 170C/Gas 5. Slice off thin rounds from the dough as required. Place on baking sheets lined with non-stick baking parchment and bake for about 10 minutes until golden and set. Cool slightly on the baking sheets, then transfer to a wire rack to cool.

**NOTE** This cookie dough will keep tightly wrapped in the fridge for up to 1 week.

## Florentine baskets

These crisp fruit and nut baskets make pretty containers for ice creams. *Makes 10*

50g/2oz unsalted butter

50g/2oz caster sugar

50g/2oz golden syrup

50g/2oz plain flour

25g/1oz mixed crystallised or glacé fruit, such as pineapple, ginger, cherries and/or angelica

25g/1oz blanched almonds or shelled pistachio nuts, chopped

¼ tsp grated lemon rind

140g/5oz plain chocolate, melted

**1** Preheat oven to 180C/fan oven 160C/Gas 4.

**2** Melt the butter, sugar and golden syrup together in a pan over a low heat. Off the heat, stir in the flour, fruit, nuts and lemon rind; mix well.

**3** Drop 3 or 4 teaspoonfuls of the mixture on to non-stick or greased baking sheets, spacing well apart to allow for spreading. Bake for 10 minutes until golden brown.

**4** Allow the biscuits to cool very slightly until starting to firm up, then quickly lift each one with a palette knife and drape over an upturned dariole mould or small tumbler. Using your fingers, carefully press into a basket shape, fluting the edges.

**5** Repeat with the remaining mixture; leave the baskets until cool and set firm.

**6** Melt the chocolate in a heatproof bowl over a pan of simmering water. Carefully release each basket from its mould, and dip the base into the chocolate to coat. Place the baskets, chocolate side up, on a wire rack and leave until set.

**7** Just before serving, fill the baskets with scoops of ice cream.

**VARIATION** Use good quality white chocolate instead of plain. Dip the rims of the baskets rather than the bases into the melted white chocolate to give an attractive edging.

### Focaccia with figs and raisins

Topped with juicy caramelised figs, this soft focaccia is made with pizza mix lightened with a little extra yeast. Serve it with soft goat's cheese or crème fraîche. *Serves 4-6*

115g/4oz seedless raisins
150ml/¼ pint medium or sweet sherry
225ml/8fl oz hand-hot water
2 tsp active dried yeast
2 x 145g packets instant pizza mix
85g/3oz demerara sugar
6-8 fresh figs, sliced
olive oil, for drizzling

**1** Oil a 28x18cm/11x7in shallow baking tin. Put the raisins in a bowl. Warm the sherry, pour over the raisins and set aside to soak.
**2** Pour the water into a bowl, sprinkle on the yeast, stir and leave to froth for 15 minutes.
**3** Put the pizza mix in a large bowl, stir in 50g/2oz of the sugar and make a well in the centre. Add the frothed yeast and mix to a soft dough.
**4** Turn out on to a floured surface and knead for 2-3 minutes until smooth. Drain the raisins, reserving the liquid, then knead them into the dough.
**5** Press into the prepared baking tin, pushing the dough to the edges. Cover with oiled plastic film and leave to rise in a warm place for about 30 minutes until doubled in height.
**6** Preheat oven to 220C/fan oven 200C/Gas 7. Make dimples all over the surface of the dough with your fingers and lay the sliced figs on top. Drizzle with a little olive oil and sprinkle with the remaining sugar. Bake for 10-15 minutes until golden and caramelised.
**7** Spoon the reserved sherry over the focaccia; cool slightly. Serve warm, with soft goat's cheese or crème fraîche.

### Pecan and maple syrup baklava

Crisp, light filo pastry layered with a mildly spiced pecan nut mixture and drizzled with maple syrup. *Makes 12-20 squares*

225g/8oz shelled pecan nuts
50g/2oz light muscovado sugar
½ tsp ground mixed spice
400g/14oz packet large filo pastry sheets
140g/5oz butter, melted
175g/6oz maple syrup, warmed

**1** Preheat oven to 220C/fan oven 200C/Gas 7. Grease a 28x18cm/11x7in shallow baking tin.
**2** Coarsely grind the pecan nuts in a food processor, then transfer to a bowl. Add the sugar and mixed spice and stir to mix.
**3** Unroll the filo pastry and halve widthways to make 2 rectangles. Place one half on top of the other and cover with plastic film to prevent the filo pastry drying out.
**4** Lay one sheet of filo in the tin, allowing it to extend up the sides. Brush with melted butter. Layer five more pastry sheets on top, brushing each with butter and trimming to fit the tin. Sprinkle with a fifth of the nut mixture.
**5** Repeat this process four more times, to give five layers of nut mixture. Cover with five more sheets of pastry, brushing each with melted butter and trimming the pastry to fit as you go.
**6** Mark the surface of the baklava into 12-20 squares with the tip of a very sharp knife. Bake for 15 minutes, then lower the setting to 180C/fan oven 160C/Gas 4 and bake for a further 10-15 minutes until golden.
**7** On removing the baklava from the oven, spoon the warm maple syrup over the surface. Leave to cool in the tin for about 2 hours. Using a sharp knife, cut into the marked squares to serve.

### Triple chocolate brownies

These irresistible rich, moist dark chocolate brownies are laden with milk and white chocolate chips, and butterscotch pieces. *Makes about 12*

115g/4oz butter, plus extra for greasing
85g/3oz good quality plain dark chocolate (minimum 70% cocoa solids), in pieces
4 medium eggs, beaten
2 tsp vanilla extract
400g/14oz caster sugar
115g/4oz plain flour
25g/1oz cocoa powder
115g packet milk chocolate drops
115g packet white chocolate drops
8 butterscotch sweets, roughly chopped

**1** Preheat oven to 190C/fan oven 170C/Gas 5. Liberally butter a 28x18cm/11x7in shallow baking tin and line the base with non-stick baking parchment.
**2** Melt the butter with the chocolate in a heatproof bowl over a pan of simmering water. Remove from the heat and stir in the beaten eggs, vanilla extract and sugar. Mix thoroughly.
**3** Sift the flour with the cocoa powder over the mixture, then beat in until evenly incorporated. Stir in the chocolate chips and butterscotch pieces.
**4** Spoon the mixture into the tin and spread evenly. Bake in the middle of the oven for about 35 minutes until set, but still moist. Leave to cool in the tin.
**5** Turn out when completely cold and cut into squares or bars to serve.

**NOTE** These delicious chocolate brownies have a characteristic fudge-like texture. For a more 'cakey' texture, bake for an extra 5-10 minutes.

# index

**acknowledgements**

The publishers wish to thank the following for the loan of props for photography:

*The Conran Shop*, Michelin House, 81 Fulham Road, London SW3 (0171 589 7401); *Divertimenti*, 139-141 Fulham Road, London SW3 (0171 581 8065); *Divertimenti*, 45-7 Wigmore Street, London W1 (0171 935 0689); *Designers Guild*, 277 Kings Road, London SW3 (0171 351 5775); *Habitat*, 196 Tottenham Court Road, London W1 (0171 631 3880); *Ikea*, Purley Way, Croydon (0181 208 5607); *Inventory*, 26-40 Kensington High Street, London W8 (0171 937 2626); *Jerry's*, 163-7 Fulham Road, London SW3 (0171 581 0909); *LSA International*, The Dolphin Estate, Windmill Road, Sunbury on Thames, Middlesex (01932 789721); *Muji*, 26 Great Marlborough Street, London W1 (0171 494 1197)